THE TRANSPARENT TRAVELER

THE

The Performance

TRANSPARENT

and Culture of

TRAVELER

Airport Security

RACHEL HALL

Duke University Press   Durham and London   2015

© 2015 Duke University Press
All rights reserved
Printed in the United States of America on acid-free paper ∞
Designed by Heather Hensley
Typeset in Scala Pro by Copperline

Library of Congress Cataloging-in-Publication Data
Hall, Rachel, [date] author.
The transparent traveler : the performance and culture of
airport security / Rachel Hall.
pages cm
Includes bibliographical references and index.
ISBN 978-0-8223-5939-5 (hardcover : alk. paper)
ISBN 978-0-8223-5960-9 (pbk. : alk. paper)
ISBN 978-0-8223-7529-6 (e-book)
1. Airports—Security measures—United States. 2. Aeronautics,
Commercial—Security measures—United States. 3. United
States. Transportation Security Administration. 4. United
States—Social conditions—21st century. I. Title.
HE9797.4.S4H35 2015
363.28'70973—dc23 2015010109

Cover art: Hasan Elahi, *Transit v4.1*, 2015. Courtesy of the artist.

For Dustin

CONTENTS

ACKNOWLEDGMENTS

I first became interested in airport security in 2006, when living and working apart from my partner, Dustin Howes. He was teaching in southern Maryland. I was teaching in southern Louisiana. During the two long years that we lived apart, I spent a lot of time alone in both major metropolitan and small regional airports. Initially, airport security grabbed my attention as an irritating obstacle: a bureaucratic apparatus separating me from the one I loved. I sought my revenge through writing. I would pass the time by jotting down observations and later developed those sketchy notes into snapshots or short, sharply focused critiques of various aspects of the performance and culture of airport security. Since those early attempts to document and mount a response to airport madness within the United States after 9/11, many colleagues have offered constructive criticism and encouraged me to keep working on it.

Kelly Gates and Shoshana Magnet gave me my first opportunity to write about airport security for an audience when they asked me to join a panel on surveillance at the National Communication Association in the fall of 2006. Later, they kindly extended me an invitation to submit a revised version of the paper to a special issue of the *Communication Review*, which has since been reprinted as *The New Technologies of Surveillance*. Brian Rusted generously attended the panel with Gates and Magnet and two other presentations given by me that year. After the third panel, he approached me and said: "You know there is a book in this, don't you?" The thought had not occurred to me, but with his suggestion in mind, I kept researching and writing on the topic.

"The Body and the Archive of Confiscated Stuff" was well received by a wonderfully rowdy audience in the Performance Studies Division at the National Communication Association in the fall of 2006 and a stimulating group of scholars and artists in attendance at the Carnal Knowledges Visual Culture Symposium at George Mason University in the spring of 2007. While most of that paper did not make it into the book, the project gained momentum from the energy generated by sharing the work in its earliest stages.

Louisiana State University has been consistently supportive. First, they hired Dustin, who joined the faculty of political science in the fall of 2008. Suddenly we were living together and working across the quad from one another! Then in the spring of 2009, the Louisiana Board of Reagents awarded me an ATLAS grant in support of the project. The grant gave me a full year of paid leave in which to draft the book, which left me no choice but to produce something. What I produced was—to borrow a turn of phrase from Anne Lamott—a "shitty first draft." That year, I was lucky enough to be in a cultural studies writing group with Jenell Johnson and Rick Popp. The two of them suffered through that unwieldy first draft. Their careful responses have had a lasting influence on the book's tone, scope, and critical intervention. During my year of leave, I was invited to present on the project in my home department. I benefited from the enthusiasm and feedback of colleagues and graduate students in the Department of Communication Studies at Louisiana State University.

A cohort of feminist media studies scholars with an active presence at the Society for Cinema and Media Studies conference has provided rich intellectual exchanges and vital professional support during the writing of this book: Carrie Rentschler, Amy Hasinoff, Jennifer Petersen, Shoshana Magnet, Margaret Schwartz, and Carol Stabile. I was honored when Magnet invited me to submit some of my work for publication in her edited volume, *Feminist Surveillance Studies*. It was through this collaboration that I met her coeditor, Rachel Dubrofsky, whose editorial influence improved my chapter in that volume and related material in this book. Magnet also offered much needed advice and feedback on the book proposal.

Courtney Berger at Duke University Press sets the bar for humane professionalism in publishing. It has been an absolute pleasure to work with her, from the start of this project to its finish. Hearty thanks are also due to Erin Hanas for her careful attention to detail and to the talented folks in the art department at Duke University Press.

I am indebted to Diana Taylor and Carrie Rentschler for agreeing to review the manuscript. The book is vastly improved for having had their eyes on it. Traces of Taylor's theoretical contributions to the field of performance studies can be found throughout this book. I hope that she finds the critical intervention offered here to be consistent with the mission of the Hemispheric Institute of Performance and Politics. Rentschler is the toughest editor with whom I have had the privilege of working. She has a keen critical mind and a talent for playing devil's advocate. Other writers should be so lucky. Both Taylor and Rentschler deserve extra special thanks for keeping the momentum going on a project that could have easily stalled out amid crushing grief. There are no words to express my gratitude for the latter, other than to put it simply: thank you for providing me with the opportunity to be nourished by work in the midst of personal crisis.

During the writing of this book I became pregnant, learned that I was having (surprise!) twins, and received the news of Dustin's diagnosis of ALS when the kids were just two years old. Many people have extended themselves in numerous ways in order to keep our family going. Before and ever since, these folks have managed to make both work and play possible. First, my family: Sharon Hall and Deed Houpt, Charles and Kim Hall, Sarah Hall and Chris Harpst, and Daniel Hall. Second, Dustin's family: Brandon Howes and Erin McCrea, Janet Howes and Edward Guisdala, Joann Stoddardt, Marilyn Kelly, Randy and Colleen Howes, Russ and Sue Vincent Howes, Jason Howes and Shannon Fisher, Cory Howes and Anna Tippen Kerr.

Thanks to friendly colleagues and students at LSU: Renee Edwards, Ruth and Michael Bowman, Patricia Suchy, Tracy Stephenson Shaffer, Jonathan Lebret, David Terry, Loretta Pecchioni, Graham Bodie and Ashley Jones Bodie, Jim Honeycutt, Andrew King, Stephanie Houston Grey, Bryan McCann, Ashley Mack, William Sass, Andrea Betancourt, Bonny McDonald, Doug Mungin, Wade Walker, Nicole Constantini, Anna Marsden, Hal Lambert, Wayne Parent, Rick and Susan Moreland, Tim Slack and Tracy

Rizzuto, Laura Moyer, Wonik Kim, Jas Sullivan, Dana Berkowitz, Leonard Ray, and Kate Bratton.

I continue to benefit from the long-distance support and friendship of my graduate mentor, Della Pollock, and my BFF from graduate school, Phaedra Pezzullo.

Thanks for amazing friends: Jennifer Smith, Kate Wentzel, Ellen Bondoc, Seth and Maureen Baldwin, Niels and Anna Rosenquist, Chris Hardy, Adam and Becky Schiffer, Alec and Emily Ewald, Greg and Jodi Petrow, Liz Markovits and Bennett Hazlip, Susan Bickford and Greg McAvoy, Erin Carlston and Carrisa Showden, Jonathan Weiler, and Ian Finseth and Stephanie Hawkins.

Heartfelt thanks to the people who have taken good care of our children and/or prepared food while we worked: Ashley Williams, Lula Cain, Ashley Brown, everyone at the University Presbyterian Day School in Baton Rouge, and the distinguished members of Rachel's Aunties. Special thanks to Amie Robinson for the excellent care she has provided for Dustin and the kids.

Finally, thanks to Dustin, Madeline, and Henry for ongoing inspiration. Dustin, I don't know how much more time we have together. Rather than give in to the dreadfully suspended present, which beckons as I write, I hope we can find a way to inhabit the richly undetermined present, teeming with the likes of you and me.

RETHINKING ASYMMETRICAL TRANSPARENCY

Risk Management, the Aesthetics of Transparency,
and the Global Politics of Mobility

A terrorist attack is a moment in space and time where none of us wants to be. But standing in line at an airport security checkpoint is also a moment in space and time. In public discourse about airport security and terrorism prevention in the post-9/11 era, these two moments are repeatedly set against one another. Not surprisingly, the threat of another terrorist attack eclipses matters of prevention. In comparisons drawn between these two "moments," the business of prevention frequently serves as a comic foil to the deadly threat of terrorism. The infamous "Don't touch my junk" discourse that erupted late in 2010 in response to the introduction of full-body scanners at airports across the United States is a case in point. While media professionals, privacy activists, and Transportation Security Administration (TSA) spokespersons publicly debated the merits and dangers of the full-body scanners and their old-school counterpart, the physical pat-down, the discussion remained safely within the comedic frame of Americans' puritanical obsession with hiding, revealing, and protecting private parts. The "Don't touch my junk" discourse articulated the only public challenge to full-body scanners and physical pat-downs as a matter of homophobic masculine pride on the order of defending one's "junk" from the locker room assaults of other boys. A popular expression of misplaced heterosexual vanity enacted a comedic reversal of male genitalia as vulnerable to sexual attack by lusty TSA screeners, underwriting the treatment of airport security as a "joke" once again.

Perhaps critiques of airport security frequently take the form of sophomoric jokes because the instrumental frame delimiting public discussions of terrorism prevention shuts sober debate down before it can begin. In serious discussions of airport security, professionals and laypersons alike evaluate prevention techniques and technologies based on a single criterion: whether or not a particular measure protects us from another attack. The impossibility of disproving that prevention works leaves the door open for security professionals and casual observers to endlessly exploit the possibility that it does.[1] In the minds of agreeable air passengers, the logic goes something like this: "Well, if it makes us safer from another terrorist attack, then I am all for it." The discourse of terrorism prevention devalues the live moment at the checkpoint and downplays the impressions it leaves in favor of the outcome of arriving safely at one's destination. People need and want to fly for many different reasons, including work, education, health care, love, death, war, business, family, friendship, and tourism, which means that passengers will likely go along with whatever new security policy, technology, or procedure the TSA imposes. As long as the instrumental frame goes unchallenged, we remain willing to view what happens at the checkpoint as either necessary and therefore unchallengeable, or as lacking in gravity by comparison to the virtual threat of another terrorist attack and therefore not worthy of serious critique or public debate. In other words, the ends will always justify the means. But given the virtual possibility of another attack, the work of prevention is not so much a means to an end as a means-without-end.[2] If we acknowledge that the work of prevention is never done, then it may become possible to hold our attention at the airport security checkpoint long enough to reflect critically on what is happening there.

This book argues that airport security is a cultural performance of risk management.[3] That is not to say that I equate airport security with stagecraft. The analysis of airport security offered here departs from the angry and sometimes witty public discourse in which writers have regularly used theatrical metaphors to criticize or dismiss airport security. For example, consultant Doug Laird, a former Northwest Airlines security director, describes airport security as "nothing more than show."[4] Anna Quindlen describes the "hustle and bustle" at airport security checkpoints as "window dressing."[5] In a letter to the editor of the *New York Times*, Nicole Woo goes further, describing the government's policies and procedures as "empty gestures" designed to assuage an anxious public: "The government's air travel rules of the past five years—from confiscating tweezers to checking passengers' footwear to the recent obsession with liquids and gels—are just reactions intended to placate a nervous public, and are clearly not security measures that have been methodically and disinterestedly decided. We should not be distracted by such empty gestures."[6] Contrary to these critics, who employ theatrical metaphors in a manner implying that performance means faking it, I understand the performance of airport security as constitutive of a culture of risk management, which exercises an enduring influence far beyond the controlled zones of securitized airports.[7]

Scholars of risk management have also turned to theatrical metaphors in order to describe the changing aspect of risk societies in terms of a notion of performance as faking it. In his book *World at Risk*, Ulrich Beck urges us to take seriously the "staging of global risk," but his use of the theatrical metaphor indicates his interest in risk as a mediated spectacle, whereas I am interested in the production and maintenance of the culture of risk management via live performances of airport security. Beck understands the practical prevention measures taken and compelled in the name of risk management to be an effect of mediated representations of risk. Our analyses share a commitment to "take the role of staging seriously."[8] We also agree on the matter of risk management's amplification of terror: "It is not the terrorist attack, but the global staging of the act and the political anticipations, actions and reactions in response to the staging which are destroying the Western institutions of freedom and democracy."[9] Where we differ is that Beck's sociological individual is imagined as a visual consumer of illusory media content, whereas I am interested in air passengers as cocreators of a shared reality.

When individuals perform the rites of airport security, they participate in what Michel Foucault called *biopolitics*. According to Colin Gordon, biopolitics "designates forms of power exercised over persons specifically insofar as they are thought of as living beings: a politics concerned with subjects as members of a *population*, in which issues of sexual and reproductive conduct interconnect with issues of national policy and power."[10] Other scholars have analyzed homeland and airports security in terms of biopolitics. In his book, *Surveillance in the Time of Insecurity*, Torin Monahan offers an analysis of how the concerns of national security have eclipsed issues of human security in the post-9/11 era. Citing Foucault's "Society Must Be Defended" lectures, Monahan writes that the nature of biopower rests in "making live and letting die."[11] In her recent book, *Terrorist Assemblages: Homonationalism in Queer Times*, Jasbir Puar includes terrorism prevention in the category of biopolitics because terrorism prevention leverages citizens' lives and their collective capacity for a shared future against the threat of death by terrorism. She argues that biopolitics is ultimately about the citizen's "capacity for capacity," where capacity is defined in terms of the citizen's ability to affirm life and futurity.[12]

This book provides a performance-based analysis of biopolitics, where performance is defined in Richard Schechner's terms as restored or "twice-behaved" behavior.[13] Puar makes passing reference to performance in her discussion of the pressure that citizens face to submit to screening by surveillance technologies: "Pivotal here is the notion of capacity, in other words the ability to thrive within and propagate the biopolitics of life by projecting potential as futurity, one indication of which is performed through the very submission to these technologies of surveillance that generate these data."[14] I argue that performance is not incidental to biopolitics; rather, performance is the mode in which the citizen's episodic affirmations of life and futurity are rehearsed, compelled, enacted, repeated, and confirmed. By definition, capacity is that which remains to be demonstrated or proven. In other words, the citizen's capacity for life and futurity has to be performed (over and over again) if it is to be believed.[15] Consequently, "the technical nature of innocence is changing."[16] The risk management approach to international terrorism compels air passengers to affirm life and futurity, but this affirmation takes the form of a negative assertion: the demonstration of (the absence of) the threat of death.

A national security program that defines innocence by negation raises a series of questions: How does one show (the absence of) the threat of terrorism? And what could such demonstrations possibly look like when bodies are infinitely variable? When air passengers are culturally diverse? When individuals are irreducibly singular in their proclivities, mannerisms, and manias? When the objects passengers carry are polysemic and multipurpose? When the space of the airport is already so charged with tension and anxiety that it is terribly difficult to sort out the emotions of one passenger from the next, or one passenger from the affective environment of the airport and the heightened energy that attends the event of flying? Finally, who can never perform innocence in this system, based on racial difference, immigration and citizenship status, disability, age, and religion?

Even these cursory references to the complexity characterizing the flows of bodies, bags, objects, and affects through airports suggest that it would be nearly impossible to establish a universal set of conventions for performing (the absence of) the threat of terrorism. And yet for over a decade, the TSA and like-minded national security programs, US citizens, and visitors to the United States and other countries with securitized airports have been engaged in an ambitious, frenetic, far-reaching, self-contradictory, and multipronged experiment to do just that. The risk management approach to international terrorism assumes that once attempted or realized, the unwanted event is likely to occur again and, based on this assumption, treats the threat of additional attacks as imminent/immanent. In other words, a particular security crisis serves a national prevention strategy once it has been lassoed from the actual past (historical terrorist attacks) or the virtual past (failed attempts and close calls) and projected into the immediate futures of securitized airports.

The terrorist threat looms in what I call the *future interior*.[17] My concept of the future interior attempts to name and describe a risk management strategy that works on time by spatializing it: security experts imagine the components of the next terrorist attack to be (in)visibly enfolded into what Brian Massumi has called the "empty present" of prevention. In *The Politics of Everyday Fear*, Massumi observes that a mind set on avoiding an accident that has already taken place inhabits neither the future nor the past but the empty present in which the accident is about to have happened (again).[18] Indeed, security cultures developed to prevent terrorist attacks routinely shift participants away from the historical past into the suspended present, where the threat of terrorism remains hidden, enfolded, or tucked away.[19] Consequently, passengers and their belongings appear to the eyes of security experts, petty officials, surveillance technologies, and alert citizens as an endless and overlapping series of mobile interiors-in-crisis. The fantasy of controlling the threat of another terrorist attack by enfolding that risk into the bodies, bags, objects, and affects that inhabit the present moment of prevention as it is defined and redefined from the perspective of those looking for trouble corresponds to Gilles Deleuze's description of the societies of control that began to replace disciplinary societies in the postwar era. In place of the disciplinary society's "organization of vast spaces of enclosure," Deleuze writes, we now have a series of "interiors in crisis." If the enclosures characteristic of disciplinary power were *molds*, distinct castings, Deleuze writes, then "controls are a modulation, like a self-deforming cast that will continuously change from one moment to the other, or like a sieve whose mesh will transmute from point to point."[20] Passengers and the things they carry transmute from threatening to innocent and back again. Enfolded with the threat of terrorism, security employees and technologies open up and flatten out passengers' bodies and bags in order to demonstrate (the absence of) the threat of terrorism. In these collaborative performances of risk management, passengers and their belongings perform the symbolic labor of embodying the threat of terrorism so that it can be demonstrably managed within securitized airports.

The Airport as Vital Place

In the mid-1990s, anthropologist Marc Augé described the airport as a utopic nonplace in which passengers enjoyed blissful anonymity or the brief experience of having been momentarily liberated from the mundane responsibilities and moral obligations of everyday life. The author writes about the experience of showing proof of identification at the checkpoint in exchange for access to the departure gates in terms of the contractual relations governing the airport as nonplace: "As soon as his passport or identity card has been checked, the passenger for the next flight, freed from the weight of his luggage and everyday responsibilities, rushes into the 'duty-free' space; not so much, perhaps, in order to buy at the best prices as to experience the reality of his momentary availability, his unchallengeable position as passenger in the process of departing."[21] But in the post-9/11 era, "unchallengeable" is no longer an accurate description of the departing passenger's position. Rather, the passenger remains suspect so long as she remains within or near a securitized airport, on an airplane, and on or near a tarmac. In place of the contractual exchange of a passport or ID card for admittance to the departure gates, we now have an elaborate, ongoing performance of passenger transparency. Like their fellow performers (TSA employees and other airport service persons), passengers endure the dull but continuous pressure of terrorism prevention as a performance-without-end. In the words of Lisa Parks, "Much more than a non-place, the airport has become a vital place where security, technology and capital collide, and spur the U.S. social body to recognize its terrorizing interiority."[22] To assert that airports have become vital places is not to say that they have come to function more like anthropological places, which in Augé's terminology references bounded cultures and societies with rich local traditions and idiosyncratic unwritten rules for getting along. Rather, post-9/11 airports continue to feel like nonplaces insofar as they are relatively generic mixed-use spaces inhabited by corporate chains and networked security agencies.

What makes airports *vital* in the post-9/11 era is the symbolic work they perform. Security cultures of terrorism prevention invest tremendous energy and resources into producing docile global suspects, who willingly become transparent or turn themselves inside out in a manner that renders them readily and visibly distinct from terrorists (an expansive category that includes all of those people unfortunate enough to be suspected of or misrecognized as belonging to the group). In the visual culture of the war on terror as brought to US media consumers by US media corporations, terrorist embodiment appears as a problem of opacity. Performed by the US military and documented by US media corporations, *opacity effects* visualize bodies, geographies, buildings, or institutions as possessing interiors and thereby allude to realms beyond the visible. Opacity effects raise suspicion merely by daring to show something that it is not totally visually accessible and immediately comprehensible to the viewer or monitor. Perhaps most significantly, opacity effects communicate the military and security state's objection to physical and psychological interiority. They picture a desire to rid the warring world of pockets, caves, spider holes, and veils. They simultaneously communicate and invite a shared compulsion to ferret out all secrets and produce actionable intelligence from detainees by any means necessary.

Opacity effects indirectly nourish a political culture of compulsory transparency in the citizenry at large. In the United States and other "paranoid empires" in which the political leadership feels besieged by the threat of international terrorism, periodic media spectacles of terrorist embodiment remind publics what is at stake if "we" do not adopt and uniformly submit to airport security regulations and surveillance technologies.[23] By this I do not mean to suggest that media spectacles of opacity are intentional efforts by US media corporations to serve as agents of propaganda for the US military or security state. Rather, I am suggesting that some military, government, and media professionals share an aesthetic orientation, which implies a global politics of mobility. If terrorist embodiment is a problem of opacity, then securitized airports treat all passengers as suspect (threateningly opaque) until they perform *voluntary transparency*, or demonstrate readiness-for-inspection. *Transparency effects* refer to attempts by the US security state to demonstrably exclude passengers from the presumptive status, terrorist, by "clearing" their opaque bodies, bags, and belongings for takeoff. Transparency effects reify the interior/exterior binary, only to perform operations of flattening upon passengers and their things, which render the interior as surface. Thus exteriorized, interiority may function as a screen for the projections of security technologies, TSA officers, and alert citizens.[24]

The colonial binary is subtly recast in the post-9/11 era. Instead of "the West and the Rest," we have docile and noncompliant suspects in the war on terror, or willing participants in the biopolitical project of risk management and those who have been excluded from that project. To be clear, I do not mean to equate or even establish a parallelism between the airport security apparatuses and prison camps established in the name of terrorism prevention and the war on terror, respectively. Rather, the project of this book is to show how these disparate security cultures are united by a common visual strategy. The extended analysis of the aesthetics of transparency offered here is meant to correct the rush by scholars in the humanities to compare airports to other exceptional spaces in the war on terror. Perhaps most provocatively, Gillian Fuller made the observation in her 2003 essay "Life in Transit: Between Airport and Camp" that the post-9/11 airport functioned as an exceptional space or a camp in Giorgio Agamben's terminology. For Agamben, she writes, "any zone where 'normal order' is suspended is a camp." After drawing the comparison between the post-9/11 airport and the camp, Fuller distinguishes the two sites based on the contrast between mobility and immobility: "If freedom of movement is, as Arendt claims, one of the most elemental of freedoms, then the camp provides the ultimate backdrop to the sublime feelings of placelessness that many experience as they wander through the airport. The camp, like the airport, is built for transit. Yet in the camp, no one moves. Both airport and camp constitute zones of exception, each are framed by a rhetoric of emergency, each are limit concepts of the other. One facilitates movement and the other denies it, yet both are zones of perpetual transit and futuristic promise."[25] Fuller and others argue that the creation or designation of exceptional spaces enables extralegal activities to proliferate at those sites. For these scholars, part of what it means to render a space exceptional is to grant it liminal status or create a state of suspended reality in which practices that would otherwise inspire protest are allowed to develop without a fight.[26]

The airport security checkpoint lacks the immediate threat of physical violence present in the interrogation and torture scenarios of the war on terror in extralegal spaces like Abu Ghraib and Guantanamo Bay (Gitmo).[27] Docile suspects' presumed capacity to perform voluntary transparency makes physical violence against their bodies seem both unnecessary and unacceptable.[28] By contrast, noncompliant suspects' presumed incapacity or unwillingness to perform voluntary transparency rationalizes the performance of forcible transparency upon their bodies by torturers and interrogators. I define *forcible transparency* as subjecting a noncompliant body presumed to be opaque to intensive questioning, duress, or torture in order to forcibly materialize the guilty party or bad intentions of the interior in the form of a verbal confession, actionable intelligence, or neutralization of the threat via the person's progressive mental degeneration. Noncompliant status need not be earned through demonstrated resistance to the US military and/or security state. Practices of racial, ethnic, religious, and risk profiling presume some groups to be noncompliant and categorically exclude them from participation in the collective, coercive project of risk management.

In this book, I make the case that the aesthetics of transparency allows citizens of paranoid empires to recognize themselves as fundamentally different from and somehow more innocent than the ordinary Iraqis, Afghanis, and other non-Westerners subjected to detention, torture, and abuse in the name of the war on terror—in many cases without probable cause. I argue that charged distinctions between populations presumed capable of performing voluntary transparency and those presumed to be irredeemably opaque have enabled paranoid empires and their citizens to make the unprecedented shift to preemptive law at home and preemptive warfare abroad without inspiring serious public debate or effective political protest.

There is another type of transparency that gets performed across the disparate sites of the detention centers of the war on terror, Israeli and US airports, and beyond, which complicates my neat recasting of the colonial binary in terms of docile and noncompliant suspects. While the general trend holds that docile suspects are presumed capable of performing voluntary transparency and detainees in the war on terror are presumed incapable or unwilling, performances of involuntary transparency occur across these sites. *Involuntary transparency* refers to the practice of reading a person's exterior for involuntary signs or clues about intentions thought to reside in the interior. A covert layer of security, involuntary transparency assumes that people lack full control over the communicative signals their bodies and faces send out into the world. According to this security strategy, people's inability to exercise total control over their performances of self in everyday life leaves room for security agents trained in behavior detection to decipher passengers' guilt, despite their feigned innocence. Unlike the performances of forcible transparency enacted in the theaters of the war on terror, performances of involuntary transparency do not require physical contact or force. But there is a crucial similarity between these two types of transparency, which separates them from all of those included in the category voluntary transparency. In the case of voluntary transparency, the object of surveillance is granted some degree of agency in his performance of transparency, even if agency is limited to the choice of whether to submit to screening by surveillance technologies or a pat-down inspection. In the case of forcible transparency, the object of surveillance's agency is presumed and subdued through imprisonment, physical force, and mental duress. But in the case of involuntary transparency, the agency of the behavior detective cancels out the agency of the suspects she is reading.

A Political Culture of Compulsory Transparency

Under the pressure of strategies designed to unfold and reveal threats thought to be lurking within the interior of passengers and their things, select domains of performance have become opportunities for passengers to demonstrate their innocence. These include passengers' object relations, interactions with security technologies, facility with security protocol, physical gestures, styles of comportment, and ability to blend in to their surroundings, as well as the absence of physiological signs of nervousness or anxiety. Framing airport security as a collaborative cultural performance enables me to begin to describe, if not untangle, the knot of consent and coercion produced when passengers perform voluntary transparency. Airport security is consensual insofar as it is a cultural performance demanded by some passengers. This is what George Carlin was getting at when he said, "Airport security is only there to make white people feel safe." Carlin's observation suggests that airport security is directed at a select audience of travelers, who imagine themselves as endangered and consequently want to see protections put in place. The reactive character of airport security proves his point. Terrorism prevention generates policies and adopts technological solutions that are made in the image of the last attack or near miss. Lessons learned from investigations of specific terrorist plots are applied to the traveling public at large. So, for instance, in response to the terrorist attacks of 9/11, the Bush administration quickly embraced the use of biometric technologies for the purpose of prescreening all international travelers wishing to enter or move through the United States. The infamous zip-top bag policy for regulating liquids, gels, and aerosols was tailored to the attempt to bring down as many as ten aircraft traveling from Britain to the United States using liquid explosives in 2006. The nearly successful attempt to blow up a plane headed for Detroit using plastic explosives in late 2009 prompted the TSA to begin replacing metal detectors with full-body scanners at the checkpoint. Finally, the TSA cites the 9/11 attacks, the shoe bomber incident of 2002, and the liquid explosives plot of 2006 in its rationales for the behavior detection officers stationed in US airports. This pattern can be understood as a reflection of the government's attempts to appease fearful members of the traveling public.

As the performance scholar Diana Taylor has noted, the Bush administration's performative declaration of a war on terror attempted to produce consent for its security policies. Once those policies are in place, she observes, people living in the United States shift from the Bush administration's saying-so-makes-it-so to the proliferation of domestic security policies, which hail ordinary people to embody that reality. Those whose consent was projected and retroactively conferred by the declaration of a war on terror gradually move from the performative construction of reality into what Taylor calls the animative performance of that reality in their everyday lives: "The way that human beings in the United States continue to live it on the ground. Albeit in different ways, we are all required to participate in the scenario, to undergo ritual acts of surveillance by showing our IDs, submitting to searches, taking off our shoes, reacting to color-coded alerts, and having our phones tapped. We perform terror every day; we incorporate it."[29]

The point is that whether or not a particular passenger agrees with the government's threat construction or genuinely fears another terrorist attack, the security state requires that person to perform *as if* the threat construction and risk management measures adopted to address it were valid. The performative construction of the threat of terrorism comes full circle once it animates citizens and visitors to the United States to perform the symbolic labor of embodying the threat of terrorism. By participating in the rites of airport security, passengers publicly perform their consent to be monitored accordingly.

Airport security is coercive insofar as the US government pressures passengers in the United States and beyond to participate in these rituals of risk management by threatening to immediately restrict their mobility and holding the long-term virtual possibility of another terrorist attack over their heads. In the first case, coercion is direct, immediate, and based not in a threat of force but in a threat of immobilization: if you refuse to participate in the performance, then you will not be allowed to fly. In the second case, coercion is based on borrowed force: the security state and its officials and experts borrow the threat of force from the terrorists. Whether they believe the threat construction or not, air passengers are positioned as potential terrorists if they do not consent to surveillance and monitoring and are therefore treated as suspects without probable cause. Demonstrating consent becomes part of their performance of voluntary transparency. Such performances are crucial to passengers' achievement of the security status: "cleared for takeoff"—a telling phrase indicative of the passengers' default status of threatening opacity.

By participating in airport security passengers actively and publicly forfeit their right to be presumed innocent under the old legal system. They trade the presumption of their innocence for the presumption of their capacity to perform voluntary transparency. No mere inconvenience, this represents a profound change to the United States and potentially international legal system and our basic conception of citizenship. The old, idealized version of democratic citizenship and what rights it supposedly granted, chief among these being the right to be presumed innocent until proved guilty and the right to be protected from unlawful search and seizure, has begun to erode. Like most of what's promised by the mythical, idealized America, these promises have applied historically only to some and not others. The developments described in this book are historically significant, granted what is novel about the situation is not so new to historically underprivileged US citizens or to citizens of other nations and noncitizens. Other populations, particularly men of color, poor, queer, transgender, and mentally disabled people, have been categorically criminalized at different points in US history. What becomes significant within the United States and far beyond in the post-9/11 security context is that the possession of US citizenship and the appearance of whiteness and middle- or upper- class status are no longer enough to grant individuals the presumption of innocence. Nor is it enough for foreign visitors to the United States to be citizens of nations that America considers to be its allies or to possess the phenotypic features typically associated with the global North.

Crucial to this historic shift is a global politics of mobility, which celebrates and protects the mobility of some at the expense of others. The new idealized performance of voluntary transparency gives rise to a new form of mobile, global citizenship: the willing suspect. What I call performances of voluntary transparency—not performances of the global northerner or whiteness or normalcy or class status per se—earn formerly privileged populations the temporary attribution of innocence they used to enjoy on a more permanent basis. Likewise, successful performances of voluntary transparency can temporarily grant members of historically disadvantaged minority groups and those who deviate from normal in some way temporary access to innocence. Transparency is the new white, if you will. The presumption of innocence is a luxury no longer available to even privileged citizens; or, rather, it turns increasingly on whether those citizens are willing to routinely submit to physical or virtual search and disclose digitally captured information about their bodies.

Those accustomed to the presumption of their innocence have experienced the shift to a preemptive legal framework as an assault on their basic rights, especially their right to privacy. The newly disenfranchised have responded indignantly. While a few groups have staged protests, many more have reluctantly submitted to the new security policies. Some have expressed their discomfort and displeasure with the new policies by sharing in a sophomoric sense of humor about the situation, which targets the TSA and blames its employees for their troubles in a manner that is decidedly classist. This response misses the point of their former privilege and callously exercises that privilege anew by heaping scorn and resentment on the relatively low-paid work performed by TSA employees. In this book, I argue that TSA employees are members of a hybrid security-service industry that facilitates the securitized mobility of those privileged passengers who are so apt to resent them.

Rethinking Asymmetrical Transparency

In critical surveillance studies literature, scholars use the term *asymmetrical transparency* to refer to governments or corporations that know more about their citizens or customers than the other way around. The problems faced by surveillance societies unfold as dramatic contests between Big Brother and his victims. This way of conceptualizing asymmetrical transparency has produced divergent schools of thought regarding how citizens might respond to surveillance overreaches by government agencies, militaries, and private corporations.

The realist position, perhaps best exemplified by the sociologist David Lyon, calls for *more transparency* on the part of data collectors as a means of restoring accountability to government agencies and corporations, which currently practice asymmetrical transparency. The Snowden/PRISM scandal in 2013 drives home the continued importance of Lyon's arguments. He identifies the key problem of surveillance societies as the way in which technical, commercial, and administrative organizations and spaces "draw a veil (intentionally or otherwise) over how surveillance actually works."[30] Because data collection and aggregation is highly consequential for individuals and groups, Lyon argues, we ought to focus on "the problem of transparency," by which he means the public's lack of information about "the modes and purposes of surveillance."

"By transparency," Lyon writes, "I refer to a quality of 'seeing through.'"[31] In other words, Lyon defines transparency in functional terms as the ability to see the inner workings of the institution or corporation in question. His call for more transparency is informed, on a deeper level, by the Enlightenment proposition that transparency guarantees justice and supports the healthy functioning of institutions in democratic societies by making leaders accountable to the publics they are meant to serve. Lyon articulates three reasons that transparency is the most important issue for surveillance societies: the appetite for personal information has increased among marketers and those working on behalf of the security state; the politics of information has everything to do with what happens to data once it is collected; and personal data cannot and should not be abstracted out from real persons to the point where we forget that human freedom and dignity are at stake.[32] Lyon accepts that surveillance is an irreversible aspect of our lives and wants to take legal and administrative steps to reduce its abuse. Accordingly, his remedy is liberal, reformist, and policy-oriented. The more-transparency approach calls for reciprocal or symmetrical exposure of states and corporations, on the one hand, and citizens or consumers, on the other. It assumes that voluntarily supplying information about oneself to a monitoring agency promotes symmetrical transparency by requiring citizens or consumers to give their consent to be monitored. As long as members of surveillance societies are aware of when and where and what types of information is being collected about them, then they are able to make informed decisions regarding whether or not to participate in commercial transactions or public forums that require such "tokens of trust."[33]

Indeed, one could argue that the Snowden/PRISM scandal has bothered US citizens because those citizens have agreed, more or less enthusiastically, to open themselves and their belongings up to unprecedented inspection and analysis in US airports for over a decade now. In this context, the revelation that the National Security Administration (NSA) has been covertly collecting data on US citizens makes what has been happening in US airports feel like security theater, in the sense of performance as faking it. It gives the impression that the US government was not getting the kinds of information it really wanted at airport security checkpoints or that the information collected there was somehow insufficient, making the NSA's additional, covert layers of security necessary. But NSA conduct may prove legal under the PATRIOT Act, even if that act is found to be unconstitutional in the long run. In other words, through their elected representatives, a majority of US citizens supported the PATRIOT Act. Given this, the Snowden/PRISM scandal exemplifies the knotted character of consent and coercion in post-9/11 security cultures.

In contrast to Lyon's call for more transparency, the antirealist position in critical surveillance studies calls for *less transparency* or strategic opacity on the part of individuals and social groups subjected to surveillance by states and corporations. According to these writers, performances of opacity protect human interiority from the registers of surveillance and strategically introduce the complexity of lived experience back into those registers. The antirealist position assumes that surveillance data is impoverished by comparison to the rich, inexhaustible, and unpredictable quality of lived experience, which includes the interior life of the imagination, creativity, memory, and desire. The performance studies scholar and theater practitioner John McGrath is perhaps the best spokesperson for strategic opacity: "The challenge of communication under surveillance," he writes, "is to develop a continual proliferation of codes, beyond any one authority's translation skills."[34]

Along these lines, the literary critic Amitava Kumar advocates a postcolonial approach to surveillance that embraces the impossibility of translation. In his poetic treatise *Passport Photos*, Kumar makes the case that in postcolonial experience subjectivity, culture, memory, and history far exceed an individual's immigration record. For Kumar, poetry and stories are the best means we have of practicing (and protecting) human freedom and dignity from the ravages of capitalism and the poverty of the information age.[35] Likewise, McGrath writes: "A key means of introducing the indeterminacy, the excess of lived space, into government and corporate surveillance spaces will be the use of code."[36]

The less-transparency position is informed by Foucault's critique of surveillance, which directly implicates Enlightenment philosophers in the development of modern surveillance societies.[37] In Foucault's interpretation of Jean-Jacques Rousseau, mutual monitoring guarantees justice. Individuals are equal because equally trapped and reciprocally disciplined by the gaze of their others. In a related formulation, Foucault calls disciplinary power simply, "mutual and indefinite 'blackmail.'"[38] Accountability requires exposure, hence no individual may be permitted to escape visibility. As Foucault famously put it in *Discipline and Punish*, visibility *is* the trap.[39] The less-transparency approach promotes strategic opacity via the use of multiple codes, which one's surveyors cannot decrypt because they do not possess all of the necessary translation keys. This approach argues that one may continue to participate in commercial transactions and public forums without consenting to more intensive and extensive surveillance. A person performs dissent to the conditions of life in a surveillance society covertly, by cynically encrypting their performance of self for the cameras, machines, or human monitors on the lookout for trouble.

Artist Hassan Elahi's work exemplifies a third, artist-led movement, which argues that in the digital age, *more transparency is less*. After a neighbor falsely accused Elahi of hoarding gunpowder in a Florida storage space, an FBI agent stopped the artist at the Detroit airport in 2002 for questioning. Elahi learned that the FBI suspected him of involvement in the terrorist attacks of 9/11. He was mistakenly added to the terrorist watch list.[40] The artist was subjected to nine polygraph tests back-to-back. The questioning lasted for six months and left Elahi afraid to go anywhere or do anything without first notifying the FBI of his plans.[41] In response to these

FIGURE I.1 *Security & Comfort v.3.0*, Hasan Elahi (2007). Courtesy of the artist.

events, Elahi's ongoing project, *Tracking Transience,* is an elaborate online installation through which the artist tracks himself across the globe. Elahi constructs an exhaustive image archive, which consists of one alibi after another, accounting for how he spends each moment of his life-in-transit. Elahi posts about a hundred images each day of where he ate, where he used the bathroom, and which rooms he occupied (figure I.1). He also posts every debit card transaction he makes and wears a GPS device, which reports his real-time location on a map featured on his website.[42]

The artist collages the images he makes while in transit for exhibition in museum and art gallery spaces. In these works, opaque series of plates of food and toilets allude to the exhaustion of an ob-scene body that is never done proving its innocence. The food and waste montages make mocking allusion to the permeable boundaries and longed for transparency of his suspect body: what was once exterior to the body is incorporated and finally shat out again. Rather than implying a depth to be accessed, the photomontages display the surface accumulation of visual information, the exhaustive collection and display of evidence that only ever refers back to the passenger's mundane bodily functions carried out in a variety of locales. The artist's use of repetition and difference (i.e., same shit/shot, different toilet) mocks the security state's desire for total control over a suspect who will prove reliably predictable. The artist pokes fun at the fantasy of the transparent body/environment "eliminated" of risk (waste) through ongoing, exhausting processes of self-surveillance.

In reference to *Security & Comfort v.3.0*, a reporter from CBS News asked the artist: "Isn't that a little too much information?" In an ironic move reminiscent of Andy Warhol's response to an interviewer, "If you want to know about me, look at the surface of my paintings," Elahi responded: "No, no, I'm all about full disclosure."[43] The artist points out that you can monitor yourself more accurately than the government can.[44] He and other artists critical of surveillance practices are part of a movement called "sousveillance," which means surveillance from below. Elahi's political strategy obeys the basic laws of economics: "I've discovered that the best way to protect your privacy is to give it away."[45] He is particularly interested in critiquing information as a commodity. According to the artist, it is secrecy that gives information value; therefore if you make your secrets public, you devalue covertly collected information about yourself. He speculates that if everyone tracked himself accordingly, the resultant information flood would make it impossible for any one person to be tracked by intelligence agencies. His site gets 160,000 hits each day.[46] In the more-transparency-is-less approach, one volunteers an excess of private information in order to sow confusion among one's monitors. Some of the artists working in this movement use transparency as a means of producing a protective layer of opacity via information overload. In other words, this school advocates a form of hyperconsent to the conditions of life in surveillance societies. Persons are encouraged to provide information far in excess of what state or corporate authorities would want or could use. Taken to the extreme, micro acts of consent become macro acts of dissent, which intentionally overload the information system to the point that the information collected becomes useless.

Each of the aforementioned schools of transparency within critical surveillance studies—more, less, more-is-less—adheres to the right-to-privacy argumentative framework. The limitation of this approach is that it tends to address the problems faced by what Paul Gilroy refers to as overdeveloped societies (or surveillance societies, as they are called by scholars of surveillance studies) in relative isolation or perhaps in comparison to one another. Insofar as perturbed passengers, as well as scholars and artists critical of the recent expansion of the surveillance state, frame the problem as an issue of the right to privacy, they have not addressed the degree to which the performance of voluntary transparency has become a symbol of distinction within overdeveloped societies as against individuals and populations that are excluded from the biopolitical project of risk management.

I suggest that scholars and artists working in critical surveillance studies consider expanding the term *asymmetrical transparency* beyond the presumed domestic contexts of surveillance societies. What if *asymmetrical transparency* referenced the asymmetrical ascription of varying degrees of transparency and opacity to populations based on a biopolitical racial norm that is not narrowly phenotypical but refers instead to the current symbolic markers of one's capacity to affirm life and futurity (reflexivity, docility, ability, efficiency, savvy, and capital) versus those qualities that mark one out as excluded from that collective and coercive project? Moving in this direction is consistent with the broader, collaborative project initiated by feminist scholars of surveillance: to shift critical surveillance studies away from matters of privacy, security, and efficiency to a consideration of the political problem of combating new forms of discrimination that are practiced in relation to categories of privilege, access, and risk.[47]

When transparency is understood as the aesthetic form currently taken by cultural performances of risk management, the ground shifts from questions of more or less transparency, where transparency and/or strategic opacity appear to be answers to the problems plaguing surveillance societies, to the questions *What symbolic work does the aesthetics of transparency do in this performance? And to which other performances of transparency (or opacity) is it networked?* A revised conception of asymmetrical transparency demands a new critical practice, which proceeds by drawing connections between diverse security cultures according to a shared aesthetic of surveillance. Consequently, I adopt a transmedial method of analysis that ranges far and wide beyond the controlled spaces of securitized airports.

First, by attending to airport architecture, personal computing, and mobile consumer devices, I am able to describe, critique, and theorize the transparent traveler as the embodiment of a cultural ideal of slick submission to surveillance in the post-9/11 era. Attention to the architectures through which the transparent traveler moves and the mobile devices that she carries with her en route enables me to draw out the broader global fantasy of privileged, securitized mobility, enabled by airport security as we have come to know it in the post-9/11 era.

Second, I analyze photography and computer-generated imagery (CGI) in news coverage of the war on terror because when one pays attention to the content of the form (medium), these "old" and "new" visual technologies communicate stasis and mobility, respectively. It is only via transmedial analysis of photography and CGI, then, that it becomes possible to see how the look of these respective technologies moralizes a global politics in which the mobility of some is premised on the immobility of others. Consequently, I follow my comparative analysis of photography and CGI from war coverage by US media corporations to a government-run informational website about Guantanamo Bay, where CGI invites US media consumers' virtual tourism of the prison camp.

Also featured in my analysis of the aesthetics of transparency are reality television, social networking sites, and surveillance cameras. I attend to these media because reality television and social networking sites (not to mention the saturation of public space by permanently installed surveillance cameras and mobile consumers' phone cameras) have generated and continue to nourish popular cultures of disclosure and exhibitionism. I speculate that the performances of voluntary transparency enacted and consumed via reality television, webcams, smart phones, and social networking sites may prepare passengers to take the performance of voluntary transparency at the airport in stride.

Finally, training videos and advertisements play a key role in the book because they provide sites for the analysis of performance pedagogy and popular fantasies in circulation about airport security, respectively. The passenger must learn to embody the lessons communicated to her in training videos and placards posted near the checkpoint. Airport security pedagogy not only provides passengers information in how to perform voluntary transparency but also reinforces a political culture of compulsory transparency. Alternatively, television commercials, print advertisements, and billboards provide commentary on airport security that issues from somewhere outside the vital place and thereby offer glimpses at the global, gender, racial, and class politics implied by the aesthetics of transparency.

Overall, the analysis deconstructs the transparency/opacity binary by unpacking the cultural and historical specificity of the purportedly neutral aesthetics of transparency. In the first chapter of this book, "The Art of Performing Consumer and Suspect: Transparency Chic as a Model of Privileged, Securitized Mobility," I argue that post-9/11 security cultures cultivate transparency chic, or the artful performance of consumer and suspect. In this chapter, I examine how the TSA's policies and procedures for monitoring the things passengers carry onto planes render suspect (and in some cases invert) consumer habits, object relations, and social relations among consumers as each of these is performed at other sites, such as the workplace, the mall, the street, or the gym. I describe the airport as akin to a maximum-security mall in which passengers shuttle between spaces of fantasy and scrutiny and are expected to shift rather effortlessly between the states of distraction desired of mobile consumers under capitalism and the state of high alert commanded from citizen-soldiers in the war on terror. I discuss the TSA's prohibition and confiscation of particular consumer items, the development of "airport-friendly" products, and the use of the airport security checkpoint as a trope of discipline and deprivation in advertising.

In chapter 2, "Opacity Effects: The Performance and Documentation of Terrorist Embodiment," I analyze the visual documentation and performance of terrorist embodiment by US state and commercial media for an audience of US consumers. If transparency effects make interiors into visible surfaces, opacity effects allude to interiors that remain inaccessible. I show how the producers of opacity effects use computer-generated imagery to reframe photography as the medium best suited to the work of documenting the opacity of enemies in the war on terror. The US government's public relations materials pertaining to the war on terror and major media corporations' coverage of the war repeatedly position US media consumers as the privileged visual subjects of the war on terror. Their virtual tourism of the war relies on the frozen stillness of the United States' enemies, captured within prisons and again within the frames of photography. Media consumers consent to the war by silently ignoring and/or virtually touring the clear-coated versions of the extralegal institutions established in the name of prosecuting the war on terror and visually consuming the war as game or intrigue.

In chapter 3, "Transparency Effects: The Implementation of Full-Body and Biometric Scanners at US Airports," I argue that submission to screening by full-body and biometric scanners provides US citizens and others traveling within the United States and select other nations the opportunity to distinguish themselves from would-be terrorists and thereby clear themselves of suspicion. The surveillance technologies adopted to address the threat of terrorism render passengers' three-dimensional bodies as flat visual patterns and/or flat outlines of human forms and eventually as a generic image of the human form. Likewise, submission to biometric capture offers foreign visitors to the United States the opportunity to become transparent in the sense of the trusted traveler. I provide an overview of the myriad trusted traveler programs in effect today. I analyze a State Department video that introduces foreign visitors to mandatory biometric capture in which the trusted traveler is visualized as a rudimentary outline of a human figure. The implicit logic of the video's aesthetics of transparency is that the territory and citizens of the United States are already transparent. In order to achieve the status of trusted (i.e., transparent), foreign visitors to the United States must submit to biometric capture.

In chapter 4, "How to Perform Voluntary Transparency More Efficiently: Airport Security Pedagogy in the Post-9/11 Era," I demonstrate that transportation security pedagogy addresses people's capacities to be trained to perform voluntary transparency, unless limited by a medical condition or disability. In this chapter, I analyze two pedagogical campaigns designed to train the traveling public in the art of efficient submission to post-9/11 security protocols. I also examine two pedagogical campaigns addressed to TSA employees. The first trains agents to be sensitive when performing physical pat-down inspections on those passengers unable to be screened by machine because of a disability or medical condition, and the second teaches TSA employees how to provide security with a smile. Across these texts, one finds a range of contradictory social models, including egalitarian, ruthless individualism and market competition, government assistance for those unable to perform reflexive governance and the good-vibes security state. Despite the different models of social relations among passengers and between passengers and representatives of the security state on offer in these campaigns, the aesthetics of transparency provides consistency. If one shifts the unit of analysis from the individual passenger or TSA employee to the airport environment, then one can begin to see how each of these campaigns promotes a transparent airport environment.

Chapter 5, "Performing Involuntary Transparency: The TSA's Turn to Behavior Detection," demonstrates that performances of transparency extend to those aspects of appearance, behavior, and mannerism purportedly beyond the control of passengers. In this chapter, I explore the TSA's program in behavior detection: Screening Passengers by Observation Techniques (SPOT). Based on select Israeli security techniques, which have been modified according to a contested school of behavioral psychology in order to meet the efficiency requirements of US airports, the SPOT program approaches the passenger/suspect as a discrete individual characterized by neurological, muscular, and skeletal processes understood to be bound up in the body. At the same time, the TSA has at least partially embraced what could be characterized as a more fluid understanding of affect as something that circulates between and among bodies, objects, the airport environment, and the event of flying or of getting through security. I argue that passengers' performances of affective transparency within the space of the airport potentially pose a threat to public participation beyond, insofar as the process simultaneously isolates members of the public, each of whom may be caught in a private experience of the terror of suspicion, and breeds conformity via the pressure to perform inconspicuousness. Finally, I draw on the resources of performance studies to offer a critique of the pseudoscience informing behavior detection.

In the book's conclusion, "Transparency beyond US Airports: International Airports, 'Flying' Checkpoints, Controlled-Tone Zones, and Lateral Behavior Detection," I demonstrate how the book's theoretical and analytical contributions are relevant beyond US airports. First, I provide an overview and analysis of how the Department of Homeland Security (DHS) has attempted to influence global aviation security policy and the degree to which it has encountered push back from international institutions and other national security programs. Second, I provide a conceptualization of the *deterritorialized checkpoint*, of which the securitized airport is merely one example. The term is useful for grouping together otherwise geographically dispersed and politically diverse contexts in which security officials and vigilantes employ the aesthetics of transparency. Third, I demonstrate how the aesthetics of transparency is at work in recent attempts to control affect in public spaces beyond airports. Fourth, I discuss how the latest version of community policing in the United States mobilizes citizens to engage in lateral behavior detection. Finally, I sketch an alternative vision of the politics of mobility to the one documented and analyzed in this book. In the process, I make pointed suggestions regarding areas for further research and new interdisciplinary collaborations that would enable the alternative vision proposed.

CHAPTER 1

THE ART OF PERFORMING CONSUMER AND SUSPECT
Transparency Chic as a Model of Privileged, Securitized Mobility

A s the events of 9/11 recede further into historical memory, performances of voluntary transparency have been elevated to a mode for producing social distinction. Executed with panache, performances of voluntary transparency require the embodiment of a brand of neocosmopolitanism, which I call transparency chic. Those who practice transparency chic appreciate the aesthetic value of transparency, arm themselves with sophisticated mobile consumer electronics as so many signs of their tech savvy, and view airport security screening as one among many of the opportunities for performing their class distinction from the masses.

Consider, for example, the cover of the May 2012 Travel Issue of *Smithsonian* magazine, which visualizes summer travel as an X-ray image of the future vacationer's luggage. The generous use of negative space and the transparent blues and yellows of the mock security image lend summer vacation a hip sophistication, which extends to the home reader dreaming of, planning, or anticipating her own vacation. Rather than signaling the stress of making one's way through an airport security checkpoint, the cool blue see-through case holds the ingredients for summer relaxation: a pair of women's sunglasses, an MP3 player and ear buds, scuba fins, flip-flops, a drink mixer, and a margarita glass (figure 1.1).

AMERICA'S BEST SMALL TOWNS

FIGURE 1.1 Cover of the May 2012 Travel Issue of *Smithsonian* magazine. Cover art by Hugh Turvey at the British Institute of Radiology.

If we had to say what transparency communicates here, it is not so much the traveler's security status with the TSA as the promise of levity in the double sense of the term: the transparent traveler packs light and is prepared for pleasure. While the image is clearly an allusion to airport security, it carries no negative connotations. The fantasy of travel being peddled here is one in which the traveler moves gracefully from her home to and through a far-off destination. The cover image begs the question: in what sort of a culture does a summer reader/traveler borrow the promise of relaxation and the quality of hip sophistication from a security image?

Is this perhaps a kinder, gentler formulation of what market researcher Jim Bulin calls "preparedness chic"? Crystallized in the suburban driver's choice of a Hummer for everyday driving, preparedness chic implies a defensive ethic of mobile citizenship: "It's about not letting anything get in your way and, at the extreme, about intimidating others to get out of your way."[1] If preparedness chic has about it a character of vigilantism: mobilizing citizens to defend their homes and families and perform their own emergency management, then transparency chic is about the privilege of securitized mobility: the immense resources deployed to secure the mobility of some at the expense of many others.

In contrast to the heavy aesthetics of the armored vehicle, transparency chic celebrates self-exposure for the sake of secure mobility.[2] An index of the first-world traveler's "privileged paranoia," or her desire to reap the rewards of mobility while avoiding the risks, transparency chic takes the form of a willingness to open the live body, its accoutrements and possessions, as well as its digital double, to routine inspection and analysis.[3] An anxious ethic of mobile citizenship, transparency chic simultaneously signifies the passenger's mobility and her capture. It expresses the traveler's desire for unlimited mobility without vulnerability, awkwardness, interruption, or surprise. In a strange new twist on the old superstitious practice of wearing a charm close to the body to protect oneself during travels far from home, the transparent traveler wears her willingness to turn herself inside-out on her sleeve, as if this state of readiness-for-inspection would protect her from harm.

The clean look of transparency displayed on the cover of the *Smithsonian* magazine may reassure US readers that they will be able to interface with new locales, strange people, places, and customs without getting messy or experiencing discomfort. Like the application that "ghetto-proofs" the GPS device in your phone so that you never accidentally end up in the wrong neighborhood, where you might have to interface with poor people, transparency promises prophylactic pleasures. Blighted areas disappear from your map as the GPS leads you to one of "America's Best Small Towns," rendering the world through which you drive more transparent, in the sense of being legible to you or encoded in a manner that is already familiar to you (i.e., "Here's the strip mall with the chain store just like the one in our hometown where we can get our favorite, standardized and therefore predictable cup of coffee"). *Parochial* is the last word the transparent traveler would ever want applied to herself. Her readiness-for-inspection is supposed to be a marker of her travel savvy and therefore her cosmopolitanism.[4] Still, she finds a mock security image of pleasures neatly contained and evenly distributed in a retro-yet-compact, hand-held suitcase seductive.

In the service of securitized mobility, transparency does not symbolize genuine openness in a manner that would signal vulnerability and therefore potential threat or future injury. Sara Ahmed has written eloquently about how understandings of openness as vulnerability have caused oppressed populations like women and African Americans to curtail their own mobility:

> Vulnerability involves a particular kind of bodily relation to the world, in which openness itself is read as a site of potential danger, and as demanding evasive action. Emotions may involve *readings of such openness*, as spaces where bodies and worlds meet and leak into each other. Fear involves reading such openings as dangerous; the openness of the body to the world involves a sense of danger, which is *anticipated as a future pain or injury*. In fear, the world presses against the body; the body shrinks back from the world in the desire to avoid the object of fear. Fear involves shrinking the body; *it restricts the body's mobility precisely insofar as it seems to prepare the body for flight.*[5]

In the service of privileged, securitized mobility, select images, gestures, object relations, and signals of openness encase members of the traveling classes and their belongings in a kind of magical, securitized force field, as a means of preparing those bodies for commercial air travel. Rather than curtail their mobility, these citizens remobilize in a more securitized fashion. Transparency, as the appearance or image of openness-to-inspection, functions as a kind of mobile enclosure—a human-size zip-top bag.

Architectures of Mobility and Mobile Consumer Electronics

In modern and postmodern architecture and the consumer electronics market, transparency holds out the utopic promise of unlimited mobility, unrestricted access, and immersive experiences. In other words, the fantasy mobilized by transparency across these actual and virtual spaces is the fantasy of virtual mobility. Much has been made in the fields of architecture and media studies of transparency's utopic aspect. One could begin, for instance, with Walter Benjamin's writing on the glass and iron structures of the nineteenth century, those phantasmagorias, which "reified nineteenth-century myths around power, the market, and urban forms in ethereal structures full of movement and light."[6] More recently, contemporary media theorists Anne Friedberg and Gillian Fuller describe an affinity between the mobile and virtual gaze of the arcade-going flaneur about which Benjamin wrote and the virtual and mobile gaze cultivated in users of postmodern architecture and consumer electronics. In particular, both writers are interested in how the aesthetics of transparency operates in the postmodern era via windows and screens. Peter Adey has also written about windows and screens within airports.[7]

For Friedberg, there are two different definitions of transparency at work in the case of windows and screens. In order to theorize the similarities and differences, she borrows a distinction, drawn by architectural historian Colin Rowe and painter Robert Slutzky, between literal and phenomenal transparency: "Literal transparency is a condition of nonopaqueness, seeing through transparent materials; whereas phenomenal transparency is a means of spatial ordering."[8] In the first case, the mobility enabled by transparent materials is visual: the invitation to observe the glass pane of a window as a spatial boundary and then be invited to look past or through it. In the second case, the mobility enabled by transparency is also visual: the screen, understood as a "window" (or more likely a cubist layering of multiple "windows"), invites views onto and perhaps the virtual movement through other worlds. Friedberg argues that the distinction between literal and phenomenal transparency "offers a parallel model for a consideration of the window as a literal architectural aperture and as a phenomenal space of viewing."[9]

In the writings of both Friedberg and Fuller, the phenomenal transparency of the computer screen retains the utopic aspirations and cubist layering of glass architecture. In the history of architecture, Fuller writes, glass was a material that promised a revolutionary approach to building that would be open to the world.[10] "Glass," writes Fuller, "appears to be the perfect match for a cultural fiction that associates commercial international aviation with lightness and airiness, rather than pollution and war, for example."[11] Likewise, Friedberg notes, "Glass is described paradoxically as a 'material' that is also 'dematerializing' because of its transparency."[12] She goes on to cite Gyorgy Kepes's definition of transparency in modern architecture: "Transparency means simultaneous perception of different spatial locations."[13] For Fuller, Friedberg, and other critics, transparent building materials create a cubist layering of spatial planes. Indeed, airports celebrate modern technology by offering vistas of huge flying machines parked just outside or taking flight, exposed tracks and raised trams, and atrium views of the sky to be traversed—each of these views onto the outside world layered upon layers of interior spaces layered, via the liberal use of transparent building materials, within the space of the airport.

Transparent building materials lend airports in Chicago, Washington, Dallas, Seattle, Indianapolis, Milwaukee, Toronto, Munich, Paris, Cologne, and Jeddah (to name a few) an open, airy feel and encourage the heroic vantage point of a people that will travel as far as they can see and beyond. In the work of architects like Helmut Jahn and Cesar Pelli, the return to iron frames, glass ceilings, and walls in the 1980s and 1990s alludes to nineteenth-century train stations. The train stations were influenced, in turn, by contemporary architectures of consumption such as the Crystal Palace designed for the first World's Fair in London and the arcades of Paris, which provided visitors a realm of escape within the everyday. Organized around atriums, Jahn's structures resemble the skylit fountains and food courts of the shopping malls that proliferated during the 1980s and 1990s.[14]

Like their nineteenth-century predecessors, these postmodern architectures are sites of conspicuous consumption. Transparent building materials produce *Jetsons*-esque visual cultures that invite passengers to check one another out as they scurry by or leisurely shop and consume beverages and food at bookstores and cafés.[15] Airports celebrate the spectacle of human mobility with expansive promenades, moving sidewalks, and transparent passageways. Fuller observes that "great glass caverns and tubes dominate contemporary airport architecture, each designed by a brand name architect—Renzo Piano, Richard Rogers, Norman Forster, Paul Andreu—each with a manifesto about light, glass, aviation, and aesthetics."[16] Indeed, such architectural features organize the flows of people through the airport, producing what she calls a "motion aesthetics at the airport" or what Peter Adey, following Rachel Bowlby, writes about as the strange forward momentum of the airport.[17] Indeed, the transparent architectures of postmodern airports not only express nostalgia for the modern era's miraculous transcendence of the laws of gravity but also enable passengers' virtual, if not actual, mobility within the airport. Business travelers model how to fly well, and consumers show they have the financial wherewithal to fly at all. In most airports the semiprivate spaces of public restrooms are the only opaque, closed-off spaces—a fact reinforced by the use of stainless steel throughout.[18]

Consumer electronics are perhaps the most important prop in the savvy traveler's performance of virtual mobility within airports. This is merely one iteration of what Kelly Gates has called tech-savvy citizenship. According to Gates, tech-savvy citizens are "people for whom technical competency and active participation in their own self-government are two mutually constitutive responsibilities."[19] In the consumer electronics market, transparency promises unlimited mobility (via compact, lightweight personal technologies) and virtual access (to information, entertainment, shopping, social networks, and business contacts). Because they are designed for maximum mobility, consumer technologies are the most coveted when they have the least material presence, when they appear almost weightless, like the aptly named Macbook Air. The designers of consumer electronics strive to discover the magic ratio that will allow them to supply more screen on less body. Consumers want their personal electronics to be lacking in material substance, and they will pay more for less. In this market, transparency expresses the desire for screens that will function more seamlessly like windows onto the world. This is no longer the literal transparency of using see-through materials (as Macintosh did in the 1990s).[20] Rather, it is phenomenal transparency: the screen as a frame or phenomenal space of viewing. Ideally, the technology's innards will become so compact and lightweight as to go unnoticed, thereby facilitating the user's interaction with the screen as though it were a window. The technology enables the roving, disembodied eye of the mobile consumer via its own charmingly diminutive stature. In turn, the miniature, lightweight bodies of consumer electronics are a credit to their owners, a visible index of the consumer's timeliness, tech savvy, and spending power.

In both airport architecture and consumer electronics, transparency facilitates the viewer/user's actual or virtual mobility, sense of access (or perhaps even entitlement), and immersion in other worlds. Transparency is therefore not only an expression of the wish to escape the monotony of everyday life but also productive of some travelers' experience of privilege. Freedom is defined in relation to others. One person's freedom to travel may well impinge on another person's freedom to live his life without being treated like a tourist exhibition. "Travel and tourism," writes Lisa Nakamura, like networking technology, are commodities that define the privileged, industrialized first-world subject, and they situate him in the position of the one who looks, the one who has access, the one who communicates. Microsoft's omnipresent slogan: "Where do you want to go today?" rhetorically places the consumer in the position of the user with unlimited choices; access to Microsoft's technology and networks promises the consumer a "world without limits" where he can possess an idealized mobility. . . . A sort of technologically enabled transnationality is evoked here, but one that directly addresses the first-world user, whose position on the network will allow him to metaphorically go wherever he likes.[21]

Insofar as the literal transparency of airport architecture and phenomenal transparency of consumer electronics facilitate the first-world traveler's virtual mobility and unchecked access, they participate in the production of her utopic fantasy of transcendence through travel (virtual or actual). Transparency figures the traveler's desire to dematerialize, become a disembodied eye, and achieve the bliss of placelessness via immersion in the surface experience of other worlds.

But in the post-9/11 era, the airport has taken on the dystopic mood of terrorism prevention, becoming a highly controlled space in which passengers and their belongings bear the burden of embodying the threat of terrorism. In the space of the airport, the externalized threat of terrorism folds in on passengers and their belongings. Perhaps transparency has become the aesthetic of choice for the biopolitical regime of risk management because it repeatedly performs the desired spatial operations of exteriorization and incorporation spontaneously and simultaneously. Transparency reveals what it enfolds. As Gillian Fuller argues, "This kind of transparency generates the opportunity for continuous fluctuations of interpretation."[22] She cites Rowe and Slutsky, who argue: "By definition, the transparent ceases to be that which is perfectly clear and instead becomes that which is clearly ambiguous."[23] Even as passengers are invited to experience airports from the inside out, as an exercise in virtual and perhaps narcotic mobility (as Fuller suggests), what I call the passenger's space is subjected to the gaze of the security state and the sideways glances of suspicious peers. The passenger's space refers to a mobile field made up of a passenger's body, bags, effects, and affect.[24] Enfolded with the threat of terrorism, the passenger's space must be interpreted, deciphered, and ultimately "seen through." As Fuller puts it: "Transparency serves both the rational and irrational, alternating between an illuminating display of the previously unseen to the dark suspicions of 'what have you got to hide?'"[25]

Suspended between sites of distraction and departure gates, passengers' roles oscillate between consumers and suspects. But these subject positions ought not to be understood as diametrically opposed in the sense of the liberated consumer on the free market and the limitations on mobility exercised at the checkpoint. Peter Adey argues that the disassembly of the passenger-prosthetic subject at the checkpoint "strips down and opens up the passenger body to the airport's wishes"—and the airport's wishes are not limited to control but also include the desire for passengers willing and ready to spend money as well as time in the airport.[26] The intention behind airport design is that affected passengers "would be more susceptible to parting with their cash in the many retail concessionaries, or they would be more submissive and obedient to direction and instructions in the security-check areas."[27] In the post-9/11 airport, the marketing and surveillance strategies of "categorical seduction" and "categorical suspicion" typically applied in segregated fashion to prospective consumers and criminalized populations increasingly overlap and are alternately (and sometimes simultaneously) applied to members of the traveling public within the space of the airport.[28]

Rather than assume that the transition from consumer to suspect and back again is a smooth or uncomplicated process, as the term *consumer-suspect*, used by some scholars of surveillance studies would suggest, I attempt to slow down passengers' movements through the controlled spaces of airports long enough to pay attention to the awkwardness of this performance of dual citizenship: consumer and suspect.[29] I ask how these performances differ, and I attempt to clarify the differences between these two forms of transparency-as-openness to the environment's wishes. Finally, I examine how consumer culture has moved to appropriate airport security's aesthetics of transparency such that the differences and perturbations separating the appearances and behaviors appropriate to the conspicuous consumer from those of the suspected terrorist are rendered more seamless and perhaps less contradictory—at least on the face of things.

It also seems important to note here at the outset the defining tension animating performances of consumer and suspect within the space of the airport; namely, passengers' simultaneous experience of privilege and suspicion. Airport security post-9/11 can be understood as an extreme effort to protect first-world travelers' privileges of mobility, access, and immersion. Ironically, in its attempt to protect these privileges, airport security has inadvertently rendered passengers' consumerist values and practices suspect. Mark Salter understands airports as heterotopias or "social spaces that are 'in relation with all other sites, but in such a way to suspect, neutralize, or invert the set of relations that they happen to designate, mirror, or reflect.'"[30] In this chapter, I examine how the TSA's policies and procedures for monitoring the things passengers carry onto planes render suspect (and in some cases invert) consumer habits, object relations, and social relations among consumers as each of these is performed at other sites like the workplace, the mall, the street, or the gym.

If the Panopticon is an ideal model of disciplinary power, the post-9/11 airport constitutes what Foucault would call a compensatory heterotopia: "another real space, as perfect, as meticulous, as well arranged as ours is messy, ill constructed, and jumbled." Airports are compensatory heterotopias insofar as they express nostalgia for well-defined and controllable territories and bodies, as well as objects readily identifiable as weapons. The props currently used to produce the visual effect of the securitized airport (gray plastic bins, blue plastic gloves, zip-top bags, and X-ray machines) bespeak a hygienist's view of security, where everything is separated, sorted, zipped, sealed, and visible because evenly distributed in space—as if a clean line of sight would guarantee detection of the terrorist threat lurking within passengers and their belongings. Indeed, Foucault understands the compensatory heterotopia as an American phenomenon insofar as he holds up the Puritans of the New World as exemplary of this spatial order.[31]

Suspicious Objects

Viewed from the perspective of one who would detect and prevent terrorism, everyday consumer goods become uncanny. Yates McKee describes the predicament well: "Have we not been told to be watchful and wary of 'suspicious packages' in public spaces, and the strangers who might leave them for us? Indeed, the discourse of Homeland Security has redefined the entire horizon of object-relations in everyday life, with all things now understood in terms of their potential for unforeseen violence—a paranoiac ontology that calls for exceptional, preemptive action of all kinds."[32] The most suspicious package is the one left unattended. But the new order of object relations casts suspicion over the entire field of objects and the passengers who carry them.

The new suspicion surrounding formerly harmless objects reenacts and attempts to correct for the surprise and terror that art supplies and common small tools (i.e., X-Acto knives and box cutters) could serve as instruments of mass destruction. Mutation is the threat enfolded into every object—its potential for unforeseen and possibly sinister uses. Lisa Parks writes about the object's uncanny capacity to mutate from harmless to destructive with no notice: "Upon the conveyor belts of airport screening checkpoints, then, there is a larger drama unfolding about the unstable position of the state not only in the war on global terror but also in a world of uncertain materialities, mutable things, and camouflaged objects, where a cell phone can be a gun, a lipstick can be a knife, a teddy bear can carry a weapon, a condom can be a vessel for drug-running, and a shoe can be a ticking time bomb."[33] The TSA attempts to control for the threat of mutation by permitting passengers to carry on board only those objects and materials that are transparent in the double sense of (1) open to inspection and (2) obvious in the sense of appearing overtly as what they are and having a singular, nonthreatening function.

Passenger performances of transparent object relations require them to participate in rites of exchange. Passengers hand over banned consumer goods with small ticket prices to TSA officers with the hope of getting something in return. Catherine Bell defines rites of exchange as "those in which people make offerings to a god or gods with the practical and straightforward expectation of receiving something in return—whether it be as concrete as a good harvest and a long life or as abstract as grace and redemption."[34] Bell goes on to note that offerings are given to "praise, please, or placate divine power."[35] If one were to describe the character of the offerings made at security checkpoints, their primary magical function is to placate the angry, invisible force of terrorism and their secondary but more practical function is to please a particular security official searching or scanning one's bags. Of course, *offering* is not exactly the right word to describe the act of handing over banned items at the checkpoint insofar as the exchange is compelled by TSA policy and enforced by a uniformed guard.

The new order of transparent object relations frequently puts the good passenger and the good consumer at odds with one another. For example, tourists are not as likely to be good consumers while abroad if they risk having their souvenirs confiscated on the way back home. Likewise, families on summer vacation carrying everything with them but the proverbial kitchen sink are viewed as nuisances from the perspective of the security state and some fellow passengers. When it comes to travel, the militaristic model of troop movement: pack light (i.e., whatever you can fit in a regulation-size carry-on and zip-top bag), has displaced the family of consumers ethic: comfort above all else (i.e., take as much of home as possible with you when you go on the road). That said, the new security regulations stimulate consumption of small ticket items. In a line that captures the anxious blurring of consumer and suspect citizenship in the post-9/11 United States, Adam Gopnik speculates about where and when he might have purchased a particular razor from the proliferation of Gillette and Schick multiblade models in his medicine cabinet: "Perhaps it got made at the inner, post-security pharmacies of airports, where one went to buy the razor one had forgotten, or been too frightened (were they banned or not?) to pack."[36]

It is no mere coincidence that passengers' gestures of submission take the form of minor material offerings made at the checkpoint. Brian Massumi tells us that the tense proper to prevention is also the tense characteristic of the consuming subject: "The future perfect—or to translate the more suggestive French term, the 'future anterior'—is the fundamental tense of the time-form constitutive of the consuming subject ('will have . . . '): also readable as an imperative, the existential imperative of capitalism in its most condensed expression). 'Will have bought = will have been': the equation for capitalist salvation."[37] It begs the question: What is the equation for salvation in the age of paranoid empire? "Will have bought and had confiscated by a TSA official = will have been saved from the terrorists once again"?

Those items that make it onto the conveyor belts are subject to screening by X-ray machines. Parks reads the X-ray sequences as simultaneously dramatizing the new terror of everyday objects and exposing "the steady pace of capital accumulation." She offers an apt description of airport X-ray sequences that captures how consumer goods simultaneously signify security and threat: "What appear on the monitors are the faint traces of consumer goods at once being protected and scrutinized as potentially dangerous objects. The x-ray machine generates a spectral slideshow of twenty-first-century consumerism, so that it becomes a gothic cousin to the television commercial, manifesting the trace of already bought and used commodities moving through the world."[38] Parks hints that the circulation of partially consumed commodities in airport checkpoints threatens to mock and ultimately undermine manufactured desire for the new. Indeed, passengers who comply with federal security regulations must get over their fear of digestion, if you will—an aversion to the slightly used, chewed, worn—like the disgust and embarrassment they may feel at the sight and smell of their slightly dingy and stinky sneakers or boots on the conveyor belt. Fear of mutation aligns with fear of human interiority insofar as mutation inheres in practices of consumption. From the physiological process of digestion, to the class of consumer goods aimed at forestalling the body's slow decay, to the unpredictable, creative practices of cultural consumers—mutation describes the aspirations of consumers wishing to be made new and the messy reality of processes of consumption, both physiological and cultural.

Liquids, Gels, and Aerosols

In response to a foiled plot to simultaneously blow up as many as ten US-bound planes with liquid explosives, Britain and the United States immediately implemented strict new security measures on August 10, 2006. At British airports, carry-on bags were prohibited altogether, placing huge burdens on security staff and baggage screening systems.[39] Passengers were allowed to board planes only with the absolute essentials such as glasses, wallets, and baby formula.[40] Over the next three months, rules and regulations concerning the dimensions and contents of carry-on luggage on British flights changed six times.[41] The TSA initially banned all liquids, gels, and aerosols from commercial flights. The agency subsequently loosened its restrictions. Beginning on September 26, 2006, passengers were allowed to bring on board containers carrying three ounces or less of toiletries. Officials said the products must fit "comfortably" inside a single, one-quart clear plastic bag that zips closed. At the checkpoint, TSA screeners and X-ray machines would examine the zip-top bags.[42] The same rules would apply for international flights with destinations in the United States. British Airlines welcomed the new American regulations and called for Britain to follow suit.[43] In response to such pressures, the Department for Transport responded that it would maintain its stricter guidelines, noting, "The threat level is different for different countries."

The European Union initially ruled out a total ban, but announced that it would permanently restrict the amount of liquids permissible in carry-on luggage.[44] In November 2006, the EU passed regulations consistent with those enforced by the TSA. Passengers would be allowed to carry small amounts of liquids, gels, and aerosols onto planes (100 ml) and containers must be placed in a "single, transparent, re-sealable plastic bag—itself no more than a litre in capacity."[45] While the EU policy enabled a loosening of restrictions in Britain, it meant the implementation of stricter regulations in every other member state. Other nations quick to adopt new regulations on liquids were Canada, India, and Australia. Transport Canada initially followed Britain's lead, banning all liquids, gels, and aerosols from flights, but followed the United States in loosening restrictions in September 2006.[46] Indeed, Canada has maintained a record of strict aviation security standards ever since the bombing of Air India Flight 182 operating on the Montreal-London-Delhi route on June 23, 1985.[47] Australia initially suggested that a ban on liquids was unnecessary, but started warning of changes in September 2006.[48] By December 2006, Prime Minister John Howard announced that Australia would join the United States, European Union, and Air India in the adoption of new restrictions for carrying liquids on board commercial aircraft consistent with those enforced by the TSA.[49]

In an effort to raise awareness regarding the new zip-top bag rule in time for the 2006 holiday travel season in the United States, the TSA rolled out its "3-1-1" public relations campaign (figure 1.2).[50] The numeric title given to the zip-top bag policy was to function as a mnemonic device for travelers being retooled for the age of aviation insecurity: three-ounce or smaller containers of liquid or gel; one quart-size clear plastic, zip-top bag holding three-ounce or smaller containers; one bag per traveler placed in the security bin. Reminiscent of a governmental service telephone number, 3-1-1 sounded like 4-1-1 or a tamer version of 9-1-1. Not exactly a sense of emergency but more of a call to public service, 3-1-1 demanded something of travelers and in so doing extended them some measure of control (one quart) over their own air safety.

Since the TSA instituted the 3-1-1 policy airport security checkpoints within the United States have regularly featured rotating displays of personal hygiene and grooming products. By putting passengers' toiletries on display, the policy inadvertently models their management of the grotesque body for the audience of their peers and the TSA officers working the checkpoint. Indeed, the hygienic appeal of the zip-top bag works with the miniaturized grooming gear it displays to promote a campy vision of flight as good, clean . . . well, not fun exactly, but security comes first!

FIGURE 1.2 Graphic from a brochure on the TSA's 3-1-1 policy.

As an added bonus, the bag protects a passenger's other belongings and luggage from unforeseen spills or leaks in transit. On a symbolic level, fluids are particularly dangerous in an era that fears the invasion of foreign bodies and mutable or indefinite matter. Travel reporter Joe Sharkey's list of "acceptable" liquids demonstrates the fluidity between the bodies of passengers and the liquids and gels they attempt to carry, ride, or wear through the checkpoint: "At first, all liquids and gels were banned. Then breast milk and baby formula were deemed acceptable, as were eye-care products, K-Y Jelly, gel-filled bras (used for both prosthetic and fashion) and gel-filled wheelchair cushions."[51]

Picking up on the anxiety circulating between passengers' bodies, prosthetic implements, and neatly zipped bags of miniature toiletries, an Australian sketch comedy show spoofed the prophylactic appeal of the zip-top bag policy by interpreting the new guidelines a bit too literally. In the *Chaser* skit, the two passengers' bodies, which are full of fluids and gelatinous substances, become the oversized, messy threats that must be contained and inspected (figures 1.3–1.4). The skit indirectly references some of the more important risk-management campaigns of the 1990s; namely, safe-sex campaigns organized in response to the AIDS epidemic.[52] In the

FIGURE 1.3 Screen capture from a skit spoofing the zip-top bag airport security policy from *The Chaser's War on Everything*, a satirical Australian comedy series broadcast on the Australian Broadcasting Corporation (ABC).

FIGURE 1.4 Screen capture of hosts riding the escalator from *The Chaser's War on Everything*, a satirical Australian comedy series broadcast on the Australian Broadcasting Corporation (ABC).

skit, the show's cohosts introduce the bit with a brief, mock-serious discussion about the zip-top bag initiative: One host remarks, "They now make you put all of your belongings in this little see-through plastic bag. It's a bit over the top, I would have thought." His cohost feigns disagreement: "No, no. I disagree. Personally, I don't think we can be cautious enough on this one." Cut to a video of the two men making their way through London Heathrow wearing only shorts and human-sized clear plastic bags.

"Is this okay? We wanted to be in compliance with the new regulations," they tell an airport employee. With some gleeful anticipation they add: "Do you think we will need to remove our shorts too?" The skit parodies the new security regulations by exaggerating compliance with the state's demand for transparency. The show's hosts deliberately take exposure too far. Showing the initiative to strip down to their shorts at home, the overzealous passengers make a mockery of the security state's attempt to train them in the art of readiness-for-inspection.

Controlled Spaces of Distraction

In practice, the layered approach to airport security virtually expands the checkpoint until its regulatory function can be said to operate throughout the entire space of the airport. In effect, there is no longer the clear division once established by the checkpoint between "sterile" and "nonsterile" sections of the airport.[53] Since 9/11, the entire environment remains contaminated. Suspicion may be concentrated at the checkpoint, but it ripples outward from there to the airport curbside pick-up and drop-off lanes, where drivers are no longer free to park for fear their automobiles will become car bombs. Suspicion follows passengers past security to the gate, where they are monitored by uniformed and remotely stationed behavior detectives and airline staff and fellow passengers, who are routinely reminded to be on alert and report any suspicious behavior or unattended baggage to the authorities.

The virtual expansion of the checkpoint throughout the space of the airport means that passengers are never done proving their innocence. In the era of the airport as nonplace, the traveler's space served, for Marc Augé, as the archetype of nonplace. This is because the traveler's mobile gaze constitutes his placeless reverie: "The ideal vantage point—because it combines the effect of movement with distance—is the deck of a ship going out to sea."[54] In the post-9/11 era, this visual relationship is reversed: the passenger's space, which includes his or her material possessions, gestures, body, and affects, becomes the object of the security state's preventative gaze. Whereas users of the airport as nonplace gained admittance to the departure gates by showing identification and passing through a metal detector and only then could partake of the pleasures of momentary anonymity, users of the airport as vital place are required to carry on performing their innocence until they leave the airport in the city of their final destination.

The liberation experienced at getting through security is no longer a welcome experience of anonymity and placeless reverie so much as a brief experience of minor relief in the midst of the dull pressure of a perpetual state of high alert. Passengers may be free to shop or eat and drink on the other side of the checkpoint, but they remain subject to state and peer surveillance and are expected to do their part for transportation security should the opportunity arise. In other words, innocence is never achieved. Just as the layered approach to airport security involves a series of moving parts, the securitized airport implies rotating roles: suspect, consumer, terrorist, and informant. Within the securitized airport, anyone can play the role of terrorist or informant. Consequently, the security technique of identity verification (e.g., checking the passenger's passport or photo ID against her boarding pass) is no longer sufficient and must be supplemented with techniques and technologies geared more toward the control of the airport as a risky site animated by the potential components of the next terrorist attack.

Despite the paranoiac ontology of material culture in the United States since 9/11, securitized airports continue to function as spaces of distraction. Scholars of urban design have noted that in the era of postfunctionalism, airports and other "junctural zones," such as train or metro stations and traffic squares or roundabouts, have become less nonplaces to move through and more destinations in their own right, places to spend time. One consequence of this trend, Justine Lloyd observes, is the incorporation of liminal spaces within junctural zones: "Distraction is increasingly evident in the inclusion of fabulous spaces within the most banal, in other words, the linking of junctural zones with liminal spaces—the airport as nightclub, the railway station as arcade, the Internet café."[55] In these trends, Lloyd argues, we see distraction becoming an end in itself: "Distraction's object is to immerse the traveler in the very surface of the travel experience."[56] Lloyd barely mentions the intensification of airport surveillance after 9/11, but it requires an amendment to her description of airports as spaces of distraction. In practice, passengers shuttle between spaces of fantasy and scrutiny and are expected to shift rather effortlessly between the states of distraction desired of mobile consumers under capitalism and the state of high alert commanded from citizen-soldiers in the war on terror. In airports across the world, consumption doubles as problem and solution. Advertisements and spaces of consumption located within airports, which once promised the mere convenience of goods and services for passengers-on-the-go, have taken on the additional burden of easing the discomfort and frustration of passengers unaccustomed to being treated as suspects.

Security checkpoints are frequently positioned within sight of places of consumption such as fast food stalls, cafés, bars, bookstores, and souvenir shops. According to Gillian Fuller and others, this arrangement produces the terminal's momentum: "Glass partitions organize a sequencing of behaviors and their accompanying spectacles according to where one is located: in customs one is searched; in the café one is served; in the departure lounge one waits."[57] For example, at Reagan National, there is a Dunkin Donuts just outside the checkpoint. It is positioned just to one side of a grand wall of windows. On sunny days, the tables in front of the stall where passengers eat donuts and drink coffee are bathed in natural light. As passengers follow the winding security queue toward the checkpoint, they turn from Dunkin Donuts to face the checkpoint head-on. Just beyond the dull, gray checkpoint, the Golden Arches beckon. Layering security and consumption in this manner gives a whole new meaning to the term *comfort food*. The spatial arrangement makes it clear that consumption has become part of the rhythm of airport security.[58] Donuts, fries, coffee, beer, or wine are the little rewards passengers can look forward to once they have made it through the checkpoint. The screening scenario creates views, framed by metal detectors and plastic partitions, of people sitting, standing, talking, drinking, eating, and browsing.

By the same token, security checkpoints are frequently and awkwardly positioned right smack-dab in the middle of things. This is the case at the Houston airport, where there is a sprawling security checkpoint positioned directly across from the food court and just out of the way of a major thoroughfare between terminals. Pedestrians and passengers being escorted to their gate on loudly beeping golf carts move through the crowd. This spatial arrangement renders the checkpoint a relatively transparent scene available to individuals who have already made it through and are nervously or leisurely awaiting their next flight. On the other side of the checkpoint, signs politely ask passengers: "Did you remember to collect all of your belongings?"

At the Toronto airport, one airline attendant offers a grave warning to passengers wishing to check in extra early: "You sure you want to go in? Once you're in, you're in." After passengers pass through security, they run into a small café, and if they keep moving in a straight line, they eventually run into a cash machine installed next to a glass box containing a currency exchange station. There is a waiting area at the money changing station, but that's about it on this side of the checkpoint. If passengers sit down for a rest, they will find themselves looking through an expansive transparent divider. Just on the other side of the massive glass wall is a walkway with a moving sidewalk and just beyond that a bookstore. It is almost like standing on one side of the street and catching a glimpse of a display window in a bookshop on the other side. The shop's flat, vertical display of books beckons passengers, but they cannot walk around or through the glass partition and enter the shop. In such visual situations, a transparent partition simultaneously communicates passengers' virtual mobility and the designed obstacles to their free movement throughout the space of the airport.

Opportunities for comfort and diversion take on additional value in the immediate aftermath of a terrorist attack or close call, when the reactionary character of risk management goes into full force, instituting new policies and procedures on the fly, an approach that inevitably leads to longer wait times for passengers. Regardless of the nature of the security incident, the first recommendation to travelers is to allow more time. While perturbing to passengers, longer wait times are good news for airport vendors. After the "Christmas Day attack" of 2009, Rick Blastein, chief executive of OTG Management, which owns and operates several restaurants and food vendors at JFK and La Guardia airports, said, "Business is stellar for us," and reports that the business saw a significant jump in sales immediately after the failed bombing.[59] If anything, spaces of distraction within airports have become more important in the post-9/11 era.

Airport-Friendly Products

Cultural theorists have long appreciated the performative dimension of consumption.[60] This tradition of scholarship raises the question of how object relations and consumer values are being reworked through the rites of exchange performed at airport security checkpoints across the United States. For instance, what new forms of peer pressure are animated by security culture's leveraging of individual mobility and national belonging in exchange for command performances of voluntary transparency? Thorstein Veblen's term *conspicuous consumption* would seem to take on new meaning within the context of the securitized airport. Rather than deriving from competitive performances for the benefit of one's peer group, the conspicuous nature of consumer habits is compelled by an external force: the TSA. In such scenarios, peers are not so much one's competitors on the consumer marketplace but potential informants, ready to turn on a fellow passenger for the sake of security or at the very least in order to punch up their own performances of voluntary transparency.

A clash of aesthetics arises in the referendum on consumer habits at the airport: the vanity of well-groomed passengers performing their best approximation of the clean, buffed, or at least well-coiffed bodies appearing in advertisments versus the stripped-down, zero-degree style of the military recruit in training. The new order of object relations displayed on conveyor belts and X-ray monitors at airport security checkpoints is caught somewhere between the old consumer trends toward luxury goods and services, sublime technology, and buying in bulk, on the one hand, and the new compulsion to pare down, miniaturize, and stop hoarding, on the other. Under the preventative gaze, consumer objects become signs not only of taste and distinction, conformity and trendiness, or material comfort but also serve as part of a mobile field of signs, made up of a passenger's body and the objects she carries. Passengers are not suspect because of their consumption per se. It is more accurate to say that their physical relationship to consumer goods constitutes the particular field under consideration at the checkpoint and gets caught up in the general aura of suspicion that surrounds passengers and their stuff as they move throughout the airport.

With time, product designers and advertisers have domesticated the threat of mutation enfolded in material objects in a manner that facilitates the coupling of security compliance and consumption of luxury goods.[61] Luxury is alternatively defined as promising the ease and efficiency of getting through more quickly and/or maintaining glamour at the checkpoint against all odds. Both versions of luxury retooled for the age of paranoid empire make class promises of exceptionalism and/or distinction. For an example of luxury as the ability to get around some of the rules and regulations of the checkpoint, consider the "airport-friendly" laptop bag—or

FIGURE 1.5 Screen capture of Skooba Design's product page.

"Checkthrough," as it is known by its creator, Skooba Design—which was developed in response to a call put out by the TSA on March 3, 2008 (figure 1.5).[62] In a video post on the TSA blog entitled "The Evolution of the Bag: Going 'Checkpoint Friendly,'" a TSA representative stands in front of a nondescript airport security checkpoint and describes the friendly-bag initiative: "The Laptop Bag Program has been an idea to get industry to give us some of their most innovative ideas for getting a laptop through screening while remaining inside the bag. We asked them to send us white papers of their best designs that they think would separate a laptop from the rest of the contents of the bag so they would give us the same image of the laptop, as if it were in a bin."

Since suspending its call for new, "airport-friendly" laptop bag designs in July 2008, the TSA has been careful to point out that it does not endorse particular brands of bags over others. The legal disclaimer posted on its website puts it bluntly: "TSA does not approve, endorse, or otherwise promote any private or commercial laptop bag design or laptop bag manufacturer. TSA will allow laptops to remain in *any* bag through security screening *provided* the bag allows for a clear and unobstructed X-ray image of the laptop, when used properly; TSA will conduct additional screening on any bag that fails to provide such an image."[63] As it turns out, an opaque laptop case is as capable of providing a good security image as a bag with a window—that is, provided the bag is of the simple sleeve variety. Zippers, straps, dividers, and pockets full of gear obstruct the view of the X-ray machine and, by extension, the TSA official. Approved bags successfully perform the function of separating the laptop out from other objects for special screening. In the spring of 2012, the *New York Times* reporter Matt Richtel endeavored to solve the mystery of why some personal electronics require a special bag or separate bin while others do not. After consulting with security experts, spokespeople for the TSA, and airline industry analysts, he concluded that the laptop rule is about appearances. An unnamed source said the laptop rule is an instance of security theater. It exists to give people a sense that something is being done to protect them.[64]

For an example of the luxury of maintaining distinction at the checkpoint, consider the feature on what is in Brazilian singer Bebel Gilberto's bag when she flies, published in the November 2009 issue of Delta's *Sky* magazine. Under beauty products, Gilberto says she only uses organic products: "Some include Dr. Alkaitis facial cleanser, EO lavender liquid hand soap, Jurlique blemish cream and my Coqui Coqui agave massage oil." As a final flourish, Gilberto notes that all of her favorite beauty products come in small sizes, "so I can carry them with no problems." Gilberto's travel tip for Delta passengers: "To go through the x-ray, I always use my Sue London slipper flats, the best slippers ever. It takes one second to take them off and put them back on."[65] Here the celebrity models consumer tricks for maintaining glamour while enduring the thoroughly unglamorous experience of getting through security.

If Gilberto offers the consuming suspect tricks for maintaining style while complying with federal security regulations, the average consumer-suspect accepts and justifies the minor deprivations of the checkpoint along the lines of: "Well, if it makes us safer, then okay, I'll pay four dollars for another bottle of water. Better safe than sorry." In contrast to these two possible responses to airport security, strategic compliance and faith in the risk management approach to terrorism prevention, there is a third option. Nonbelievers openly mock airport security regulations, but only when they are outside the vital place. A few months prior to the TSA's call for airport-friendly bags, the *Better Living through Design* blog, which describes itself as "an online resource for people interested in great design," featured a bag that may not be friendly but definitely has a sense of humor. It is an opaque canvas shopping bag with an X-ray image of the bag's pretend contents printed on its surface (figure 1.6).

Better Living Through Design > PERSONAL > **Bags** > Exposed Bag

Exposed Bag

Search by Category

Bags

Bicycles

Clothing

Gadgets

Jewelry

Packing and Travel

Personal Accessories

Written by Kris on October 26, 2007. Permalink

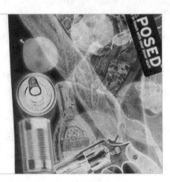

Cheeky shopping bag.
"Reveal your inner deviance with an X-ray look into your bag – featuring your usual cellphone, ipod and keys, alongside your not-so-usual Jack Daniels, brass knuckles and snub-nose revolver. Made of durable non-woven plastic fiber and available in a shoulder bag or grocery tote, it makes for an intriguing accessory for everyday use… unless, of course, you're planning on any airline travel!"

[posted by kris]

FIGURE 1.6 Screen capture from the *Better Living through Design* blog's review of the Exposed bag.

The writers at *Better Living through Design* encourage readers to "reveal your inner deviance with an X-ray look into your bag—featuring your usual cellphone, iPod and keys, alongside your not-so-usual Jack Daniels, brass knuckles and snub-nose revolver. Made of durable non-woven plastic fiber and available in a shoulder bag or grocery tote, it makes for an intriguing accessory for everyday use . . . unless, of course, you're planning on any airline travel!"[66] The bag treats transparency as an aesthetic effect, which may also function as an opaque surface for concealing what's inside, rather than facilitating acts of seeing or showing through. The truth inside is likely more mundane than the provocative faux interiority displayed on its surface. Rather than design for security's sake or design for the sake of more efficient security (as in the case of the airport-friendly bag), the Exposed bag is design for design's sake. It is the work of a designer with a vision of what a bad security image might look like.

The choice represented by the airport-friendly bag and the Exposed bag—one literally transparent and the other "transparent"—neatly encapsulates the range of possibilities for those who are subjected to the preventative gaze and must therefore demonstrate (the absence of) the terrorist threat. The consumer who buys the airport-friendly bag wants to make a show of compliance with post-9/11 federal security regulations. Her performance of voluntary transparency doubles as a performance of good citizenship. Arguably, the consumer who purchases this bag is also buying into what John McGrath has called the ideology of crime: "If you haven't done anything wrong, then you have nothing to fear." By contrast, the Exposed bag's surface image of faux interiority—at once banal and threatening—performs a reflexive critical commentary on the visual culture of airport security. It mocks the TSA's mandate of transparent citizenship by putting on transparency with a vengeance. The consumer who buys this bag likely takes pleasure in being perceived as a bad subject. If this bag could talk, it might say something like: "There's stuff in my bag, but you can't see what it is." Despite the Exposed bag's rebellious spirit and outlaw identification, the curators of the *Better Living through Design* blog do not expect a consumer to wear this bag to an airport, where the joke is likely to bomb.

Sexing the Checkpoint

Over time, the security checkpoint has become a freely circulating trope of discipline and deprivation used to stimulate uncritical practices of consumption based in outlaw identifications and overt sexualization of the checkpoint. Take, for example, a 2009 Dolce & Gabbana ad campaign that expresses the cosmopolitan traveling class's resentment of the new airport security procedures by appealing to popular nostalgia for a time when airport security was aimed at catching drug smugglers. There are two versions of the television commercial titled "Go Heist for D&G Time and Jewels." They are virtually the same, but one shows a female model trying to get through security, and the other features a male model. The commercial is shot in the visual style of a 1970s cop drama but also bears the cinematic traces of the 1970s period film *Blow*. Considering the cine matic reference, seventies-inspired fashions, and extreme thinness of the models, the ad reads as an allusion to the glamorous and dangerous lives of cocaine smugglers. The heist scenario also plays to countercultural nostalgia for the domestic terror groups of the 1970s like the Symbionese

Liberation Army or the Baader-Meinhoff gang, only there is nothing politically subversive about the fashion-plate couple starring in this commercial. The fact that our protagonists stole the jewels they are attempting to get through security makes them more sympathetic: outlaws rather than elites, or more accurately, elite outlaws. But smuggling designer jewelry through security during an economic recession does not a Robin Hood make.

The commercial opens with a four-way split screen of surveillance video stills, representing cameras positioned throughout the airport and labeled Camera A, B, C, and D, respectively. Two figures start running in the Camera B shot located in the upper right quadrant of the screen. A 1970s made-for-TV funk soundtrack begins. The surveillance angle on the action expands until it fills the whole screen. The couple is young, hip, and sexy. As they run through the airport they notice a security camera looking at them and later collide with another passenger, who knocks the woman's designer bag to the floor. A load of jewelry and watches spills out across the floor. They bend down and quickly put the loot back in her bag. Cut to an overhead security shot of the couple rushing to a spot where they stop briefly to put on the watches and bracelets, tucking them beneath their long sleeves. The couple put on dark sunglasses in synchronized fashion. Cut to another overhead surveillance video shot of them racing up to the checkpoint. She goes through first and sets the alarm off. She then removes her sunglasses and jeans and walks through again in nothing but a leather jacket, long shirt, white cotton panties, and metallic heels (figure 1.7). She sets the detector off again as though setting off down the runway.

This time a female security guard meets her. In a tight waist-level shot, we see the guard wave her wand over the passenger's wrist (figure 1.8). The sensor goes crazy. The guard takes the young woman by the wrist, pushes her sleeve up, and raises her wrist up to her face, revealing the watches and bracelets hidden there (figure 1.9). The scene is reminiscent of a lesbian seduction/fight scene from a 1970s B-movie.

The final shot zooms in on a gray plastic bin holding an Italian passport with a boarding pass tucked inside and a silver watch. The words "D&G / Dolce & Gabbana / TIME" appear over the security still life in white letters (figure 1.10).[67]

The consuming suspect races against time and adorns her body with layers of designer products in order to deter the buzz-killing sobriety of the security state and ultimately the great leveler, mortality. Her excess pro-

FIGURE 1.7 Screen capture from Dolce & Gabbana ad. Female model going through security.

FIGURE 1.8 Screen capture from Dolce & Gabbana ad. Wand over model's wrist.

duces inefficiency, which protects her from the prospect of being subject to the clock like everyone else. She will battle the fascist security state by arming herself with D&G accessories. In the fantasy world of high fashion, material deprivation means not being able to wear three pieces of designer jewelry on each wrist, and there is nothing objectionable about stripping down. Her wealth is prohibited not just because it is stolen but also because it produces distinction in a historical context of economic hardship.

The model attempts to exploit the protocols of the checkpoint. Because she is attractive, she will use stripping as a diversionary tactic to help her smuggle the D&G contraband through security. The fully uniformed fe-

FIGURE 1.9 Screen capture from Dolce & Gabbana ad. Security guard exposes model's jewelry.

FIGURE 1.10 Screen capture from Dolce & Gabbana ad. D&G logo layered over security bin.

male guard's performance of antidesire while holding our barely dressed lithe young antiheroine by the wrist as if the two were in a choreographed fight/dance scene intensifies the ad's erotic charge. A model of unattractiveness, the guard is immune to all manner of temptation and diversion. She deflects the passenger's erotic charge without responding to it. Sexiness belongs exclusively to the thin, young, and fashionable protagonist and humor to the viewers rooting for her to make it through to the other side with her contraband undetected. The ad thumbs its nose at the inappropriateness of conspicuous consumption in a recession. In a reversal of fortunes, the elite market for Dolce & Gabbana accessories is outlawed. You can still get away with it, the ad promises, just be discreet about it: tuck in your excess so that the ugly and déclassé officials running the checkpoint don't catch you. Who feels like shopping? In the commercial's final image, the confiscated watch glamorizes the gray security bin.

The digital layering of the D&G logo over the gray security bin mimics its actual use as advertising space. In December 2006, the TSA granted companies permission to sell the bottom of bins as ad space. In return for the business, ad companies must share revenues with airports and supply the TSA with gray plastic bins, carts, and stainless steel tables. The idea of a St. Petersburg–based firm, SecurityPoint Media, the twelve-by-seventeen-inch ads are glued to the bottom of the bins. The company's president, Joe Ambrefe Jr., says they came up with the idea because passengers, who must put their valuables into the bins, watch them "like hawks" until they are able to retrieve them on the other side of the checkpoint. Some airport security experts worried the ads might slow down airport security traffic, but pilot programs suggest the ads do not have an adverse effect on the efficiency of airport security.[68]

Fascinating Fascism and the Aesthetics of Transparency

In a rare case of advertising inspired by the war on terror and then installed just outside a checkpoint, passengers at the Charles De Gaulle Airport in Paris in the summer of 2009 were greeted by a glossy backlit Longchamps billboard (figure 1.11). It is difficult to imagine a more perfect visualization of airport security as an extravagant effort to uphold the privileges of mobility, access, and immersion enjoyed by some passengers. Context is important here. De Gaulle is one of the more luxurious airports in the world, with high-end boutiques around every corner. On the most basic level, the billboard announces the practicable experience of a Longchamps shopping experience awaiting wealthy passengers on the other side of the checkpoint. But like any good ad, the billboard signifies in excess of a realizable consumer experience.

The advertisement's visual content and positioning on site at the checkpoint promise the luxury and sexual appeal of a feminine, heterosexual passenger being physically carried through security by masculine, uniformed soldiers. The blond model being supported by the officers wears the vaguely fascistic gear of a horsewoman: black leather gloves, fitted black patent leather pants, and spike-heeled black patent leather boots. While she

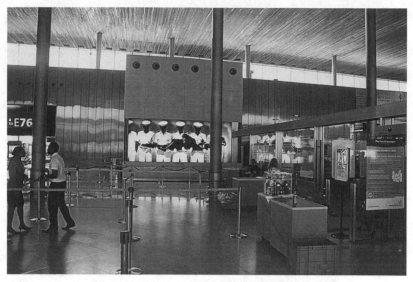

FIGURE 1.11 Photograph of airport security checkpoint at Charles De Gaulle Airport. Backlit Longchamps billboard in background. Photograph by Dustin Howes (2009). Courtesy of the photographer.

resembles a Hitchcock heroine, her escorts appear like the stiff, faceless figures of a cinematic fantasy or dream sequence, heads slightly bowed, white hats floating surreally above blacked-out faces. The ad's erotic appeal issues from the contrast between background and foreground, masculine and feminine, white and black. The officers' fitted white uniforms strike poses of varying degrees of readiness behind the full-color pop-out of the fully covered centerfold. The visual contrast suggests a physical (and possibly economic) relationship between the masculine anonymity of military service and the feminine distinction of conspicuous consumption. There are the dark, receding voids where one expects to see faces on a group of uniformed soldiers clad in bright white, and there is the model's floating white face, which is thrust forward by the reflective, black patent leather shell of clothing tightly encasing her body. But these political and economic relations are arguably upstaged by the glossy, saturated, full-color suggestion of a sexual fantasy of mutual opacity (read: anonymity)—a fantasy enabled by uniforms. The image projects the possibility of a series of sexual exchanges involving different forms of submission: blind, group submission to military authority, on the one hand, and feminine sexual submissiveness in/to physical discomfort and material luxury, on the other.

In her essay on Leni Riefenstahl's aesthetics, Susan Sontag writes: "Fascist aesthetics . . . flow from (and justify) a preoccupation with situations of control, submissive behavior, extravagant effort, and the endurance of pain; they endorse two seemingly opposite states, egomania and servitude. The relations of domination and enslavement take the form of a characteristic pageantry: the massing of groups of people; the turning of people into things; the multiplication or replication of things; and the grouping of people/things around an all-powerful, hypnotic leader-figure or force."[69] It is not much of a stretch to see these dynamics at work in the "characteristic pageantry" of the material regulations governing securitized airports. The TSA and marketers of securitized commodities group people and things around the hypnotic force of the threat of terrorism. If the transparent architectures of postmodern airports communicate the environment's openness to consumers' wishes, then the fascist aesthetics of the checkpoint, distilled in the Longchamps ad, endorse the egomania of travelers' privileged paranoia via TSA employees' performance of anonymous servitude. The Longchamps ad is rather brilliant and daring (if mockingly so) in posing the question, on site at the checkpoint: Who's submitting to whom in this scenario? Rather than stick with the knee-jerk response that passengers are being made to submit to surveillance technologies and representatives of the security state, one could argue that TSA employees are being made to submit to passengers' demands for efficient, low-risk mobility. Perhaps the ad's staging of egomania and submissiveness alludes to the relations enacted over and over again between privileged members of the traveling classes, who resent being treated like suspects, and TSA employees, who labor in the service of the former group's privileged paranoia so that they will feel more comfortable with the experience of being treated like suspects.

In the translators' foreword to the Belknap edition of Walter Benjamin's *Arcades Project*, Howard Eilan and Kevin McGlaughlin argue that part of Benjamin's interest in the arcades was that as transparent architectures they were at once the street and the interior and as such a privileged site for his study of the commodification of things, which he understood as an insidious process by which capitalism invaded "the most intimate areas of life and work." They write: "In this 'projection of the historical into the intimate,' it was a matter not of demonstrating any straightforward cultural 'decline,' but rather of bringing to light an uncanny sense of crisis *and* of security, of crisis *in* security."[70] For Benjamin, the nineteenth-century interior was a mollusk's shell stuffed full of material belongings as signs of comfort. Comforting stuff accumulates to the point of crisis or signifies a crisis *in* security.

In the twenty-first century the crisis *in* security is no longer merely a crisis of accumulation. It is also a crisis of mobility. When carried onto airplanes, material belongings turn from signs of comfort into signs of threat. So instead of the mollusk's shell crammed full of stuff, we have the neatly packed airport-friendly laptop bag. At once public and private, the transparent bag reveals the interior to be empty of nonregulation material objects and arrays regulation objects for inspection by a routine screener and/or X-ray machine. Exceptional consumer-suspects find ways of being at ease with comprehensive monitoring of their passenger spaces, self-consciously understood as a series of troubling folds or interiors-in-crisis. As passengers become more comfortable with opening themselves up to the airport's wishes, with the help of TSA employees and marketers of securitized commodities, it becomes important to ask how these developments within the culture of airport security are shaping the character of citizenship and public life in other contexts. Over time, performances of voluntary transparency have become opportunities to produce one's social distinction from the traveling masses. Airport security becomes one among many diverse sites in modern life, where neoliberal subjects prove to be more or less savvy in the ways of the world. Exceptional performances of traveler savvy require money and special, securitized consumer implements. In this context, literal transparency has taken on new aesthetic value as a marker of the hip sophistication of those who remain unruffled by post-9/11 security measures.

CHAPTER 2

OPACITY EFFECTS

The Performance and Documentation of Terrorist Embodiment

B rought to US consumers by US-owned media corporations, coverage of the war on terror employs the aesthetics of transparency to persist in mapping the world as visually accessible and physically penetrable by the US military abroad and domestic security officials at home. In this context, the aesthetics of transparency expresses a paranoid imperial longing to reproduce the former visual and positional privilege, which the West has long enjoyed. Anne McClintock writes: "What was genuinely new about the aftermath of the 9/11 attack was that, for the first time, control of the technologies of the image-world swiveled in orientation: instead of the West looking at the rest of the world through the God-eye of modern visual technologies, it was as if the globe had swung on its axis and the ex-colonized world was now gazing at the West with technologies of vision believed for centuries—by the West—to be under the West's control."[1] Since at least the time of Columbus in the Americas, the aesthetics of transparency has served colonial powers in their efforts to see through their populations and evaluate deceit. In the post-9/11 era, military and security experts perform the "diabolical opacity" of enemy bodies, and US media corporations document those performances for distribution to an audience of US consumers.[2] If transparency chic figures an idealized version of docile, suspect citizenship in the post-9/11 era (chapter 1), mediated spectacles of diabolical opacity figure its opposite: the stubbornly noncompliant, noncitizen suspects in the war on terror. There is not a direct, causal relationship between media consumption of the war on terror and voluntary transparency on the part of US media consumers. It is more accurate to say that US media corporations impart an aesthetic orientation to consumers, which prepares them to perform voluntary transparency if and when the opportunity presents itself.

US media corporations position consumers as the privileged subjects of a mobile and virtual gaze of high-tech warfare. "War is, then, the subject of these images," writes Nicholas Mirzoeff, "but it is also a means of creating subjects, visual subjects."[3] The question is: *What is the political character of the visual subjects thus produced?* US media corporations address consumers as exceptional in their technological sophistication. The media consumer's presumed virtual mobility, rather than his political power, guarantees and is proof of his privilege. A proof, Lisa Nakamura notes, which is often inversely proven by anachronistic images of frozen others.[4] Within the new regime of preemptive warfare and imprisonment, consent takes the forms of visually consuming the war as game or intrigue and silently ignoring or touring the clear-coated versions of extralegal institutions established in the name of prosecuting the war on terror.

The US media consumer's unlimited virtual mobility is premised on the enemy's stillness, via detention in the prison camps of the war and frozen by the frames of photography. Across a range of media depictions of ordinary and iconic enemies in the war on terror, photography connotes opacity and promotes immobility as the proper treatment of the diabolically opaque, whereas CGI connotes transparency and enables the mobility of the visual subjects of the war. Photography is used to allude to the interiors of enemy bodies, cave dwellings, and prisons, whereas CGI is used to provide architectural models, which render those interiors accessible to virtual tourism by the consumers of state propaganda and commercial media. The contrast between photographs full of details and empty or otherwise transparent virtual spaces and geographies underwrites a politics of vision and mobility that clings to the Enlightenment fantasy of seeing, knowing, and ultimately controlling the bodies and spaces thus surveyed. Within this paranoid imperial fantasy world, terrorist embodiment visually communicates the message that opacity will not be tolerated.

Two media images from the war on terror offer a particularly poignant

FIGURE 2.1 "Deposed Iraqi President Saddam Hussein entered and left his underground hiding place near his home town of Tikrit through this small hole in the ground in Ad Dwar, Iraq, seen in this Dec. 15, 2003 file photo." © AP Photo / Efrem Lukatsky, file.

example of how photography, in particular, may be used to document terrorist embodiment as a problem of opacity. These images visualize interiority as the true enemy in the war on terror: photographs of Saddam Hussein's spider hole (figure 2.1), taken from above, looking down into the darkness, and images of his "medical examination," featuring the dark cavity of his mouth being pried open by an inspector (figure 2.2). In the first image, the darkness of the spider hole signifies the limits of US military vision and invites trespass. It shows the Western audience an image of what was once an obstacle to transparency at the moment the cover has been removed, allowing the light of day to break through. There is a strange doubling across the two images: the dark cavern in the first signifies US mastery over the rest of the world; the dark cavern in the second signifies dominance over an enemy of the state.

In the two images, US mastery is revealed to be both visual and spatial: American soldiers can see in the dark, where they perform opacity effects on the enemy's body. Darkness may be shown only once it has been defeated, at which point it signifies a victory rather than a challenge or threat. These images of darkness and interiority demonstrate to the US viewing public that it needs the military to do its seeing for it and that the visual

FIGURE 2.2 Captured former Iraqi leader Saddam Hussein undergoes medical examinations in Baghdad in this December 14, 2003, file photo (in this image from television released by the US military).

payoff is being taken along for the ride. The featured black holes compensate for all of those other dark spaces that the US military has not been able to master or penetrate.

In the image of Saddam Hussein's medical inspection, his inspectors reveal the body's materiality. His body has an inside and an outside, held together by human flesh. Unlike the imposters that showed up in the news while he was in hiding, this body is real (really Hussein's body). US soldiers confirm the reality of his body by showing its depth and penetrating its surface. "We" get to see the dark cavity of his mouth and extreme close-ups on his teeth. The medicalization of this encounter signifies Hussein's physical submission to US authority, connotes his animality, and—to the Eurocentric viewer—may suggest a benign version of US imperialism, which has science, medicine, and the Enlightenment on its side. This painstakingly documented and widely circulated medical exam thus rehearses what Robert Stam and Ella Shohat have called the "animalizing trope" of Empire or "the discursive figure by which the colonizing imaginary rendered the colonized beastlike and animalic."[5]

For US viewers, Saddam Hussein's body must be revealed in all of its materiality, and this materiality must be exaggerated because his body has to represent both himself and another, who was still missing at the time (Osama bin Laden). Hussein's body comes to stand in not only for bin Laden, in the sense of a body double or substitution, but also potentially reads as a synecdoche of the Middle East—the region to be unilaterally "enlightened" and democratized by the US military. If Iraq is to be forcibly democratized, the medical exam connotes the primary discursive statement of Operation Iraqi Freedom: "This is for your own good, Iraq." By extension and according to the neoconservative ideologies that promoted and produced the war, it is also for the good of the entire region of the Middle East as it is imagined and misunderstood by the United States.

Virtual War Tourism

CNN's online Special Report "Saddam Hussein: Captured" offers an interactive reenactment of Hussein's capture (figure 2.3). Users may view slide shows composed from video footage of the press conference held when Hussein was captured. They may also view still photographs of the hideout or take a virtual tour of it. If they click on the audio show titled "The Raid," they will see the talking heads at the press conference interspersed with images of Saddam Hussein's medical examination and hear L. Paul Bremer, US civilian administrator in Iraq, speaking: "Ladies and gentleman [pregnant pause], we got him." Cheers and applause can be heard from offscreen. Lt. Gen. Ricardo Sanchez speaking: "This is Saddam as he was being given his medical examination today." Again cheers and applause are heard from offscreen. Sanchez proceeds: "After uncovering the spider hole, a search was conducted and Saddam Hussein was found hiding at the bottom of the hole. The spider hole is about six to eight feet deep and allows enough space for a person to lie down inside of it."

Within the microcosm of CNN's Special Report, the transparency of the US military and the Western media is communicated via CGI technology, whereas the opacity of the aging tyrant is pictured in photographs. If the user clicks on the interactive feature provocatively titled "Explore Saddam's Hideout," she gets a pop-up window with a documentary photograph of the compound on the left, duly captioned, and an interactive graphic on the right (figure 2.4).

"Explore Saddam's Hideout" is a mix between the documentary conven-

FIGURE 2.3 Screen capture of the main page from CNN.com's online Special Report, "Saddam Hussein: CAPTURED."

tions of reenactment and a video game. The user gets a bird's-eye view of the hideout and a virtual tour of the spider hole (figure 2.5). On the interactive map, the hole signifies the limits of US military vision. It establishes a temporary boundary, which may be crossed by the user if she clicks on the black square that marks the hole. At first a boundary, the hole is made to reinforce technological transcendence of the barriers that stand in the way of mere mortals. The interactive report invites US media consumers to view and virtually enter into the hole.

If the user clicks on the photo gallery titled "Saddam caught 'like a rat' in a hole" and then a tab labeled "The capture," she will see a series of still photographs taken inside the hut above ground and adjacent to the spider hole (figures 2.6–2.7). As Hussein slips from spider to rat, the clean CGI images of the hole become the messy photographs of the hut's interior. Accompanying the slides of the hut's interior are moralizing captions.

The nine-month manhunt for ousted Iraqi leader Saddam Hussein ended December 13, 2003, when he was captured in a hole beneath a small walled compound on a sheep farm about nine miles from his ancestral home of Tikrit.

Explore Saddam's hideout: Use the arrows to navigate, then click on the soldiers, the hut window and hole for details.

FIGURE 2.4 Screen capture of the interactive feature, "Explore Saddam's Hideout."

FIGURE 2.5 Screen capture of the virtual tour of Saddam's "spider hole."

The visual relationship established between "Saddam" and the user enacts a neocolonialist set of looking relations between the Middle East and the West. Hussein's history of moral reprehensibility serves as an alibi for the US media and by extension the users of CNN's website. A neocolonialist vision is rehearsed in a manner that pretends to be only about a singularly evil individual. The Online Special Report departs from previous productions of the colonized, racialized body by making the capture

FIGURE 2.6 A rudimentary kitchen stands along one wall of the small hut where Saddam was captured. © AP Photo / Efrem Lukatsky.

FIGURE 2.7 Dirty dishes clutter the hut. © AP Photo / Efrem Lukatsky.

of the colonial subject into an interactive game of narrative reenactment. Hussein is figured as the stubborn, misbehaving outlaw, who must be physically, forcibly subdued. The scene of capture is akin to a scene from an early reality television program like *Cops* or some other true-crime show. The climactic scene of this genre features cops violently subduing animalized suspects. Such programs rehearse the drama of a predictable power dynamic between individuals coded as inferior based on their race, class, and lack of education, and the rational cops, who know how to handle them. While we don't get to see Hussein taken down, the images and video of his medical exam accomplish a similar spectacle of dominance and submission.

At the risk of overstating the difference in what digital photography and CGI presently picture in news reports published by US media corporations, it is a matter of time versus space. Photography can attest to the ravages of time: the beard, the grime, the scratches, and the dirty clothes, the accumulation of dirty dishes—all evidence of time spent underground. But CGI can animate the space of the spider hole. It takes us there, not in the sense of documentary, but rather in the terms of a mobile graphic that simulates a tourist attraction and lends a strange architectural, if not surgical, precision to US military operations.[6] Whereas the CGI rendering of the spider hole offers users a relatively empty environment through which to move, photographs like those of Hussein's medical inspection overwhelm us with the fullness of even one fragment of space and time. CGI is clean technology to photography's messy capture of bodies and places. Within this visual economy, CGI signifies the technological prowess and superiority of the West and the US military in particular, whereas digital or remediated photography serves as evidence of the primitive status of the other. We are told that the photographs and video made of Hussein's medical examination were circulated to prove to Iraqis that he had in fact been captured. The reason given reveals the cultural assumption that citizens of the United States and Iraq possess differential levels of technological sophistication. The implication is that US citizens inhabit the digital era (and are therefore beyond photography as a guarantee of anything), whereas Iraqi citizens remain stuck in the age of mechanical reproduction.

In CNN's online Special Report, users are neither flaneurs nor rubbernecks.[7] They are more like visitors to an interactive display at a museum of science and technology on the National Mall in Washington, DC. The special report encourages users to identify with the US military under the guise of a democratic encounter with information made possible by new and improved media technologies. Virtual imaging technologies enable users' vicarious participation in the prosecution of the war as game, entertainment, celebration, and proof of the fact that technology is on "our" side.

Virtual Prison Tourism

An informational video available on the government-run Guantanamo Bay Prison Camp website demonstrates how the aesthetics of transparency can be strategically mobilized in order to "clear-coat" the objectionable and/or extralegal sites established in the name of persecuting the "war on terror" for an audience of US citizens.[8] The website uses the aesthetics of transparency to address reservations that US citizens and other Western viewers of the site might have about the prison and what happens within its walls.[9] The video prominently uses the word *transparent* in its tagline, "Safe, Humane, Legal, Transparent."

First, CGI is used to map the world as menaced by the threat of terrorism from the all-knowing perspective of US security experts, thereby visually justifying the existence of prison camps like Gitmo. The technology is also used to create the appearance of an open and therefore purportedly democratic institution into which "we" the viewers are invited to peer. In this manner, the aesthetics of transparency lend a democratic veneer to sites where radically undemocratic practices thrive. If declaring a state of emergency or establishing a camp brings exceptional spaces into being, as Giorgio Agamben argues, then the rhetorical practice of clear-coating attempts to render those same spaces thoroughly unexceptional when it is politically expedient to do so.

The video opens on a black screen with the true-crime television convention of typing letters in an old-computer font onto the screen. This effect equates the video screen with a computer screen at mission control. White letters appear across the top left corner of the screen: "The Global War on Terror" (figure 2.8). As the letters appear, there is a high-pitched clinking sound of "computer typing." A male voice comes in: "The United States and its allies are currently engaged in a war against terrorism that spans the globe. Joint Task Force Guantanamo plays a vital role by con-

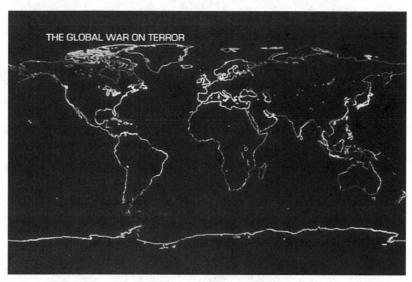

THE GLOBAL WAR ON TERROR

FIGURE 2.8 Screen capture of the "Global War on Terror" map from Joint Task Force Guantanamo Command Video.

ducting the safe, humane, legal and transparent custody of detained enemy combatants."

Once the title appears, a blurry image takes over the entire screen and quickly snaps into focus. A cool blue map of the world in outline overlays the black screen. The borders of countries and continents are incandescent and appear as mere outlines for the nations and land masses they mark. Here the transparency effect of the cool blue outline produces the opacity effect of the world as a dark, menacing place enfolded with threats unknown to the video's viewers. A thin yellow line comes across the screen from the right and meets another line coming in from the left. Where the lines meet pinpoints an area on the map. A small square of light flashes up (signaling interactivity/ information/ illumination), and then the box goes black again as the yellow outline rapidly grows larger until it disappears beyond the frame of the video screen. The effect is repeated in exactly the same manner, only this time the yellow square enters the screen from the left. The effect is repeated at different points on the screen five times in quick succession. The last time the box of light grows until the white flash covers the entire screen. A video still of the guard tower at Guantanamo comes into focus out of the bright white screen. There is an American flag displayed prominently on the guard tower. One man stands guard in fatigues. As the voice-over continues, the video is set in motion. Birds fly into the frame from somewhere in the distance behind the tower, then turn, and fly toward the tower passing just behind and over the tower, flying freely out of the frame.

The video proceeds to make the case that detainment produces intelligence that saves lives. It offers a brief history of the prison camp and furnishes visual proof that the detention center at Guantanamo is humane. The viewer learns that "following the attacks of September 11, 2001, there was a need to detain enemy combatants to keep them off the battlefield and to maintain access to them for intelligence value." Detainee operations began January 11, 2002, when "the dormant facilities of Camp X-ray, which had originally been constructed to isolate disruptive migrants, were re-opened." An overhead shot of the prison camp flashes up over the entire screen then shrinks to become the contents of a yellow box. "CAMP X-RAY" appears on the yellow line next to the box. The narrator tells the viewer: "Now detainees are housed at camp Delta, which includes communal living, medium security facilities, as well as maximum security facilities modeled after those existing in the United States." The whole screen flashes to white as if a bright light were being shined in the viewer's face, then the light stream narrows to a thin horizon line across the map of the world, the horizon becomes a yellow line, and the white letters "GITMO FACILITIES" appear over the top and centered on the screen. The screen whites out, shining light in the viewer's face again, and then up comes a video still of the barbed wire fence at Camp Delta. The camera zooms in on a sign attached to the fence: "Honor Bound to Defend Freedom."

Within the context of the video, the thin yellow frame creates the transparency effect of giving the viewer a window through which to view the closed institution. The combination of CGI and photography efficiently communicates that the prisoners, not the institution, are opaque. The yellow frame surrounding photographs of the prison's interior relays the message: "We have nothing to hide. In fact, we are proud of the quality of care that we provide for our prisoners." The minimum-security unit shot is of clean, made-up cots. On the surface of the cots, someone has neatly stacked the goods rationed to detainees: blankets, clothing, and so on. The maximum-security image features a big man with his back to the viewer, who stands guard on a cellblock. If the still images of the prison's interior are meant to demonstrate the virtues of the "transparent" institu-

FIGURE 2.9 Screen capture of inmates at Guantanamo Bay Prison Camp engaged in outdoor recreation from Joint Task Force Guantanamo Command Video.

tion, the photographs showing prisoners use a variety of visual techniques to produce opacity effects. For example, the viewer is offered a glimpse at "detainee living conditions." A yellow box displays overhead surveillance video of two detainees walking in a dirt yard. They wear white short-sleeve shirts, khaki pants, and flip-flops. The polo shirts, baggy pants, and flip-flops connote a relaxed, tropical vacation spot (figure 2.9). The figures shown walking in the yard on a bright sunny day are meant to appear ambulatory and to communicate the message that they are free to move about the yard on their own, yet they are pictured with their backs to us. The overall effect is to communicate the transparency of the institution and the opacity of the prisoners housed there.

In another image, which is meant to provide evidence of prisoners in "undisturbed prayer," we see the prisoners bent over in prayer, with their heads covered (figure 2.10). The image is there to help the video make the case that Guantanamo is a culturally sensitive institution. The viewer learns that prisoners are afforded undisturbed prayer daily and receive specially prepared meals according to their dietary needs. Detainees receive "unsurpassed medical care," which is available "24-7." The video cuts to interior shots of the camp's medical facilities, which are pictured as totally empty spaces featuring displays of the latest medical technology.

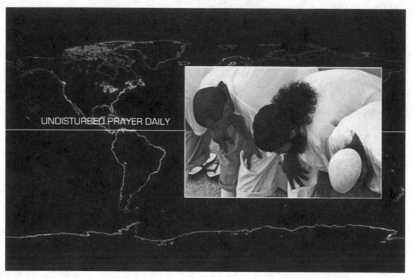

FIGURE 2.10 Screen capture of inmates in prayer position from Joint Task Force Guantanamo Command Video.

The caption "Full preventative care" appears on the screen. The narrator makes the case that detainee medical care is comparable to that provided to service members.

Although images like this are intended to humanize the prison and document the humanity of those who run the institution, they are addressed to a US audience. As such, they may simultaneously reinforce the prisoners' cultural and religious opacity in the eyes of the more xenophobic members of that audience. Arguably this effect is invited in the photograph above via signs of difference including the covered heads (connoting cultural or religious otherness for a majority-Christian audience), the contrast between the dark skin and hair and the bright white clothing, and the capture of the prisoners' bodies assuming a prayer position, which prevents the viewer from seeing the prisoners' faces.

Thinking beyond what is visible within the frame, one could argue that the blinding white of the prisoners' garb works to cancel cultural memories of the bright orange jumpsuits featured in that other, widely circulated image showing prisoners at Gitmo undergoing sensory deprivation during in-processing at the facility on January 11, 2002. In that other image, the prisoners wore orange jumpsuits, industrial earmuffs, and blackout goggles. Their hands were cuffed behind them, and they kneeled in the prison

FIGURE 2.11 Screen capture of military boots crossing the threshold at Guantanamo Bay Prison Camp from Joint Task Force Guantanamo Command Video.

yard as guards stood over them. As a result of the circulation of that image, the orange jumpsuit has become an important sign of the illegality and inhumanity of the institution in countless silent protests of the facility's use in the war on terror performed at events across the United States since 9/11.

In the video's next segment, titled "GWOT Intelligence," the narrator asserts: "Valuable intelligence has prevented terror attacks." This statement is accompanied by video footage of an American soldier in the theater of war with a "local" helper. The soldier removes weapons from a cache, followed by a shot of one soldier letting another soldier into the gate at Guantanamo, as if he'd been out in the field collecting information to bring back to headquarters (figure 2.11). The narrator continues: "The intelligence gathered from these detainees has prevented numerous attacks against coalition forces and is used for the force protection of those who work inside the wire." There is a slippage from the narrator's assertion that detainee information has protected soldiers in the field to the caption's claim that "valuable intelligence has prevented terror attacks."

The video concludes with two short segments on military commissions and freedom of the press. Transparency surfaces as the virtual offer to come view the facilities, which are pictured as empty courtrooms, and in the image of open cooperation with members of the press. Near the end of the video we see an exterior shot of a reporter being filmed doing a story on location at Gitmo. The video ends with a shot of the ground near the entrance gate of the prison camp. The viewer watches as soldiers' feet leave and enter the gate. The guards are proxies for the video's viewers, reenacting "our" having virtually crossed over the prison's threshold. As "we" are escorted back across the threshold and out of the prison, "we" see only the guards' feet. The prison guards are the ones who are allowed to remain the most opaque within the video. The video subtly communicates that the guards are mere functionaries of the institution. The gate closes and the video returns to the establishing shot of a guard tower.

The Terrorist Grotesque: A Photographic Exhibit

Media depictions of terrorist embodiment as a problem of opacity have also been used to communicate a moral argument for quiet submission to the new rules, regulations, protocols, and technologies of airport security in the post-9/11 era. Gendered and sexualized depictions of terrorist embodiment, in particular, moralize voluntary transparency. For example, in its coverage of Umar Farouk Abdulmutallab's nearly successful attack on Northwest Flight 253 from Amsterdam to Detroit on December 25, 2009, ABC News depicted the would-be terrorist as a grossly undisciplined woman. The news organization posted government photographs of the accused bomber's underwear.[10] In the photos, the suspect's briefs have been turned inside out to reveal a packet of explosive powder sewn into the crotch (figure 2.12). The garment figures the terrorist's opacity in the visual and linguistic registers of failed feminine hygiene.

Public exhibition of the government photos begs the question of whether al-Qaeda has not intentionally or otherwise crafted a brilliant, interactive durational performance art piece spoofing the deepest, darkest recesses of the American psyche. The article refers to the suspect's "underpants"—a garment worn by women and children in the United States. Indeed, there is an uncanny resemblance between Abdulmutallab's underwear, which features a secret explosives compartment, and a pair of women's underwear outfitted with a maxi pad or panty liner. The tattered, torn, and stained underwear connotes the shame of soiling oneself and arouses in the viewer the fear of losing physical control over the body and the nightmare of being publicly exposed in a compromised state. The photos call to mind the old parental admonishment "Make sure you have on clean un-

The bomb packet is a six-inch long container of the high-explosive chemical PETN, less than a half cup in volume, weighing about 80 grams.

In the second photo (right), the packet of explosive powder has been removed from the underpants and displayed separately.

A government test with 50 grams of PETN blew a hole in the side of an airliner. That was the amount in the bomb carried by the so-called shoe bomber Richard Reid over Christmas 2001.

UNDERWEAR WITH EXPLOSIVE PACKET

The underpants bomb would have been one and a half times as powerful.

Acid in Syringe Was Detonator

The packet of PETN explosive powder is shown separately here.

Tragedy was averted only because the detonator, acid in a syringe, did not work.

"It's very clear it came very, very close," said Rep. Pete Hoekstra, R.-Mich., ranking minority member of the House Intelligence Committee. "The explosive device went off, but it became an incendiary device instead of an explosive device, which is probably what saved that airplane."

UNDERWEAR AND EXPLOSIVE PACKET

The acid in the melted plastic syringe, pictured below, caused a fire but did not make proper contact with the PETN.

Abdulmutallab told FBI agents he received the bomb from and was trained by al Qaeda in Yemen over the last few months.

PETN PACKAGE

FIGURE 2.12 Screen capture from ABC News with forensic photos of Farouk Abdulmutallab's underwear, with explosive powder sewn into the crotch, packet removed from the underwear, and PETN packet.

derwear in case you are in an accident." The public shaming was reprised in the fall of 2012 when Lee Ferran of ABC News reported that the bomb failed to detonate because Abdulmutallab's underwear was dirty.[11]

Abdulmutallab's race is not marked explicitly, and his body remains out of frame, but it is the articulation of Orientalism and the female grotesque, in this case, which implicitly demands and condones his public emasculation. Feminist philosopher Mary Russo conceptualizes the female grotesque as that cavernous figure associated "in the most gross metaphorical sense" with the female anatomical body. She writes that the word *grotesque* "evokes the cave—the grotto-esque. Low, hidden, earthly, dark, material, immanent, visceral. As bodily metaphor, the grotesque cave tends to look like (and in the most gross metaphorical sense be identified with) the cavernous anatomical female body."[12] In the underwear photos a secret compartment, lurking just beneath the surface of the crotch panel, visualizes terrorist embodiment as a problem of grotesque folds and hidden depths. The series pictures the bomb smuggler as an enigma, resulting in a new hybrid construction: the terrorist grotesque.

In addition to depicting Abdulmutallab within the visual codes of failed female hygiene, the public exhibition of the terrorist's "underpants" queers him. As Puar has observed: "The depictions of masculinity most rapidly disseminated and globalized at this historical juncture are terrorist masculinities: failed and perverse, these emasculated bodies always have femininity as their reference point of malfunction, and are metonymically tied to all sorts of pathologies of the mind and body—homosexuality, incest, pedophilia, madness, and disease."[13] The photographic exhibit repeats this pattern of visual representation. The not-so-subtle final shot in the series displays only the packet of pentaerythritol tetranitrate (PETN). The article explains: "Tragedy was averted only because the detonator, acid in a syringe, did not work." The photo displays the packet lengthwise right beside the tape measure. ABC News explains: "All photos include a ruler to provide scale." Earlier in the article, ABC News reported: "The bomb packet is a six-inch long container" of the highly explosive chemical, "less than a half cup in volume, weighing about 80 grams." The final shot queers the aspiring terrorist by indirectly referencing his willingness to tuck his penis between his legs in order to make room for a substitute phallus.

The photographic exhibit documents a deliberate process in which select government officials displayed, lit, and shot the underwear and PETN packet, first together, then separately. The forensic authority visually communicated by the exhibit connotes the would-be terrorist's abject degradation in the face of that authority. In the photographs, the underwear appears to have been ripped or cut off of Abdulmutallab's body, and in the second photo, the PETN packet has been removed, exposing a hole burnt through the crotch of the underwear. Ostensibly the hole communicates the irrational extremism of a person who would strap a bomb to his body, but it may also signify the threat of penetration—a threat that extends beyond Abdulmutallab's individual body to the bodies of every suspect in the war on terror. As Jeremy Packer first observed: "Citizens become bombs, not simply by choice or through cell propaganda and training, but by Homeland Security itself."[14] Abdulmutallab's failed attempt to become bomb extends outward to all air passengers, who are treated as potentially explosive until they perform voluntary transparency.

The Privilege of Becoming Bomb

Mediated spectacles in which US military and government officials perform opacity effects on enemy bodies communicate a threat of physical force. In the moment of their consumption, such images appear to apply exclusively to figures of diabolical and stubborn opacity. Later, those scenes may be indirectly referenced in a manner that extends them outward until they include the traveling public at large. When government and security officials introduce new surveillance technologies to securitized airports, they defend the technology on the grounds that it offers a digital and/or no-touch solution to the problem of international terrorism. Advocates sell the public on the new technologies by placing them on a continuum that runs from less to more invasive of the passenger's space, thereby linking the new surveillance technologies back to mediated spectacles of US military and government officials forcibly subduing noncompliant suspects in the war on terror. This rhetorical move positions air passengers as fortunate by comparison to those who must be physically subdued and searched. Security experts talk as though passengers ought to feel reassured and perhaps even flattered that so much effort and money has been spent on the development of ways to process them as terrorist suspects without physically touching them.[15]

In security cultures of terrorism prevention, the capacity to risk and to have one's risky ventures securitized is a marker of the privilege of transparency. In addition to white privilege, in which white people are presumed innocent and people of color are presumed guilty, there is the new privilege of transparency. No one is presumed innocent. Some enjoy the privilege of being presumed capable of demonstrating (the absence of) the threat of terrorism. Others are presumed incapable, unwilling, or non-compliant. Charged distinctions between high- and low-tech surveillance, machine and human, vision and touch, divide populations presumed capable of performing voluntary transparency from those presumed to be irredeemably opaque. Ironically, surveillance technologies first tested on incarcerated populations are now capable of producing distinction from incarcerated populations when used to securitize the privileged mobility of air passengers.[16] The unstated presumption that technology is on "our" side (the side of those waging war on terror) subtly exerts pressure on docile suspects to submit to screening by new surveillance technologies in a manner that demonstrates that they are also on the side of the technology and, by extension, the side of those waging war on terror.

In this context, the high-tech screening of air passengers in securitized airports is one of the ways in which their difference from animalized suspects in the war on terror is symbolically performed and reinforced. In contrast to the stubbornly noncompliant and grotesquely opaque bodies featured in the mediated spectacles of terrorists analyzed in this chapter, the docile suspects moving through securitized airports are presumed to be self-subduing or capable of performing voluntary transparency. Air passengers need only wait to be told what to do, proceed calmly toward the machine, wait their turn, step on the footprints, lightly place their fingertips on the scanner bed, or hold still for the retina scanner until a border protection officer tells them that they are free to go. Despite the TSA's insistence that visual technologies for scanning the body, iris, and fingertips render human contact between TSA screeners and passengers unnecessary, these technologies serve a hybrid method of surveillance, which combines vision with touch.[17] TSA guidelines stipulate that TSA screeners must scan any body or belonging by a machine before they handle it.[18] Touch is defined as human-to-human contact and does not include human-to-machine contact. Arguably, the threat of physical force rationalizes each new technological solution and energizes passenger performances of voluntary transparency staged as public encounters between humans and machines. When air passengers allow their bodies to be scanned by these machines in full view of their fellow travelers, they lend their tacit support to preemptive law at home and (as distinct from) preemptive warfare abroad.

CHAPTER 3

TRANSPARENCY EFFECTS

The Implementation of Full-Body and Biometric Scanners at US Airports

In political cultures of compulsory transparency, periodic spectacles of terrorist embodiment promote the application of new surveillance technologies to the traveling public at large. In the immediate aftermath of Abdulmutallab's failed attempt, US security officials and influential media corporations framed full-body scanners as *the* security solution that would have stopped Abdulmutallab before he boarded his flight to Detroit.[1] The photographic exhibit of the aspiring terrorist's underwear (chapter 2) offers an over-the-top example of the moralizing function of opacity effects. The implicit comparisons invited by the photographs hail the US media consumer to perform good global citizenship, which is imagined, in comparison to the terrorist grotesque, as less voluminous, dank, and dirty. The exhibit presumes the media consumer's difference from and moral superiority to the opaque body on display. By portraying the would-be terrorist according to the conventions of the female grotesque, the exhibit implicitly invites US and other Western media consumers to distinguish themselves from this contemptuous figure by rendering their own bodies less grotto-esque. Indeed, the full-body scanners proposed as the solution to the threat of plastic explosives promise to clear passengers of suspicion by rendering transparency effects on their bodies. Imaged by the new surveillance technologies, docile suspects' bodies appear as flat, hollow, unadorned, or otherwise unmodified outlines.

Within the first few days of the attack, former TSA director Edmund S. "Kip" Hawley and former homeland security secretary Michael Chertoff were calling for the "rapid installation of a new generation of whole body scanners that can look underneath clothing to search for hidden weapons or explosives, which officials consider the single most significant aviation threat today."[2] First developed for use in US prisons, full-body imaging technologies were introduced on a trial basis at Tulsa International Airport on February 17, 2009.[3] On January 7, 2010, when President Barack Obama detailed the new policies that would be adopted by the DHS in light of Abdulmutallab's failed attempt, in addition to reforms in the intelligence community and better management and use of terrorist watch lists, he called for the speedy installation of $1 billion in "advanced technology equipment for screening of passengers, including body scanners at American airports and to work with international airports to see that they upgrade their own equipment to protect passengers on flights headed to the United States."[4] Since the decision to fast-track the new scanner machines, their actual usefulness as a means of terrorism prevention has been consistently called into question by reputable scientific studies and amateur experimental stunts alike.[5]

In this chapter, I analyze two surveillance technologies designed to produce transparency effects on the bodies of passengers by rendering their bodies less inscrutably grotto-esque: full-body and biometric scanners. While there are important differences between these technologies of surveillance—the first functions as a technology for imaging the body as literally transparent; the second functions as a technology of identification—both produce passengers' bodies as transparent via operations of flattening.[6] Full-body and biometric scanners attempt to control mysterious bodily folds and interiors by rendering them as ephemeral and networked flat surfaces, respectively. Full-body scanners treat the body as an opaque medium of contraband. Using X-ray and backscatter technology, the machines virtually strip passengers' clothing away in order to reveal bodies pictured as flattened, transparent outlines. In this case, security experts claim that the surveillance images produced are not stored or networked but immediately erased. Likewise, biometric scanners treat the body as an opaque bearer of transparent biological information. The machines digitally capture the unique visual patterns of fingerprints and faces and then network that information with patterns already collected in traveler, criminal, and terrorist databases. Both technologies elicit performances of voluntary transparency from passengers, who are expected to quietly submit to screening and digital capture by the machines.

Governmental and public discourses pertaining to the implementation of these surveillance technologies have conceptualized them narrowly in terms of the politics of the domestic body. By the domestic body, I mean to reference two different valences of the term *domestic*. I refer to the presumption that these technologies are objectionable because they represent an assault on the body's privacy, understood narrowly within the terms of sexual privacy. Second, I refer to the presumption of US citizenship with its typical support for or disinterest in the politics of new screening technologies and procedures selectively applied to foreign visitors to the United States. As a result, public critique of full-body scanners has been limited to a sexual privacy critique, while the new biometric technologies used to capture data on foreign visitors to the United States have been implemented with little to no discussion from US citizens. I demonstrate the extent to which the discourses of terrorism prevention assume that bodies coded as domestic are more transparent than queer and/or foreign bodies.

US public discourse domesticates full-body scanners via gendered and sexualizing scripts of being seen through as a form of romantic love, attraction, and/or repulsion. In so doing, these discourses frame the new technologies as yet another opportunity to succeed or fail at attractively imaging one's body for the male gaze. In this manner, US public discourse about the scanners suppresses the fact that the differential application of high- and low-tech surveillance methods is organized according to a racial norm, where race is understood not in the narrow terms of phenotype but in the broader terms of which populations are presumed capable of participating in the biopolitical project of terrorism prevention and which populations are written off as irredeemably opaque.[7]

Surveillance Is Sexy

Media discourses domesticated full-body scanners by reference to the norms of US media and consumer cultures, which celebrate Euro-American standards of beauty, health, and fitness. Consider a graphic titled "Technology

Published: December 27, 2009

Technology That Might Have Helped

The Transportation Security Administration has techniques that might have detected the explosives taken on board a trans-Atlantic flight Thursday, but they are in limited use in the United States and around the world. Related Article »

X-ray backscatter

Reveals concealed items through high-resolution X-ray imagery. The T.S.A. has purchased 150 backscatter units that will be installed next year. The image resembles a chalk etching.

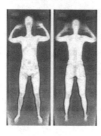

Millimeter wave screening

Reveals concealed items without exposure to ionizing radiation. There are currently 40 of these units in use at 19 airports in the United States. The image resembles a fuzzy photo negative.

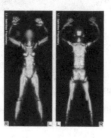

FIGURE 3.1 *New York Times* graphic depicting body images produced by X-ray backscatter and millimeter-wave screening technologies.

That Might Have Helped," published by the *New York Times* two days after Abdulmutallab's failed bombing of Flight 253 (figure 3.1).[8] The graphic pictures the images produced by X-ray backscatter and millimeter-wave screening machines, respectively. In addition to showing readers the differences between the images produced by the two types of technology, the *New York Times* describes the differences in terms of visual technologies with which the reader is already familiar. The image produced by backscatter machines "resembles a chalk etching," whereas the image produced by the millimeter-wave machines "resembles a fuzzy photo negative." It could also be said that the elongated heads and spindly fingers on the backscatter image resembles a humanoid alien from a midcentury science fiction film, while the sleek metallic perfection of the figure in the millimeter-wave image is reminiscent of the star robot in Fritz Lang's *Metropolis*. Note that both of the sample body images on display appear hollow, flat, futuristic, slender, fit, relatively young, and able-bodied—not to mention the fact that the images picture all bodies, regardless of skin tone, as fuzzy white or metallic silver outlines.

Full-body scanners examine the rough outlines of the passenger's anatomical form in order to identify "objects against bodies," or "forms that aren't traditionally part of the human physique."[9] Of note here is the telling use of the term *traditional* to describe "the human physique" (in the singular). Like whiteness or heterosexuality, transparency claims the ground of neutrality, while in fact the transparent body desired by the security state is not neutral but, more accurately, *normate*, the term Rosmarie Garland-Thomson has used to refer to what is understood as the generalizable human being or the body type thought to be normal.[10] In the context of post-9/11 security cultures, the appearance of normalcy takes on the characteristics of transparency, defined as that which we do not see or notice, as opposed to those signs of bodily difference from the norm, which register visually in the form of stigmata.[11] A generalizable body type provides a standard of transparency, which makes it possible to efficiently clear those passengers whose bodies conform to type.

The new standard of transparency also promises to discipline the female grotesque as defined by US media and consumer cultures. Consider a flirtatious piece of gonzo journalism titled "Reporter Faces the Naked Truth about Full-Body Scanners," for which Andrea Sachs of the *Washington Post* undergoes a full-body scan by a millimeter-wave machine so that she might "experience the technology's prying eyes first hand." Rather than report on which firms stand to profit from the technology's adoption or raise questions regarding its use, the reporter models for the reader how to make the adjustment to a new layer of security. The article's tone oscillates between sexual teasing and self-punishing narcissism. Sachs stresses the threat of being found unattractive in the images produced by the new machines. The reporter narrates the experience of having one's clothes virtually peeled away by the new scanner machines in terms of vanity and sexual attractiveness or repulsion, rather than as a process that renders each body suspect.

Even as Sachs worries about what she considers to be her major corporeal flaw (a belly button placed too high on her torso), she mock scolds herself to put vanity aside, for the sake of homeland security: "Get over yourself, honey: The full-body scanning machines at airport security checkpoints weren't created to point out corporeal flaws but to detect suspicious objects lurking beneath airline passengers' clothing." Sachs's commentary reassures passengers that once scanned, the body becomes nothing more than a medium or environment. But her self-admonishment, "Get over yourself, honey," presumes passengers' feminine vanity and irrelevance in scenarios of terrorism prevention. In other words, what feminist philosopher Mary Russo conceptualizes as the female grotesque (chapter 2), circulates here as a comic foil to the diabolically opaque terrorist. While the enemy's stubborn opacity rationalizes physical penetration and punishment of his body in the theaters of the war on terror, the mock vanity of the female grotesque reduces serious critique of the full-body scanners to a self-deprecating joke. In the end, Sachs tells the reader that the security expert conducting her scan eventually erased the image, but it stuck with her. She concludes the article by expressing her support for the new technology, given the very real threats terrorism poses to America's safety. "In the end," Sachs writes, "I found it comforting to know that the body scanner would uncover items missed by older equipment and that we travelers have one more layer of protection against those exceedingly crafty terrorists."

There is a politics to feeling afraid of another "crafty" terrorist attack and comforted by the installation of full-body scanners at US airports. It comes down to who gets to establish the codes and conventions of transparency and based on what type of threat construction. In the context of airport security, performing voluntary transparency is coded as hip in the postfeminist spirit of agency and empowerment via preparation of the body in anticipation of the male gaze. Because the new norms of airport security culture borrow from the norms of US consumer culture, they presume a passenger, who sees her body as a project. In their essay on how celebrity white women tweet and how those tweets are read on gossip sites, Rachel Dubrofsky and Megan Wood update Laura Mulvey's theory of the male gaze for the postfeminist digital era: "The recipient of the gaze is a participant in creating the image on display, and actively fashions the body for consumption."[12] They point out that it is only white women celebrities who are granted agency in the form of producing their bodies for the male gaze. Famous women of color are regularly discussed, critiqued, and celebrated on gossip sites, but their bodies are consistently treated as natural and therefore beyond their control. The bodies of famous white women, on the other hand, are an ongoing project or life's work of which those white celebrities can be proud because they attest to the effort put into producing the body as attractive by the standards of the male gaze.[13] Building on these observations, I argue that the good passenger operates according to a gendered and racialized model of reflexive governance. In short, the good passenger acts like a vain white woman from the United States, who labors to stay fit so that she will be ready for sex. Indirectly, then, the new surveillance technologies envision the terrorist threat by reference to (1) the figure of the female grotesque, who fails to prepare her body for the male gaze and/or the woman, who refuses male sexual advances and (2) the figure of the terrorist grotesque, a queer man of color wearing dirty bomb underwear (chapter 2).

In this context, fear of humiliation and judgment at the checkpoint is the passenger's fault. Failure to master the body project leaves "her" at risk of humiliation, not the human screener or surveillance technology's prying eyes, per se. Another *New Yorker* cartoon from the January 18, 2010, issue explores the threat of humiliation posed by the full-body scanners. In the cartoon, the passenger suffers not only the humiliation of bodily exposure but also the embarrassment of a comforting travel companion revealed. The grown man has a teddy bear hidden beneath his clothing and strapped to his waist (figure 3.2). Instead of TSA agents viewing his body image in a closed, off-site location, as they do in actual practice, the cartoon agency projects life-size full-body images of the passenger onto the wall of the airport just to one side of the checkpoint, where passengers waiting to be screened laugh and point at the unlikely revelation.

Note that while the passenger's live body is drawn straight and narrow with the slim hips of a man, his security image is drawn in the "pear shape" fat-phobically associated with the female grotesque in US popular culture. The security image functions like a funhouse mirror. The question is whether the distortion is supposed to read as a projection of the passenger's body dysmorphic disorder or as a critique of the security state's filters, which threaten to feminize and infantilize the passenger, according to this cartoon.

In reality, full-body scanners may unnecessarily expose a medical condition such as a colostomy bag, rather than a teddy bear. Feminist scholars Shoshana Magnet and Tara Rodgers argue that the body scanners may create terror and dread for passengers, "especially if these technologies 'out' individuals in their communities, violate their religious beliefs, or single them out for public humiliation, stress, and harassment."[14] The authors make a compelling case that these new surveillance technologies disproportionately affect "Othered bodies, including the intersections of transgendered, disabled, fat, religious, female and racialized bodies."[15] The *New Yorker* cartoon alludes to the threat of public humiliation but domesticates that threat via the figure of the ordinary white male traveler, who fails to be hip or sexy while proceeding through the checkpoint. He becomes the sympathetic, comic foil to the ideal of transparency chic. The cartoon invites ordinary readers to identify with him, rather than with those othered bodies for which the stakes of exposure via full-body scans run much higher.

FIGURE 3.2 Artwork featured on page 47 of the January 18, 2010, issue of the *New Yorker*. © Michael Crawford / The New Yorker Collection / The Cartoon Bank.

Ultimately, Sachs models feminine heterosexual acquiescence to the new surveillance technologies. This framing of the new surveillance technologies resonates with a romantic view of the security state as the terrified passenger's knight in shining armor and finds its precursor in American comic books and films featuring a lusty, muscle-bound superhero with X-ray vision. Consider the following iconic scene from the 1973 film adaptation of *Superman*:

On a balmy night in Metropolis, Lois Lane interviews Superman on her terrace. She wears a billowy, flowing white gown and cape. (You know what he's got on.) As Lois questions Superman about his special powers, she learns that he has X-ray vision but cannot see through lead. "What color underwear am I wearing?" the probing reporter asks frankly. A lead planter stands between them. His response is delayed. It is not until she steps out from behind the planter that he answers her. By this time, Lois has moved on to other probing questions. "Pink," he says flatly, chastely. "What?" she asks, looking confused. "They're pink, Lois." She turns to him for clarification and finds him staring at her crotch. "Oh," she nods in understanding and blushes slightly. A few minutes later as they are flying over the city together, Lois continues her interview with Superman in her head, posing additional questions in a whispery, childlike voice full of wonder: "Can you read my mind?"

In this romantic sequence from *Superman* (1973), acts of seeing and showing-through double as sex acts for the human/superhero couple, expressing the romantic longing for a super man capable of recognizing and potentially fulfilling feminine desires. Superman's ability to literally see through Lois's evening gown extends, metaphorically, to his magical capacity to read her mind. In the terms of 1970s popular psychology, his X-ray vision is not only a superpower but also a metaphor for true love or what it means to be "in sync" with another person. The superhero's X-ray vision produces pleasure for the intrepid reporter who secretly wears pink underwear. The experience of being "seen through" feminizes Lois, temporarily softening the tough-as-nails city reporter. At the end of the flight scene, Superman drops Lois off on her terrace, leaving her in what appears to be a blissful, postcoital trance so that he can return to the thankless work of fighting crime.

Sachs's article represents a widespread pattern of media representation that relied on gendered and sexualized scripts of encounters between passenger-suspects, on the one hand, and technologies or representatives of the security state, on the other. One can see this media narrative neatly encapsulated in the December 6, 2010, cover image of the *New Yorker*, which upends the romantic formula of *Superman* by reversing gender roles to comic effect (figure 3.3).

In so doing, influential US media outlets like the *Washington Post* and the *New Yorker* participate in and promote what Shoshana Magnet has called "surveillant scopophilia," which refers to the ways in which new

FIGURE 3.3 Cover art for the December 6, 2010, issue of the *New Yorker.* "Feeling the Love," by Barry Blitt.

surveillance technologies produce "new forms of pleasure [for some] in looking at the human body disassembled into its component parts while simultaneously working to assuage individual anxieties about safety and security through the promise of surveillance."[16] This selective treatment aligns the new technologies with US popular cultures of surveillance, where sex appeal (or the tragic lack thereof) is the only story being told. The "sexy" or comically asexual exposed-body is uniformly white. In this manner, the sexualization of the new surveillance technologies in US discourse domesticates the machines while obscuring the global racial norm used to determine which bodies are presumed capable of reflexive governance via high-tech screening and which bodies are presumed incapable or unwilling to practice reflexive governance and must therefore be forcibly subdued.

Cookie Cutter

The biopolitical racial norm delineating which suspect populations are appropriately managed via visual technologies and which populations may be physically handled was subtly reinforced in the white, heterosexual indignation expressed by some US citizens, who voiced their objection to the enhanced pat-downs performed on those passengers unable or unwilling to undergo scanning by the machines. A member of the House reportedly told TSA Chief John Pistole at a hearing on the scanners and the new pat-down procedures that he wouldn't want "his wife to be subjected to that."[17] Indeed, the parental furor raised by the TSA's announcement that children who refused to be scanned would undergo a modified physical inspection (without releasing any more details about what constitutes a modified pat-down "for security reasons") demonstrated both the presumption of the right not to be treated like a suspect and the threat of sexual abuse inherent in the physical pat-down.[18] For an example of this discourse at its most homophobic, consider San Diego software programmer John Tyner, who became a folk hero of sorts in the fall of 2010 when he belligerently told a TSA officer, "If you touch my junk, I'll have you arrested." The incident was caught on a cell phone video and quickly went viral. The homophobic indignation of a man angry at the loss of his privacy appeals to the sophomoric sense of humor in those privileged passengers who have only recently become the objects of state surveillance and thoroughly resent it. The sophomoric brand of humor wrongly assumes that TSA employees are the enemy and, consequently, makes them the butt of the joke.

Taking its cue from the "Don't touch my junk" incident, the only organized protest against the full-body scanners and enhanced pat-downs staged within the United States adopted the sexual privacy frame. Tyner's statement informed the We Won't Fly protest campaign, which uses the same rhetorical strategy (figure 3.4).[19] Their motto is "Stop flying until the scanners and gropers are gone."[20]

In anticipation of the 2010 Thanksgiving holiday weekend,[21] the group organized a National Opt-Out Day, which encouraged participants to forgo the scanner machines and opt instead for the enhanced pat-down inspections performed on those passengers who refuse to be scanned.[22] While organizers state that they do not wish to inconvenience other travelers, the political strategy is to attract critical public attention to both human and machine forms of bodily inspection by jamming up airport security flows on the busiest travel day of the year. Significantly, the protest refused to buy into the racist logic that understands no-touch, high-tech surveillance as a mark of distinction from those populations to which low-tech, hands-on surveillance methods are routinely applied. Media coverage of the National Opt-Out Day characterized protestors as in the statistical minority, citing a CBS News poll which found that 80 percent of Americans approve of the machines. Reports uniformly declared the

WE WON'T FLY
Act Now. Travel with Dignity.

HOME | NOV 24: NATIONAL OPT OUT DAY! | BLOG | ABOUT | TELL YOUR STORY

FIGURE 3.4 Graphic circulated in support of National Opt Out Day boycott of airport scanners, held on Wednesday, November 24, 2010. WeWon'tFly.com.

protest a bust, reassuring viewers that holiday travelers did not experience additional delays. Perhaps the protest failed, but roughly two years later major news outlets in the United States reported that the TSA had been quietly removing X-ray body scanners from major airports and replacing them with millimeter-wave machines. The TSA claimed the switch was intended to speed up lines at airports. Despite public claims that the move was about security efficiency, media reports suggest that the TSA was under legislative pressure to implement privacy software on all machines and to commission an independent analysis of the X-ray scanners' potential health impact.[23]

Given the sexualized media narratives surrounding the rapid installation of full-body scanners in US airports beginning in early 2010, it is perhaps not surprising that the major objection voiced by major US media outlets concerned the protection of passengers' sexual privacy.[24] In response to the charge that the new machines violate sexual privacy, the TSA stressed that the security images produced cannot be saved or stored. In order for the next passenger to be scanned, the previous image must be deleted. TSA

Chief John Pistole assured the public that no mobile phones or cameras are permitted in the remote viewing rooms, where agents inspect the full-body images.[25] In other words, the TSA understands the privacy violation in terms of the politics of information rather than the politics of performing submission to comprehensive surveillance—or the live experience of being produced as one of the security state's many suspects.

The TSA stresses the measures it takes to de-eroticize the body images it makes. The organization notes that faces are blurred or blocked out, no hair is visible, and human monitors are of the same sex as the passengers being screened (the TSA appeals to this same heteronormative logic when it describes and defends its organizational procedures for conducting physical pat-downs). In the arguments made for why these images are not pornographic, we learn by negation what is sexualized: faces, hair, and heterosexuality. The TSA's insistence that these are asexual images because "no hair is visible" is an instance of the Victorian postmodern. In the Victorian era, women's hair had to be braided or otherwise wrapped, worn up, and tucked in because hair was understood to be a sign of adult women's sexual power. In contrast to this, the stylization of the sexy body in contemporary pornography involves the meticulous grooming of body hair and produces the effect of the genitals as a smooth, clean, visible surface.[26] The sex industry and advertising more broadly present skin as an appealing and totally accessible surface. Contrary to the TSA's claim that body scanners produce asexual images, security images that render the body hairless are consistent with current trends in American pornography and popular grooming habits in anticipation of sex. Which raises the question of whether aesthetic additions to the pubic area would show up in the full-body images produced at the checkpoint and if so, would they be treated as problematic from the perspective of the security state?[27]

In early 2011, the TSA debuted a software patch on millimeter-wave machines at Las Vegas International Airport. The patch translates the body images produced by millimeter-wave machines into a gray, cookie-cutter outline of a human form.[28] The generic quality of the figure is designed to alleviate privacy concerns. Despite the variety of bodies scanned by the machines, the software patch pictures them all according to the same, generic outline. The lack of graphic detail serves as a control on the potential eroticism of full-body images. This is a body image designed to do nothing for the spectator—nothing, that is, other than sanitize the technology and, by extension, the security state's relationship to passengers' bodies.

The automatic detection software highlights suspicious regions with a yellow box on that part of the generic body image. This cues the TSA officer to physically inspect only that region of a passenger's body. Significantly, the generic body image appears on a screen attached to the scanning booth. The TSA officer stationed beside the machine and the passenger moving through the machine look at the screen together and wait for the green light or "okay" signal, at which point the TSA officer waves the passenger along. In January 2013, the TSA announced that it would be removing all backscatter machines from US airports, not due to health concerns but because the machines' manufacturer, Rapiscan, had failed to develop a software patch to translate detailed images of passengers' bodies into a generic outline of a human form.[29] Developed so as not to offend passenger privacy, the cookie-cutter aesthetic is honest and revealing in the sense that it pictures precisely what these technologies produce: a new normate body.

The Trusted Traveler

According to the risk-management mind-set, the territory of the United States is transparent, all things being equal, and foreign visitors to the territory are presumed to be more opaque than US citizens. In other words, the symbolic burden of embodying the terrorist threat is not born evenly by all passengers.[30] The United States compensates for its inability to trust foreign passengers (the euphemistic name for members of the voluntary Global Entry program, "trusted travelers" notwithstanding) by capturing the body's presumably transparent biological information.[31] Social sorting of passengers based on place of origin, selects non-US citizens for compulsory biometric data capture at the border, which currently takes the form of digital fingerprint scans and face and iris images.

To borrow Shoshana Magnet's definition, biometrics is "the application of modern statistical techniques to measure the human body and is defined as the science of using biological information for the purposes of identification."[32] But in the context of post-9/11 cultures of terrorism prevention, racial and ethnic profiling sneak in the back door with science as the security state's alibi and under cover of biometrics as a strategy of individualization.[33] Biometric technologies are crucial to what Magnet refers to as the outsourcing of the US border, where the bodies of foreigners are made to function symbolically as the mobile borders of foreign territories threatening to encroach on the domestic territory of the United States. The United States externalizes the threat of terrorism and inscribes it on othered bodies and bodies that reside outside the nation.[34] Insofar as the United States mandates biometric capture of foreign visitors and invites US citizens to volunteer biometric data as a means of expediting their passage through airport security, the technology's differential application to these mobile populations becomes a way of marking who does and does not belong in the territory of the United States. From the perspective of the security state, biometrics is preferable to an infinitely more complex and harder to access postcolonial sense of each passenger's multiple belongings to various places in the world.[35] Place is processed by the security state, not in the diachronic sense of one's story, culture, or background. Rather, place is affixed to the body as national identity, which takes on the status of intelligence value to security experts who perceive some states as harboring more terrorists and persons with terrorist leanings than others. In this manner, place becomes part of the technologically accessible space of the passenger.[36]

The history of using biometric technologies to outsource the US border begins with the US-VISIT program. First introduced in early 2004, US-VISIT aimed to create a "'virtual border' using computer networks, databases, fingerprints, and other biometric identifiers."[37] The program was a direct result of federal legislation implemented after the terrorist attacks of September 11, 2001. The PATRIOT Act, the Enhanced Border and Visa Entry Reform Act, and the Aviation and Transportation Security Act all mandated some kind of biometric identifier for foreign visitors to the United States as the best available means to enhance transportation security and border control.[38] Officially named the "US Visitor and Immigrant Status Indicator Technology," the program went by a different name in promotional and informational materials aimed at laypersons: "US-VISIT: Keeping America's Doors Open and Our Nation Secure." In March 2013, the US-VISIT program was replaced by the Office of Biometric Identity Management (OBIM), which is overseen by the Department of Homeland Security.[39] Through OBIM, Customs and Border Protection (CBP) officials have the ability to instantly check the name of a passenger, whose identity has been biometrically verified, against databases and terrorist watch lists using the Interagency Border Inspection System.[40]

The security state conceptualizes foreign passengers' bodies as opaque carriers of transparent biometric data there for the taking. As Magnet argues: "The knowledge generated by biometrics to test identity is asked to perform the cultural work of stabilizing identity—conspiring in the myth that bodies are merely containers for unique identifying information which may be seamlessly extracted and then placed into a digital database for safekeeping."[41] In this rite of exchange, passengers leave the security state a "token of trust" in the form of information on the biological life of their bodies in exchange for the privilege of flight to, from, or within the United States.[42] Giorgio Agamben argues that the United States' turn to high-tech collection of information about biological life crosses a new threshold in social control: "Electronic filing of finger and retina prints, subcutaneous tattooing, as well as other practices of the same type are elements that contribute towards defining this threshold. The security reasons that are invoked to justify these measures should not impress us: they have nothing to do with it. History teaches us how practices first reserved for foreigners find themselves applied later to the rest of the citizenry."[43] Indeed, this shift has already taken place as the United States and other nations turn to trusted traveler programs, which promise to expedite the screening process for passengers willing to pay a subscription fee and submit to biometric capture and background checks.

Foreign (and increasingly domestic) passengers may perform voluntary transparency by submitting to biometric capture at the border and thereby clear themselves of suspicion. Within post-9/11 security cultures, biometric capture acts as a means of domesticating foreign bodies. Run by US Customs and Border Protection (CBP), the Global Entry program is a voluntary program that promises to provide expedited clearance for "pre-approved, low-risk travelers upon arrival to the United States." Approved or trusted travelers proceed to the nearest Global Entry kiosk and present their "machine-readable passport or US permanent resident card, place their fingertips on the scanner for fingerprint verification, and make a customs declaration."[44] According to the website, "Global Entry is open to U.S. citizens, lawful permanent residents, Dutch citizens, South Korean citizens and Mexican nationals. Canadian citizens and residents may enjoy Global Entry benefits through membership in the NEXUS program." The NEXUS program "allows pre-screened travelers expedited processing by United States and Canadian officials at dedicated processing lanes at designated northern border ports of entry, at NEXUS kiosks at Canadian Preclearance airports, and at marine reporting locations." In addition to biometric data capture, approved applicants are issued a proximity Radio

Frequency Identification card that includes a photo.[45] Other, analogous programs recognized by Global Entry include the Free and Secure Trade program, a commercial clearance program for shipments entering the United States from Canada and Mexico; the Fast Low-risk Universal Crossing program, which is open to US and Dutch citizens; the Secure, Electronic, Network for Travelers Rapid Inspection (SENTRI), which expedites entry into the United States from Mexico; Smart Entry Service (SeS), a trusted traveler program operated by the government of Korea; SmartGate, which streamlines entry into Australia for eligible travelers; Smart Traveler Enrollment Program, which allows US citizens traveling to or living in a foreign country to enter information about their trip abroad, "so that the Department of State can better assist you in an emergency," and TSA Pre-Check, which expedites screening for US citizens who are members of Global Entry, NEXUS, and SENTRI "trusted traveler" programs. Benefits of the TSA Pre-Check program "may include no longer removing the following when going through airport security: shoes, 3-1-1 compliant bag in carry-on, laptop from bag, light outerwear/jacket, belt."[46] These programs are exemplary of the efficiency-through-technology approach to border security, using biometric technologies to "instantaneously pre-screen international travelers" to the United States.[47]

The International Civil Aviation Organization (ICAO) is presently working on a global electronic passport program, which would standardize and consolidate what are now separate programs. In the latest or third edition of Document 9303, "Machine Readable Travel Documents," the ICAO establishes a "globally interoperable standard for biometric identification of the holder and for the storage of the associated data on a contactless integrated circuit."[48] The current standards are based on studies conducted on the US-VISIT Program and Germany's Easy Pass Program. What was at one time a projection of science fiction becomes reality: "The body, in conjunction with biometric recognition technologies, becomes its own technology of verification."[49] To put it more succinctly, as David Lyon does, "Bodies become passwords."[50]

At the inception of the US-VISIT program, Agamben remarked that these so-called emergency measures effectively establish a new normal biopolitical relationship between global citizens and the US government. He argues that the separation of naked life from life-in-form is a procedure for constituting naked life as "the ultimate and opaque bearer of sovereignty," which can then function as the unquestionable ground for medical, scientific, and, we might add, security authority.[51] Naked life appears to offer a way around the mediation of the encounter by cultural codes, which may be indecipherable to the Border Protection Officer or TSA employee. As Magnet argues, this is a primary way that biometric technologies fail: "Biometric renderings of the body come to be understood not as a 'tropic' or 'historically specific' bodily representations, but instead are presented as plumbing individual depths in order to extract their core identity."[52] When naked or biological life becomes the new opaque ground for scientifically authorized security procedures, passengers' bodies are effectively turned inside out. Instead of interiority being a realm of mystery, possibility, and even threat, it becomes available as the new ground on which social control is organized and made to function in a smooth and efficient manner.

Modeling the Trusted Traveler

In this section, I analyze a State Department video produced to introduce international travelers to the US-VISIT program.[53] The video remains salient in the context of the global expansion, standardization, and integration of trusted traveler programs around the world. It employs the aesthetics of transparency to dematerialize the new border security procedures and de-emphasize the program's object: mass surveillance of travelers. First, the federal government puts on transparency in order to guard itself against the charges of domestic surveillance and racial profiling; second, images of transparency instruct global citizens in how to maneuver through purportedly transparent screening procedures and acts of image capture; third, images of transparency demonstrate good global citizenship and compel foreign visitors to the United States to become legible (i.e., transparent) security images.

The opening segment of the video introduces the viewer to the main characters, highlights key moments of action, and establishes the setting in which the action will take place. Perhaps most importantly, the opening sequence familiarizes the viewer with the simulated world of the video in which a generic figure makes his way through customs (figure 3.5). The video looks like the sort of informational or safety video you might have to sit through on a plane or a ship. It simulates camera work, offering the viewer level, overhead, and point-of-view shots on the action and equipment. Viewers of the video see most of the process from the visitor's perspective. For a brief period, viewers see things from the border official's

FIGURE 3.5 Screen capture of passengers moving through the border inspection process from a State Department video on the US-VISIT program.

perspective as he examines the finger scans and passenger's picture on a computer screen and at another point, from the perspective of a mounted surveillance camera. The video also offers viewers overhead shots of the finger scanners. Periodically, nondiegetic diagrammatic inserts interrupt the action much like they might in an educational video for schoolchildren.

The narrator kicks off the opening sequence: "Thank you for choosing to visit the United States. Our Department of Homeland Security has implemented a multilayer security system, the purpose of which is to ensure travel is simple, convenient, and secure." From the perspective of a mounted surveillance camera, we watch a simulation of international visitors smoothly and efficiently making their way through the inspection process. The video cuts to a shot of an international traveler facing a border protection official, who stands in a gray cubicle. A glass partition surrounds the official, separating him from the visitor, while still allowing the two to speak to one another and pass documents back and forth over the top of the partition. They never touch. The narrator continues: "This video will help you understand US-VISIT, the layer of security that uses biometrics, such as digital fingerprints to establish and verify international travelers identities." As the narrator pronounces the word *biometrics*, the

FIGURE 3.6 Screen capture of passenger submitting to biometric capture at the border from a State Department video on the US-VISIT program.

simulated passenger places four digits of his right hand on the finger scanner (figure 3.6).

Next we see the border protection officer push a camera shaped like an eyeball toward the international traveler. The next shot is of the officer's computer screen, which features the biometric data just captured: eight digits, two thumbprints, and a head-and-shoulders shot of the passenger (figure 3.7). As we look at the computer screen, the narrator says: "Unlike names and dates of birth, which can be changed, your biometrics are unique and virtually impossible to forge." During this last statement, the camera quickly pans out from a tight shot of the computer screen to an over-the-shoulder shot of the border protection officer looking at the biometric data captured on his computer screen.

In the next shot, a border protection officer passes a non-US passport back to the international traveler (figure 3.8). The narrator reassures viewers that biometric capture protects, rather than threatens, the passenger's privacy: "By using biometrics we protect your privacy and prevent the theft of your identity." The video suggests that the government collects biometric data as a public service designed to protect the passenger's digital privacy.

Next the video cuts to a nondiegetic, diagrammatic insert showing three

FIGURE 3.7 Screen capture of a border official viewing a passenger's biometric data on his computer screen from a State Department video on the US-VISIT program.

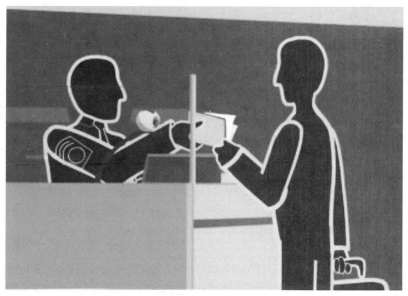

FIGURE 3.8 Screen capture of border official returning a non-US passport to a passenger from a State Department video on the US-VISIT program.

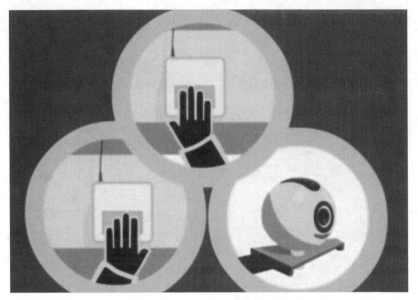

FIGURE 3.9 Screen capture of biometric technologies diagram from a State Department video on the US-VISIT program.

overlapping gold circles, each of which frames a device used in biometric capture at the border (figure 3.9). The narrator informs the viewer: "If you are between the ages of fourteen and seventy-nine, holding a non-US passport or visa, you will provide your biometrics during the entry inspection process."

The video returns to the opening shot of international travelers moving smoothly and efficiently through customs as the narrator asserts: "Biometrics allow us to expedite secure travel for you and the millions of legitimate international travelers we welcome each year."[54] The video then moves through entry and exit procedures at US air- and seaports. The video frames the inspection process during entry to and exit from the United States as "simple, efficient, and secure," and in the interest of the international passenger's privacy.

Stylistically, the video is minimalist and uses a cool, neutral blue-gray monochromatic scheme throughout, with green and yellow accents framing the technology and its products. For instance, green frames the spot on the finger scanner where the visitor is supposed to put his thumb or fingers and yellow frames his captured headshot, thumbprints, and fingerprints as they appear on the official's computer screen. While the technology and the images it produces are highlighted by the contrast of green and yellow against cool blue and gray backgrounds, the "people" featured in the video are de-emphasized in terms of color. These figures are evaporated, weightless; they match the color of the screen when it is empty (before and after the video plays). The CGI characters in this video are cool blue outlines, which is why I am tempted to refer to the star of the video as Stick Man. Actually, the best name for him might be Blueprint Man. He looks like a trace, a carbon copy of a slightly filled-out stick man drawn on another surface we cannot see. There are no blueprint women in this video. There is one blueprint child, who appears briefly in the background of the exit procedure section.

The US-VISIT video's look communicates a difference between the new, cleaner, and less invasive identification technologies and the older, messier identification technologies like film photography and ink-based fingerprinting. Writing about nineteenth-century identification technologies, Tom Gunning describes fingerprinting and photography as bodily traces because of their indexical—that is, material—relationship to the individual's body. In this video, we are ushered into a new era in identification technologies where digital imaging severs the indexical relationship between the image and the referent. A visitor no longer has to dirty her fingers to be fingerprinted. Screens and scanner beds mediate between eyes and bodies, bodies and eyes. One wonders if the US-VISIT procedures would have inspired more protest if visitors were being fingerprinted using the ink method.

"Trace" no longer seems the appropriate term. Rather than bodily traces, the new identification technologies capture image-sections of the body's surface. The new technologies do not serve a forensic project of reading a crime scene by the material traces of actions that occurred in the past. Rather, the new technologies serve a preemptive legal project of collecting data on each person's body, which may execute acts of terrorism at some undetermined point in the future. The video pictures this process of preemptive data collection as a computer simulation of a carbon copy. Blueprint Man is like a carbon copy, only cleaner. There is no tracing involved, no pen to paper, no smudging, and no dirty hands for either the visitor or the official. This clean blue-gray and neutral space is all surfaces and outlines. There are no bodies to leave traces. In fact, a real fingerprint left on the surface of the small scanner bed inhibits the proper capture of a digital "print." Experts say the cleanliness of a finger scanner determines how effectively the technology works. The more often the official cleans the surface, the more likely she is to find a match.[55]

In the State Department video, transparency is not only the desired quality of the ideal visitor to the United States, it also serves as the State Department's alibi. The video's aesthetics of transparency defends the US government against charges of racial profiling. Here transparency is transferred from the blueprint men to the blueprint border protection officers who scan them. The blue-gray monochromatic world of the ideal airport diffuses tension and racism and by implication racial profiling through sameness: transparency is the great equalizer, the guarantor of justice. Hence the video's aesthetic functions at once to project a more orderly traveler population to which its viewers should conform and defends the US government against charges of discrimination. Contrary to the video's image of democracy as a clean blue-gray field, the American Civil Liberties Union (ACLU) notes that US-VISIT was initially billed as a replacement program for the National Security Entry-Exit Registration System or NSEERS (aka the special registration program) instituted in the fall of 2002, which was widely criticized for racial profiling of Arab and Muslim men based on national origin. The ACLU argues that US-VISIT is meant to supplement, not replace, the previous program and that racial profiling is likely to continue. In a TSA operating manual accidentally leaked to the public in late 2009, the federal agency stipulates that passport holders from Cuba, Iran, North Korea, Libya, Syria, Sudan, Afghanistan, Lebanon, Somalia, Iraq, Yemen, and Algeria should face additional screening.[56]

Photography is conspicuously absent from the video, which projects an airport world in which everything is externalized: the space of the ideal airport is merely a series of visible surfaces through which the camera and by extension the viewer move with ease. The blueprint people produced by the video's aesthetics of transparency provide a way to abstract from social differences. The blueprint people are uniformly male, raceless, hairless, faceless, odorless, silent, disconnected, evenly distributed in space, unperturbed, unflappable, and so on (figure 3.10). While the blueprint people have lost most distinguishing characteristics, they retain nationality. Or more accurately, the video's narration and images reinforce the difference between insiders (US citizens) and outsiders (the rest of the world). Foreign visitors and US citizens alike are offered images of swift movement and efficiency. There is no impatience, hunger, boredom, frustration, or anxiety in this airport. There are no petty officials or victims of discrimi-

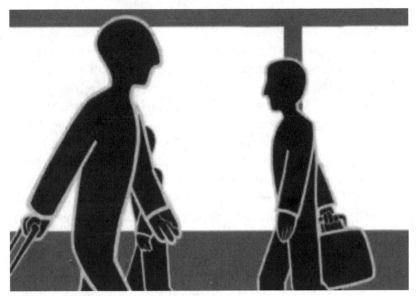

FIGURE 3.10 Screen capture of passengers moving through the airport with ease from a State Department video on the US-VISIT program.

nation: only blue outlines proceeding swiftly, but at an even pace, where they need to go.

Due to the aesthetics of transparency employed, the US-VISIT video's airport feels low on affect: just bodies and spaces here, nothing to worry about, please move on. And yet there is the "low punctum" of the Blueprint Man.[57] The video's attempt at universal signage collapses figure into ground in a manner that may communicate a sense of anomie and alienation. Or perhaps it retains affective traces of the sad and violent traditions to which this reduction belongs. The collapse of figure into ground via the video's aesthetics of transparency is vaguely reminiscent of the conventions of ethnographic photography later adopted by advertising and fashion photographers, which equate natives with their landscapes. The new aesthetics of transparency assigns the visual reduction of figure to ground positive security value. As Benjamin Muller observes: "The performance of the *trusted* traveler is rather different than simply that of the traveler, in so far as the trusted are constituted through the surveillant gaze of technology, where one's inconspicuousness is prized above all else."[58] In the instructional video, model passengers blend into the space of the airport, presumably making it easier for the TSA screener to spot the would-be terrorist.

What is perhaps most striking about the State Department video is its naive look, especially when one considers that it is selling "advanced technology" as the answer to the problem of securing the United States against terrorist threats. While looks can be deceiving, in this case they are not. Assessments by investigators at the Justice Department, scientists at the National Institute of Standards and Technology, and researchers at Stanford University have found the program to be less than satisfactory. The biggest challenge is technological in nature. The US government has already spent $1 billion for a program projected to cost up to $10 billion, which is "built on top of aging computer databases and software that government scientists concluded [three] years ago are out of date, poorly coordinated and ineffective."[59] Networking and compatibility issues are also to blame. Investigators at the Justice Department concluded that the program's effectiveness has been compromised by chronic delays in the integration of the FBI fingerprint files with the databases used by border patrol officials.[60] What is more, the US-VISIT program is not compatible with the border-crossing cards issued to Mexican visitors and workers because the two systems were not designed to interact.[61] So far, the program has been most effective at catching foreign visitors with criminal records. As a means of stopping terrorists from entering the United States, the program is less reliable. Rep. Jim Turner (D-Texas) wrote that a Stanford University study found that terrorists on the watch list who alter their fingerprints with a film of rubber gum will be caught 53 percent of the time. Other critics of US-VISIT argue that the program will not catch terrorists, who are unlikely to have fingerprint records on file with the FBI. A former deputy director in the State Department's Office of Counterterrorism makes plain the incongruity between the program's stated goals and its practical outcomes: "The reality is the universe of fingerprints for terrorists is really small. There haven't been that many major terrorist attacks."[62] One federal official said: "If we ever catch a terrorist, we will only catch an extremely dumb terrorist."[63]

If US-VISIT and subsequent trusted traveler programs have accomplished anything thus far, it has been to normalize the social spectacle of mandatory biometric data collection at US airports and seaports—to create the expectation, if not the acceptance, of such encounters between foreign nationals (and, increasingly, US citizens) and US border officials. Even if the program is not effective in catching terrorists, it has effectively introduced the idea of virtually networking global criminal databases, terrorist watch lists, and biometric data on travelers. The program has normalized the notion that it is the US government's prerogative to collect, keep, and selectively share biometric information on innocent foreign nationals and willing US citizens.[64]

Rape Jokes and the Threat of Bodily Penetration

While public discourses about new surveillance technologies voiced concern about the possibility of TSA officers abusing their authority, they rarely if ever articulated the threat of penetration by body-cavity search.[65] This is likely due to the fact that security experts sold the new surveillance technologies as no-touch solutions to the problem of international terrorism. In a context of privileged, high-tech transparency, the producers of television commercials have come closer than other cultural commentators to openly acknowledging the threat of physical penetration inherent in the performances of voluntary transparency compelled from passengers in securitized airports. Airport security–themed television commercials exaggerate the alienated erotics of the securitized airport, staging striptease and humorous scenes of sexual exploitation between passengers and security guards. Airport security–themed commercials stage actors in moments of visual confrontation between individuals and the state (represented by the architecture and technology of the checkpoint and the uniformed security guard "manning" the station). Significantly, airport security–themed ads consistently reference sex and/or sexual violation. They express popular fantasies of contaminating the sterile space of the checkpoint; at their most outrageous, they hint at a connection between border control and bodily violation.

In an Australian ad for men's underwear, an airport security guard abuses her power in order to objectify a passenger, producing visual pleasure for herself, while on the clock. Read next to similar American ads, the Australian ad suggests a transnational culture of risk management that expresses anxiety about the new technologies in terms of sexual attraction and violation. The commercial is not an attack on security guards or the state. In fact, the ad humanizes the state through the figure of a sympathetic security guard (i.e., "Who can blame the security guard for wanting a passenger this attractive?"). An Australian commercial called "Strip Search" opens on a security checkpoint. A handsome, well-built male passenger in jeans and a fitted black T-shirt drops his bag on the conveyor belt. As he approaches the metal detector, a female security guard steps into his pathway just beyond the metal detector and in order to get a better look at him. She assumes an officious posture, places her feet hip distance apart, pushes her hands into her pockets, and tilts her head back slightly in a show of suspicion. The passenger steps up to the metal detector and fills it completely with his tall, fit form. The detector goes off.

Cut to a shot of the security guard, who directs the passenger, saying, "Shirt," in a flat tone and motioning for him to take it off. Cut to a close-up on the passenger, who expresses doubt, raising his eyebrows as if to say, "Really?" He steps back and removes the shirt revealing a torso intentionally sculpted by routine weightlifting and toning exercises. The guard stares longingly and smiles slightly, then quickly regains her composure.

The passenger attempts to pass through, only to set off the detector again. "Um, pants, please," says the guard. The actor playing the passenger acts as though he is playing the role of an innocent abducted into the pornography industry, who has been asked to strip for the cameras for the first time. He steps back and reluctantly removes his pants. As he takes off his belt and pulls down his jeans, the camera moves in for a close-up of his Underdaks briefs. The Underdaks jingle chimes in as the guard looks at her fellow employee. The second guard, who works the X-ray machine, drops her chin as she stands up to get a better look at the man coming through security.

This time, the passenger makes it through and passes closely by the security guard, looking her straight in the eye as if to say, I know you want me. The second security guard reaches into the first guard's pocket and pulls out the device she was using to remotely set off the metal detector. In the final shot of the commercial her look says, "Caught you."

The underwear ad is S&M lite. The female guard is dominant. She tells the passenger what to do. She commands him to remove his clothing. Within the frame of the fantasy, he may want to question or even object to her orders, but he will capitulate. The potentially abusive slip from risk management to sexual exploitation is disarmed through a gender reversal: a homely female security guard objectifies a handsome male passenger. The ad is purportedly funny, rather than offensive, because it is clearly framed as fantasy. Casting a male model worthy of the cover image on a romance novel in the role of victim lets the viewer know that she inhabits a fantasy space. Within the frame of sexual fantasy, the gender reversal renders sexual exploitation at the security checkpoint laughable. But sexual harassment at the checkpoint is no mere fantasy or joke. As Lisa Parks points out, "Thousands of complaints have been filed" against the TSA.

What is more, she writes: "There have been letters to newspaper editors and articles re-telling stories about TSA screeners looking down the back of women's pants, cupping their breasts, or groping body parts during physical searches."[66] It bears mentioning that a similar gender reversal to the one enacted in the Underdaks commercial informs the sexual humiliation scene staged as a joke in the infamous Lynndie Englund photo out of Abu Ghraib in which the soldier holds the end of a leash. At the opposite end of the leash, a naked male Iraqi prisoner of war is down on his hands and knees, assuming the position of a dog.

First aired during Super Bowl XXXVII, a Sierra Mist commercial starring Michael Ian Black, Kathy Griffin, and James Gaffigan mocks TSA employees as corrupt and incompetent individuals. Like the police caricatured in teen comedies, who confiscate drugs in order to do them, these TSA officers take passengers' property not because it presents a threat but because they want to keep it for themselves. The passenger (played by Black) has just passed through the metal detector and is picking his bag up from the conveyor belt. He is carrying a bottle of Sierra Mist. The first TSA agent (played by Griffin) runs a security wand over Black's body and makes a beeping noise with her mouth each time the wand gets near the bottle of Sierra Mist.

"Sir, we have to take that," she says in an officious voice as she puts out her hand to receive the beverage.

Black: "I'm sorry, what?"
Griffin: "What is that, sir?"
Black: "Sierra Mist."
Griffin: "Thank you."
Gaffigan: "Please hand it over, sir. Want."
Black (calling Griffin out as a phony): "You're just going 'wah wah' when you put the thing over the Sierra Mist."
Griffin: "Wah wah. No I'm not, sir." [to Gaffigan, who plays the second TSA officer] "Boss, we have a troublemaker—wah."
Gaffigan (ominously snapping the fingertips of his blue plastic glove one by one): "Just give me the word, Wendy."
Griffin: "Wah."
Black (raises his arms in surrender): "Oh, I'm good," and walks on.

In this commercial, corrupt and incompetent TSA officials use terrorism prevention as a rationale for harassing the passenger and seizing his property. In this and other television commercials discussed in this book, close-sensing technologies like metal detectors and handheld wands become extensions or remote expressions of the security guard's body. The device's sound of alarm doubles as the body's involuntary expression of arousal. It signals banned material and a physiological change in the body of the security guard. In both commercials, the technology sounds off in response to what the guard (home viewer) wants. In the Australian underwear ad, the guard uses a remote control for the metal detector to express her physical reaction to the presence of the passenger's body at the checkpoint. In the Sierra Mist commercial the obviously fake or prop wand functions like a prosthetic sexual device or dildo held by Griffin, and the alarm goes off every time the wand is near the bottle of Sierra Mist.

But the heart of the joke in the Sierra Mist commercial is the moment when Gaffigan snaps the fingertips of his plastic gloved hand. This gesture references the medical examination and serves as visual shorthand for the threat of a security state that would go so far as to physically enter the passenger's body. Gaffigan's posture, movements, and expression communicate that he will gladly perform a body-cavity search on Black if he doesn't hand over the soda and walk away from the security checkpoint. This moment in the commercial is akin to a homophobic prison-rape joke.[67] It simultaneously references the nightmare scenario of the privileged viewer's abject fear and dissolves it: "Prison rape is funny because I am not, nor will I ever be, in prison." Or, in the Sierra Mist commercial, "Body-cavity searches are funny because I am not, nor will I ever be, mistaken for a terrorist." In other words, the commercial presumes an audience of viewers who are *not* members of the new identity category consolidated on 9/11, which "groups together persons who appear 'Middle Eastern, Arab, or Muslim'"—or at least does not care to let them in on the joke.[68]

Perhaps TSA screeners are the objects of resentment and scorn in US popular culture because, however vaguely, they allude to the inspectors, interrogators, and torturers working in prison camps in Iraq, Guantanamo Bay, and other undisclosed locations around the world. Like the comedic cinematic figure of the incompetent detective (who makes sense and produces laughs only in comparison to his ideal counterpart, the smart, hard-boiled detective), the TSA worker is portrayed as a harmless buffoon, who is hopelessly *not* up to the job of protecting "us" from the terrorists. This comedic public image of failure is culturally legible in reference to those offstage inspectors, interrogators, and torturers whose authenticity derives from their ruthless use of violent force and the threat of death.

Using sex to obscure race and ethnicity in US public discourse about post-9/11 security cultures is not a minor oversight. Rather, it is a tragically superficial distraction, which supports the unthinking adoption of a differentially applied preemptive legal framework at home and abroad. Viewed narrowly through the lens of sexual privacy and/or property rights, the new surveillance technologies appear to be Big Brother's latest assault on the citizen's individual rights. This response refuses a reflexive take on risk and thereby misses the opportunity to engage in a more challenging critique of global asymmetries in cultures of risk management. As long as transparency and opacity effects are asymmetrically ascribed across populations sorted on the basis of their presumed capacity or incapacity to participate in risk management, then the citizens of paranoid empires are content to do battle with Big Brother within the territories of nation-states and to ignore how the turn to preemptive law at home is networked to heinous extralegal practices abroad.

CHAPTER 4

HOW TO PERFORM VOLUNTARY TRANSPARENCY MORE EFFICIENTLY

Airport Security Pedagogy in the Post-9/11 Era

The transparency effects produced on and by passengers' bodies in US airports ought to be vaguely familiar and perhaps even comforting for media consumers and Internet users conversant in reality television and social networking sites. To put a spin on what Mark Andrejevic has called "the work of being watched," in reference to reality television and webcams, media savvy air passengers are perhaps not all that uncomfortable with the work of performing voluntary transparency at the checkpoint. For these passengers, partially disrobing and submitting to virtual strip-search by full-body scanners may be understood by reference to other overtly sexualized or disciplinary scenarios, like the dance club, the catwalk, or the confessional booth of a makeover reality television show. For example, the dreaded "360-degree mirror" of *What Not to Wear* serves as a useful analogy for the full-body scanners stationed at security checkpoints.

Within popular cultures of disclosure and exhibitionism operative in reality television and social networking sites, transparency involves the cultivation of one's body, face, personality, and professional and social life as surfaces rendered for spectators to read. If there is any discrepancy, it arises in the comparison between two surfaces performed for different cameras or audiences, which opens up a space for interpretation between surface and depth, or strategic performances of self versus the notion of an abiding, authentic self.[1] The voluntary transparency rehearsed via reality television, webcams, smart phones, and social networking sites may prepare passengers to take the performances of voluntary transparency required by airport security officials in stride. In the context of the computer software interface, Gillian Fuller goes so far as to define transparency in terms of the habitual or taken-for-granted quality of our interactions with computers: "When things become habitual they become transparent."[2] In other words, transparency refers to that which no longer attracts our attention because we have become accustomed to it. Indeed, the culturally specific character of transparency, as an aesthetic effect and valued social attribute in the West, becomes more apparent when the security state's turn to transparency is considered within the context of related trends evident in US popular media.

In his work on reality television, Mark Andrejevic makes the point that "interactivity" increasingly functions as a form of productive surveillance or "the work of being watched." He notes the desirability of transparency for commercial as well as security cultures: "The role of making oneself seen is central to the emerging surveillance economy in which the transparency of the subject has an increasingly important role to play in the rationalization of production."[3] Reality television has a special role to play in the new economy insofar as it models transparency as a desirable social attribute and potential shortcut to fame and fortune. Reality TV's promise of interactivity, he writes, "works neatly as an advertisement for the benefits of submission to comprehensive surveillance in an era in which such submission is increasingly productive."[4] A shortcut to fame and fortune in the genre of reality television, transparency promises to confer status and ease one's passage through the security checkpoint in the genre of transportation security pedagogy.

Taking its cue from US consumer and media cultures, the TSA adopts the ruse of interactivity in order to promote reflexive governance at the checkpoint, whereby passengers assume responsibility for making the checkpoint function in a smooth and efficient manner.[5] Transportation security pedagogy trains its sights on passengers as civil security workers, who are ideally adept at the gestures of efficient submission to comprehensive surveillance. The TSA frequently reminds the public that passengers are the last line of defense against terrorism. The honor of becoming part of the security apparatus is bestowed on passengers only after they have been demonstrably seen through by the security state. In order to fly/serve, passengers must demonstrate (the absence of) the terrorist threat. A passenger's first duty in the war on terror, then, is to perform voluntary transparency for and according to the performance standards set by the TSA. At the security checkpoint, this translates as follows: passengers are mobilized to become active participants in the production of their bodies and belongings as transparent, but their role in this production is to execute the appropriate gestures of submission to security technologies and human monitors. In these collaborative performances, TSA employees are neither as threatening as armed police officers nor as inconsequential as mall security guards. In fact, they perform the contradictory labor of simultaneously monitoring passengers (as representatives of the security state) and helping passengers open themselves up to surveillance by the security state (as members of the security-service industry). This dual role mirrors passengers' contradictory, dual performance of suspects and consumers. Passengers and TSA employees have to learn how to move and act in this new genre of performance.

In this chapter, I examine four pedagogical campaigns authorized by the TSA. In the first part of the chapter, I analyze two pedagogical campaigns designed to train the traveling public in the art of efficient submission to airport security protocol. In the second part of the chapter I turn to two pedagogical campaigns designed to teach the TSA workforce how to provide friendlier customer service and accommodate the needs of those passengers needing assistance due to disabilities and/or medical conditions, respectively. Transportation security pedagogy models the performance conventions of efficient transparency on the part of passengers, and a customer-service approach on the part of TSA employees. It communicates that there is a right way and a wrong way to conduct oneself as a passenger-to-be-screened. Likewise, it communicates that there is a right way and a wrong way for TSA employees to conduct themselves. As Mark Salter observes, airports not only control mobility but also serve a pedagogical function. In support of this claim, Salter cites Mika Aotola's argument that "airports are places where authority is recognized and instructions given for making 'proper' judgments and acknowledgments are given. . . . Airports teach people the central rituals of acknowledgment that are needed to navigate the Byzantine structures of the modern hierarchical world order."[6] In recent years, public pedagogy has been analyzed through the Foucauldian framework of governmentality. My approach to transportation security pedagogy expands that treatment to include both the instructional texts created by a governmental agency for the purpose of training passengers and TSA employees in the new protocols (the conduct of conduct) and what performance studies scholars and practitioners call performance pedagogy or the hands-on experience of learning how to do something by doing it.

Synchronized Submission

In late 2007, the TSA began holding passengers partly responsible for the general mood and smooth functioning of the checkpoint. From the perspective of the agency, airport security could be made more civil and further streamlined if passengers would arrive at the checkpoint ready for inspection. The first public relations campaign designed to train travelers in preparedness for airport security screening was introduced on November 19, 2007, just prior to the busiest weekend for air travel within the United States, the Thanksgiving holiday.[7] A TSA spokeswoman explained that the SimpliFLY campaign was intended to help passengers avoid the extra time and hassle of having their bags searched by hand. Thomas Frank reports that the TSA sent airports and airlines posters and the sixty-second video to be screened near the entrances to checkpoints. The campaign was brief, lasting only through the 2007 holiday travel season.[8]

The SimpliFLY video (figure 4.1) promises the customer service of shorter wait times to passengers capable of performing self-service prior to their arrival at the airport. The sixty-second video is subtitled "The Art of Packing Smarter to Get through Security Faster." It opens with an establishing shot of a security checkpoint in fast motion. The high-speed video matches the quick, almost frenetic tempo of the a capella background music, which layers percussive human voices singing: "Dom dom dom do dee dom dom dom do dee dee / Dang dang dang de diddle ee dang dang dang de de dang dang deedle ee dang dang." A young woman does the voice-over: "Transportation Security officers need to quickly determine whether or not a bag possibly contains a threat." As she begins, the video cuts to a shot of a carry-on being placed in a gray security bin, another similar shot, and then to choreographed line shots of passengers moving through security together in perfect time like synchronized swimmers. In one shot a line of five passengers simultaneously place zip-top bags into gray

FIGURE 4.1 Screen captures from TSA SimpliFLY video.

plastic bins aligned on the table before them. The queue is masculine—the passengers are mostly dressed in suits.

True to the genre of the musical, the video then cuts to a mirror shot featuring a line of women placing their shoes into the gray bins, again in perfect synchronization. Each time, as the passengers perform the move, the thudding sound of their stuff hitting the bottom of the plastic bin adds an additional layer of percussion to the video's background music. While I have compared the video to the film genre of the American musical, fascist propaganda films are also a fair comparison, given that the choreographed actors model the synchronized submission of the traveling masses to the authority of the US security state.

Following this is a shot of the checkpoint from the perspective of passengers, the video is sped up again to show passengers passing quickly through the checkpoint, then it slows to real time as a conventionally attractive blond woman struggles to remove her shoes while talking on her cell phone. The character of the inefficient passenger conforms to a familiar Hollywood brand of femininity: hopelessly cute and attractively inept. The passengers behind her look annoyed. Her bag looks too big and makes a heavy thud as it hits the conveyor belt at the same time the woman doing the voice-over pronounces the word *threat*.

On the other side of the checkpoint, the clueless passenger sits casually on the stainless steel tables designated for people to put their belongings back together and puts her shoes back on as if she were at home in her bedroom. As a TSA official goes through her sloppily packed suitcase, the voice-over continues: "*You* already know you're not a threat. *Show us* by packing smart." As the announcer says, "Show us," the video cuts to the hands of a TSA official searching through the passenger's messy bag. Next, the announcer tells us to "think layers: one layer of clothes, one layer of electronics. That way, it's easier for us to determine what's in your bag." As she instructs viewers on the proper way to pack for security, the instructional video demonstrates the technique she describes. The black suitcase is brand new, clean, and jet-black. So are the two pairs of women's shoes, two sweaters, and personal electronics devices that go into the bag, one layer at a time.

A final layer goes on top: a preppy argyle sweater in pink and yellow and black pinstripe pants. The hands packing the bag are those of a white woman wearing department store jewelry and a wedding band and engagement ring. Each layer of packed clothes is folded neatly. The thin cashmere sweaters look like a display in a J.Crew or Banana Republic catalog or storefront.

The video cuts back to the beginning of the checkpoint where a male African American officer asks the hapless passenger (who almost walks right past him without even noticing it because she is too busy talking on her cell phone) for her "boarding pass and ID." The announcer says: "Also, being prepared when you approach the checkpoint will make the whole process a lot faster." In the next shot, the hapless passenger's oversized red leather handbag is on top of the podium where the TSA officer is stationed. As she rifles through her handbag and leans on the officer's workstation with little regard for him, other passengers become impatient. When she finally leaves the ID checkpoint and the next passenger approaches for screening, the young African American woman is visibly annoyed by her fellow passenger's obliviousness.

The SimpliFLY video employs peer pressure to enforce efficiency standards for passengers. It does so by making a democratic appeal to the equalizing force of the queue. The problem with the hapless protagonist is that she does not think the rules apply to her. She exercises her privilege by being oblivious to others around her and ignorant of the rules governing the space of the checkpoint. Casting is crucial here. Viewers are encouraged to dislike the inefficient protagonist because she is conventionally attractive. The skit performs a comedic reversal whereby the woman who looks like a business traveler and therefore ought to be savvy in the ways of the security checkpoint turns out to be, well, inconsiderate and inept. Within the story world of the video, blondness connotes the cluelessness and inconsiderateness of the privileged. The video plants questions in the minds of viewers: Does this woman think the rules do not apply to her? Does she think she is better than everybody else or somehow above the rules and regulations? The video depicts her behavior as ridiculous at best and downright un-American at worst. It communicates the message that preparedness, efficiency, and subordination are national priorities and moral values. The video appeals to viewers: Please get with the program, if not for the sake of security, then out of a sense of common decency with respect to your fellow passengers.

The video invites viewers to identify with the African American TSA officer and passenger in line behind the inefficient white woman. Their shared common sense communicates the kind of peer relationships the video wants to promote. Significantly, the video portrays the TSA officer, who is a representative of the federal government and the law, as though he were just another in a group of passengers annoyed with the hapless protagonist. The casting of the TSA agent as African American is reminiscent of stand-up comedian Faizon Love's observation, made in the context of a critique of post-9/11 racial politics, that African Americans "only get to be Americans when [the nation] needs something from them."[9] However subtly, the video resonates with what anthropologist Lanita Jacobs-Huey has called the "Arab as new nigger" observation that emerged in black stand-up comedy clubs after 9/11.[10] Jokes in this category draw the audience's attention to the ways in which African Americans have been Americanized by the exclusion and criminalization of Arab Americans in the preemptive war on terror. While some comedians sardonically celebrated this turn of events, others used the observation to critique American collective identity as persistently exclusionary.

The final shot of the SimpliFLY video shows the white protagonist running to catch her flight after taking so long to get through security. The announcer leaves viewers with a final reminder that "we" make the difference between how fast or slowly "we" move through the checkpoint: "So next time, simpliFLY your bags and you could get through security a little faster." The announcer chuckles slightly as she delivers her final line, amused to the very end by the ridiculous woman who is the object of her (and by extension "our") scorn.

Transcripts of the SimpiFLY video are available on the TSA website in eleven languages other than English: Arabic, Dutch, French, German, Hebrew, Italian, Japanese, Korean, Portuguese, Punjabi, and Spanish. The

How To Pack	How *NOT* To Pack

FIGURE 4.2 Photograph on TSA website: "How To Pack / How *NOT* To Pack."

transcripts feature one screen shot from the video of the neatly packed suitcase viewed from above (displaying argyle sweater and pinstripe pants) and one image from the 3-1-1 campaign and two still shots of neatly and sloppily packed belongings (figure 4.2). On the TSA's website, these images are labeled "How To Pack" and "How *NOT* To Pack," respectively, and captioned as follows: "The images below show a group of items packed two ways: the items on the left are packed neatly and the items on the right are loose and cluttered. In these images, you can clearly see what all the items are, but our Transportation Security Officers don't see your bag like this—they see an X-ray image on a screen. And they have to quickly determine if your bag contains a potential threat. You know you're not a threat, but our TSOs don't know you, and seemingly innocent items can actually appear to be potential threats in an X-ray image, simply by the way they're packed."

While these images are not as overtly encoded into the visual language of US consumerism as those in the SimpliFLY video, they retain the assumption that the traveler is an avid consumer of personal electronics. Less directly, the flip-flops and beach towel connote a vacation traveler and collapse the morality of efficiency with the fun morality and casual style of the American middle class. The permanent markers and Palm Pilot or BlackBerry suggest a business traveler who knows how to play as hard as he works.

Despite the egalitarian ethos of the SimpliFLY campaign, at the time of its release and distribution to airports across the United States in November 2007, experts in airport security expressed doubts regarding whether or not your average traveler was capable of retooling herself according to the efficiency standards promoted by the video. Across the board, commentators differentiated business from periodic travelers and doubted the efficiency capabilities of the latter. David Castelveter, spokesman for the Air Transport Association said the program might not make much of a difference over the holiday weekend: "This is one of the holidays where you're dealing with the less-savvy traveler." According to the reporter, Frank, the new suggestions urge passengers to make sure "clothes [are] folded, electronic devices organized and wires coiled." TSA spokeswoman Howe explains the reasoning behind these packing tips: "If you eliminate clutter, it helps us get a cleaner look at the contents of a bag" on X-ray machines. The Business Travel Coalition supports the TSA's efforts, but the organization's chairman, Kevin Mitchell, is not optimistic that non-business travelers will catch on: "The message is a pretty sophisticated one, and it's a lot for the average person who is traveling for the first time in months to remember."[11]

Black Diamond

In February 2008, the TSA instituted a pilot program at Salt Lake City and Denver International Airports. Black Diamond was designed to test whether passengers would voluntarily sort themselves into separate security lanes based on how quickly or slowly they think they can perform the drill of taking off shoes and jackets, removing laptops from cases, and displaying liquids, gels, and aerosols in a clear plastic bag.[12] According to the TSA, the idea for the program developed out of focus groups the TSA conducted in New York City, Washington, Chicago, and Minneapolis. Participants were offered a free dinner in exchange for discussing their travel experiences with TSA researchers. Assistant Administrator Mo McGowan noted that the TSA had left passengers out of its layered approach to airport security.[13] One veteran TSA executive, Gale Rossides, said, "One of the things passengers said to us was, 'I'm a very experienced traveler. I've got just a carry-on bag. Let me get through security in a way where I'm not slowed up by other passengers.'"[14]

Spokespeople for the TSA sold the pilot program on the basis that it gives a measure of control back to passengers. The TSA security chief in Denver, Dave Bassett, said the program's success hinged on managing travelers' expectations and giving them a sense of increased control over the process: "A passenger can think, 'If I've got one bag, I should be able to get through

What Is Your Lane?

Families and Special Assistance
· small children; strollers
· groups
· assistance needed
· new to flying

Casual Traveler
· familiar with TSA procedures
· multiple carry-ons

Expert Traveler
· expert at TSA procedures
· always ready with items removed
· flies more than twice a month
· travels light
· elite frequent flyer member

Transportation
Security
Administration

got feedback?
www.tsa.gov/blog

FIGURE 4.3 TSA signage: "What Is Your Lane?"

a little faster.' It's calmed things down."[15] Along similar lines, Nicole C. Wong reports: "The program speaks to how stressful the air experience has become since the Sept. 11, terrorist attacks—for both passengers and security screeners. Giving a bit of control back to travelers might ease the tension and speed up the screening process, too."[16]

In the Black Diamond program, color-coded signs direct travelers into one of three lanes "based on their travel skills and knowledge," the TSA says (figure 4.3).[17] Posters designating the expert, casual, and family lanes borrow from ski resort signage, using a black diamond to designate expert lanes, a blue square for casual lanes, and a green circle for families and those with special needs.[18] The ski resort metaphor suggests that the separate security lanes of the Black Diamond Program reference different skill levels. It is experience and practice that produce distinction rather than innate bodily differences or diverse health conditions. But the agency's reliance on an elite outdoor sporting metaphor reveals its presumption that while there may be a range of skill levels out there on the slopes, everyone has the potential to ski the expert slopes if they just summon the courage and try hard enough.

Black Diamond presumes relatively young, healthy, and fit passengers able to modify their performance of voluntary transparency in order to bring it up to the efficiency standards set by the agency. If, historically, transparency reflected the Western ideals of rationality and scientific progress, more recently, José van Dijk argues, it has come to connote "perfectability, modifiability, and control over human physiology."[19] Transportation security pedagogy extols the virtues of a mobile and infinitely malleable passenger who is adept at self-exposure for the sake of security. In a global economy that rewards reflexive submission to security technologies and officials, as well as detachment from and a competitive attitude toward fellow citizens, slick submission to comprehensive surveillance is a sign of passenger empowerment, savvy, and productivity.

By encouraging passengers to sort themselves into the appropriate security lane, Black Diamond facilitates differential monitoring practices tailored to the appearances and behavioral characteristics associated with different types of passengers. For example, the TSA's adoption of ski resort signage sets up a distinction between two passenger stereotypes: the high-flying consultant and the toddler-toting mom. If mobility is the engine of global capitalism, the business traveler or consultant has become a popular icon of mobility-as-virtue. Consider George Clooney's character in *Up in the Air* (2009). Ryan Bingham is a corporate downsizing expert obsessed with status—all those special cards and perks one earns as a frequent flier. The most important perk being the privilege of breezing past long lines because you have special status that grants you constant, immediate access to the fast lane. His prepackaged lecture encourages businesspeople to lighten their load materially and emotionally in order to render themselves fitter for business. As he delivers his talk, a backpack sits on a table next to his podium. The backpack serves as a metaphor for the business traveler's necessary detachment given the utter ruthlessness of capitalism in times of recession. Bingham's firm hires him out to businesses across the United States that cannot stomach firing their own workers so they bring him in for a day to quickly and legally clean house. During his lecture, Bingham asks seminar participants, "What's in your pack?" Projected onto two large screens behind him are rotating images of transparent, empty backpacks.

From the TSA's perspective, savvy businesspeople who travel light are model civil security workers.[20] With preexisting training and skills suited to the information economy, they quickly rise to the top of the heap to become members of the highest-efficiency group: Black Diamond. This elite group has the special privilege of getting through security more quickly because its members are capable of a high degree of self-organization for the security state. In other words, they take on more of the burden of responsibility for rendering their bodies and belongings transparent (i.e., for producing good security images), thereby freeing up TSA workers to help less savvy passengers like mothers with small children, who are regularly pictured in journalistic and state-authored descriptions of the program as examples of less-than-efficient travelers.

The demand for efficient transportation security combines the militaristic, pack-light readiness model of the soldier with the technological prowess, information access, and efficiency standards of the business class.[21] The resultant ideal of slick submission to security screening rewards the unbearable lightness of the masculine business traveler. The point is not just that mothers with infants are regularly pictured in the slow lane, even as the slim, skirted "expert" silhouetted in all of the TSA signage is strategically feminine—like a photograph of Amelia Earhart reproduced in an Apple print advertisement prompting consumers to "Think different." As Mary Russo argues in reference to Earhart and other figures of the aerial sublime, "'Women's liberation' as so imaged, is imbricated with the history and ideology of bourgeois exceptionalism which marks off categories of irregular bodies to leave behind." Instead, Russo suggests combining the female grotesque and the aerial sublime, such that categories of irregular or "heavy" bodies don't get abandoned. In other words, she insists that we rethink the aerial sublime as an embodiment not only of possibility but also of error.[22]

In its rather flippant reliance on ski resort signage, the Black Diamond program offers a wealth of lessons *not* learned from 9/11. The Black Diamond passenger reflects the transcendence of gender, age, physical limitations, and all other attributes that slow bodies down or catch them in webs of dependency. The desired suspect aspires to transcend the physical body, has an aversion to material reality as a series of obstacles to mobility and access, and exercises ruthless independence (each passenger packs for himself and carries his own stuff). Perhaps most disturbingly, the business traveler hailed as a model civil security worker by transportation security pedagogy is readable as a miniature, mobile model of the United States as an extreme and extremely autonomous political and economic actor in the world: all access, unilateral action, and no looking back. The business traveler is adept at self-exposure, the better to move about as if she were untouchable and left no tracks. Virtually everywhere and nowhere, her lithe, translucent figure zooms down the white slopes, with a shimmering special access card in her transparent, super-lightweight pack.

Black Diamond ranks families (read: the young, the elderly and their caretakers, including all of those generally lacking travel savvy) lower than the business traveler and promises them longer wait times. Advocates of the program insist that separate security lanes make each passenger feel more comfortable as he performs the drill at his own pace. "The goal of the program," says TSA spokeswoman Sari Koshetz, "is to keep everyone happy and relaxed." Koshetz explains: "The expert travelers who know to whip out their laptop and (liquid container) bags get stressed out by people moving slow. The people in front of them get stressed out by people pressuring them."[23] The overall effect, proponents argue, is to render the affective environment of the checkpoint calm. "The basic tenet of this program," says George Naccara, the TSA federal security director overseeing Logan International Airport in Boston, "is to provide a calming experience for every traveler."[24] Louis Miller, the executive director at Tampa International Airport, says the new system should speed security and lower anxiety: "Families like it, they don't want to feel like someone's standing behind them tapping their foot. It's better for business travelers, quicker and they're not waiting. It's better for everybody."[25] Of the program's introduction to Hartsfield International in Atlanta, spokesman Robert Kennedy cited Atlanta's history of long wait times and said, "We had to do this to make the customer experience better. People come to the airport to catch a plane. They don't want to stand in line."[26] The idea of taking pressure off "families" by giving them their own, slow lane seems humane, but one has to ask: What's at stake in a federal program that establishes hierarchies based on how efficiently individuals self-sort according to gender, age, and able-bodied physical stereotypes and calmly submit to being seen through by the security state?

Since the program's inception and subsequent expansion to airports across the United States, TSA representatives report that the expert lane has been "experiencing throughput gains of as much as 30%."[27] While wait times for experts have been reduced, wait times in the family-friendly lanes are higher. TSA executive, Gale Rossides stresses the reduction in the number of baggage screening alarms in the family lane.[28] Expert lines are moving 21 percent more travelers through security in an hour than under the "one-size-fits-all system." Family lines are slower, but "the rate at which their carry-on bags set off X-ray machine alarms is down 11 percent."[29] At the end of 2008, the TSA announced that it would be expanding family lanes, then officially dubbed "Family and Medical Liquids Lanes," to every airport in the United States.[30] More recently, it has been renamed the "Family and Special Assistance Lane."

Airports in the United Kingdom have begun to adopt a similar, self-sorting approach to prevent traffic jams at security checkpoints. Gatwick Airport, which experienced some of the worst delays following the foiled liquid bomb plot of 2006, was purchased by Global Infrastructure Partners in 2009 and subsequently underwent major renovations. The new layout combines what were three separate security areas into one checkpoint featuring nineteen lanes. Two are "premium" lanes, and two are designed for families on holiday and equipped with extra staff to assist these less-than-savvy travelers.[31]

Life in the Family and Special Assistance Lane

Transportation security pedagogy addresses people's capacities to be trained to perform voluntary transparency, unless limited by a medical condition or disability. By definition, reflexive governance presumes a citizen in full control of his body. Those unable to open their bodies or belongings up for inspection in keeping with agency protocol may require the assistance of more able-bodied traveling companions or TSA employees poised to help those passengers unable to help themselves. Those passengers who are unable to participate fully in the project of reflexive governance by quickly opening their bodies and belongings for inspection and analysis are segregated to their own lane so as not to put undue pressure on them or slow everyone else down. The TSA has presented the system of separate security queues to the public as an effort to reduce impatience and frustration at the checkpoint. Whether it is framed as customer service or as security necessity, the bottom line is that the program segregates members of the traveling public based on ability.

The transparent traveler desired by the US security state is independent, healthy, and able-bodied. Physical ailments, disabilities, limitations, chronic medical conditions, or forms of social and/or familial dependency may prevent a particular suspect from being adequately self-subduing via submission to individual scanning by surveillance technologies like full-body scanners or metal detectors. This state of affairs requires the TSA officers on duty to substitute or supplement technological mediation with a physical search. For example, a passenger who relies on a mobility device cannot assume the proper position required for screening by the full-body scanners: standing with arms above head. This person fails to perform transparency insofar as she is unable to assume the proper position and produce the correct gestures in a performance that culminates in the production of a particular type of security image of her body. Likewise, cyborg passengers with implanted defibrillators cannot pass through metal detectors because their devices set off the metal detector and therefore defeat the purpose of this method of scanning passengers for contraband. Paradoxically, medical cyborgs are at once too vulnerable and too advanced for metal detectors. The TSA refers to the condition of such passengers as a "hidden disability," a visual description that casts further suspicion on them.

Where metal detectors and body scanners prove insufficient, TSA workers must substitute or supplement technological mediation with physical contact. Transparent mediation by close-sensing technologies becomes a semipublic, intimate physical encounter with a TSA official. Physical pat-downs and searches performed on such passengers typically happen in a designated area just to one side of the queue for the metal detectors and X-ray machines. Interestingly, these areas are frequently cordoned off by a series of glass or plastic partitions. This creates a situation where passengers proceeding through the regular screening process can watch as TSA officials handle passengers pulled for additional screening. The function of the transparent partitions communicates voluntary transparency on the part of the TSA, even as it heightens the theatrical aspects of the encounter, now enticingly framed by a glass box.

Sometimes these inspections go horribly wrong, as in the case of Thomas

Sawyer, a sixty-one-year-old man and cancer survivor who said a TSA pat-down inspection broke his urine bag. Sawyer suffered the further indignity of having to board his flight covered in urine without the benefit of an apology from the TSA officer involved in the incident.[32] Sawyer's experience (and that of countless others who have been subjected to physical search because of a medical condition or disability) raises the question of whether or not physical pat-downs constitute a violation of the Health Insurance Portability and Accountability Act of 1996 (HIPAA) or the Americans with Disabilities Act of 1990. The Department of Health and Human Services lists law enforcement agencies among those organizations *not* required to follow HIPAA's privacy and security rules.[33] During a national or public health emergency, the secretary of health and human services may waive certain provisions of HIPAA even for those organizations required to follow its privacy and security rules. So the answer to the first question would seem to be no, public physical inspection of passengers with medical conditions does not constitute a violation of HIPAA so long as terrorism prevention continues to be framed as a national emergency.

The question of whether or not public pat-downs of passengers with medical conditions and disabilities constitutes a violation of the Americans with Disabilities Act is more difficult to answer. The act "prohibits discrimination on the basis of disability in employment, State and local government, public accommodations, commercial facilities, transportation, and telecommunications."[34] The TSA proclaims that its commitment to customer service extends to all passengers, "regardless of their personal situations and needs." In an effort to meet the needs of passengers with medical conditions and disabilities, the agency established a coalition of over seventy disability-related groups and organizations "to help us understand the concerns of persons with disabilities and medical conditions."[35] This research has informed the TSA's approach to passengers with "all categories of disabilities (mobility, hearing, visual, and hidden)."[36] Coverage by the program indicates that TSA screeners have been briefed on the range of conditions they may encounter. It also references specialized travel tips for passengers with medical conditions or disabilities and/or their traveling companions. The general theme of these disability-specific tips is that passengers with medical conditions or disabilities and/or their traveling companions are responsible for initiating communication about their condition with TSA officers. The presumption of able-bodiedness thus further burdens passengers with disabilities and their caretakers with the affective and psychological burden of educating the TSA about their difference from the presumed norm.

In some cases, the travel tips offered attempt to head off charges of privacy violation and discrimination in one fell swoop. For example, those who dislike the exposure of a pat-down inspection at the checkpoint are advised to "request a private area for your pat-down inspection if you feel uncomfortable with having a medical device being displayed while inspected by the Security Officer."[37] In the case of passengers with medical conditions or disabilities, off-site inspection is offered as a less stigmatizing option to undergoing physical inspection at the checkpoint before an audience of one's peers. By contrast, the prospect of being transferred from the public checkpoint to an off-site location for further inspection and interrogation implies the threat of physical harm and/or arrest to those suspected of terrorism. That is not to say that passengers with medical conditions or disabilities are presumed innocent. In what is perhaps the most harrowing section of advice for passengers with medical conditions and disabilities, the TSA addresses the visual problem of dressed wounds:[38]

- Whenever there is a metal detector alarm in the area of a dressing, the Security Officers will conduct a gentle limited pat-down of the dressing area over top of your clothing.
- Clothing will not be required to be removed, lifted, or lowered during the pat-down inspection.
- The Security Officer will not ask you to, nor will he or she, remove a dressing during the screening process.
- In the event a Security Officer is not able to determine that a dressing is free of prohibited items via a pat-down, you will be denied access to the sterile area.

Particularly striking is the use of the term *sterile* in reference to the securitized area just beyond the checkpoint in the context of a discussion of how to treat a passenger with dressed wounds. The final bullet point pits the sterility of the securitized zone against the sterility of a passenger's dressed wound. One form of sterility demands exposure, while the other requires a protective covering. In its treatment of the range of medical conditions and disabilities TSA officers may encounter, the agency's tone is alternately insistent and tender as it communicates its unwavering commitment to expose what might otherwise be hidden by the pretense of a medical condition or disability.

Service with a Smile

Spokespersons for the TSA regularly state that the agency considers its two most important jobs to be security and customer service. This was not always the case: "When we started we had more of a military thing," said Lori Potoczek, a screening supervisor at O'Hare International Airport in Chicago. "Now we need to be more businesslike."[39] In her statement "businesslike" is code for greater efficiency and a consumer-friendly orientation. It was not until late 2005, amid sharp public criticism and widespread discontent with the long wait times at airport security checkpoints, that the agency reframed its mission in terms of customer service. As part of its move to better serve the traveling public, the TSA hired industrial engineers and efficiency experts to help streamline the screening process. This involved upgrading the equipment used at checkpoints as well as efficiency training for TSA officers. For example, at Potoczek's checkpoint a Chili's restaurant was pushed aside "to make room for 48-inch screening lanes, which allow faster passengers to scrunch past stragglers, as opposed to the former 36-inch lanes, which often became bottlenecked." O'Hare also began experimenting with widening screening lanes, creating separate paths for workers to recycle plastic bins from one side of the checkpoint to the other, reducing the size of areas devoted to additional screening of passengers with hand-held metal detectors, and installing new, faster machines for screening bags.[40]

These and other efficiency measures were instituted alongside the agency's new customer-service approach. Regardless of measurable efficiency gains, the agency's investment in customer service promised to ease the process of getting through security and thereby shape passengers' perceptions of efficiency in airport security. As to the matter of whether or not efforts had actually shortened wait times, reporters Jeff Bailey and Jeremy Peters of the *New York Times* observed in late 2005: "If the screening process seems no faster, it does seem at least less confrontational these days—less like being pulled over by a police officer, for the agency preaches kindness to its workers." They go on to quote Richard Larson, a professor at the Massachusetts Institute of Technology and queuing expert, who said that "sour handlers increase anxiety among those in line, making the wait seem even longer. Traveling recently, he said, 'they seem to be much more friendly now.'"[41] According to Potoczek the TSA's veneer of friendliness takes considerable effort to cultivate: "The hardest part," she said, "is 'trying to smile.'"

In November 2008, the TSA joined with the Ad Council to launch its first national public awareness and education campaign "designed to build awareness of check point security procedures in an effort to better prepare passengers for airport travel." Like previous efforts, the campaign was launched in conjunction with the Thanksgiving holiday. TSA officers nationwide underwent training in how to be calmer at the checkpoint by the Thanksgiving 2008 deadline. According to TSA executive Gale Rossides, "The training gives them enhanced communication skills. How to speak in a calm voice, how to make eye contact in order to say, 'I'm here to assist you through this.' We will give officers wireless communication devices, so they can call for a bag check or call for a secondary screening without having to yell at each other."[42]

The Ad Council's press release states that the public awareness campaign "aims to improve security by compelling airline passengers to become better prepared for security processes, thereby resulting in less frustration and a more positive experience."[43] The campaign bills itself as offering greater transparency regarding security regulations. Ad Council president and CEO Peggy Conlon says: "Research shows that Americans are more willing to comply when they understand why certain measures are in place. Therefore, we have a great opportunity to educate them on their important role in the airline security process." The Ad Council has produced a series of videos explaining the rationale behind different security regulations: *Why ID, Why Liquids, Why Shoes, 3 Simple Steps, Lanes, Laptops,* and *Traveling with Children.* Each video opens with a direct address segment delivered by an attractive African American woman in a TSA uniform. She explicitly expresses understanding of traveler frustration with the new policies and calmly explains why they exist.

In addition to these public relations videos, the TSA website offers several short instructional videos. If one clicks "For Travelers," and then "How to Get through the Line Faster," and then "Helpful Videos," one finds a series of short instructional videos about the details of the screening process. These videos are strikingly different from the SimpliFLY campaign. They are quiet, slow, deliberate, and relaxed. They feature empty airport spaces and calm, hassle-free interactions. There are no queues. There is no need to hurry. There is music in only one of the videos; it is Musak. There is no longer the sense of peer pressure that was at work in the SimpliFLY video, and there are no attempts to be humorous.

Blending In

A series of contradictions emerge across the airport security pedagogy campaigns analyzed in this chapter: Is security a great leveling force or has it produced a new global class system based on nationality and/or physical and technological facility with the new security procedures and technologies? Does the TSA treat disability as a drag on the agency's efficiency standards or with the tenderness of an organization that mandates sensitivity training? Is the TSA a military operation or part of the service industry, there to cater to the passenger's desire to be comforted as she opens herself up to inspection?

Despite the different models of social relations among passengers and between passengers and TSA employees on offer in these campaigns, there is a way in which the aesthetics of transparency pulls them all together in a manner that makes the contradictions disappear into thin air. If one shifts one's analysis from the unit of the individual passenger or TSA employee to the airport environment, then one can begin to see how each of these campaigns promotes a transparent airport environment. The SimpliFLY video promotes mechanical transparency. It employs a borderline fascist visual aesthetic of choreographed bodies modeling coordinated mass submission to the rules and regulations of airport security. All the while, the video's plotline holds up the democracy of the queue in order to pitch its message: well-behaved passengers know and follow the rules and thereby avoid drawing unnecessary attention to themselves. The video pictures conformity and obedience and uses narration and plot to frame these qualities as democratic virtues. The problem with the protagonist is that she fails to mechanically blend in to the airport environment.

Black Diamond signage tells passengers: You get to decide where you belong. But be honest: accurate self-evaluation promotes security. Like an inexperienced skier who accidentally takes the lift to the top of an expert slope and must be helped down by a ski instructor, passengers who do not understand the system or misjudge their efficiency level may be helped along or redirected by TSA workers stationed at the checkpoint. Voluntary transparency extends, then, to the practice of on-the-spot self-assessment, which is a measure of one's ability to mechanically blend into one's appropriate lane (i.e., social group) at the checkpoint and thereby avoid causing an unnecessary and possibly lethal distraction.

TSA workforce training initiatives in customer service are designed to improve the passenger's experience of airport security so that he remains unruffled during the process. In other words, customer-service training aims to improve the mood of the checkpoint, thereby promoting affective transparency at the airport. Sensitivity training that teaches TSA employees to be aware of the perspective and physical limitations of passengers with disabilities is calibrated to manage a wide range of disabilities. The TSA's efforts to manage how the agency's employees handle disabled persons aim to render even those bodies that fail to conform to the transparency standard of the new normate body (chapter 3) more predictable in their deviations from normal. In other words, the program endeavors to render a wide range of disabilities more, if differently, transparent to the security state. In some cases, the goal is to shift disability from a visual stigma that pops out from the background of a sea of normates (a potentially lethal distraction) to a familiar, if differently, transparent body. Or the goal is to render "hidden disabilities" accessible to the haptic vision of human monitors working the checkpoint. Finally, the Ad Council's public relations campaign models the ideal airport as empty and serene.

Each of these campaigns is designed to retrain passengers and TSA employees in the art of calm submission to screening and calm performance of inspection, respectively. These efforts are packaged as customer or public services, but given the TSA's turn to behavior detection as a method of control (chapter 5), passenger preparedness and self-sorting exercise a normalizing function at the checkpoint. The TSA trains passengers to be ready for inspection in order to render their behavior at the checkpoint more transparent in the sense of being predictable and orderly. Self-sorting demands a moment-to-moment, trip-by-trip, group-by-group practice of almost instantaneous self-assessment and organization for the purpose of creating a sense of calm control and reassuring efficiency. Customer service and sensitivity training aim to produce a calming effect at the checkpoint, which extends to those passengers whose disabilities and medical conditions make high-tech screening impossible and therefore render physical contact between human screeners and disabled passengers necessary. The TSA has learned to set the mood at the checkpoint, promoting good vibes and inviting passengers to tune in to its mechanical and affective demands on what feels like their terms.

CHAPTER 5

PERFORMING INVOLUNTARY TRANSPARENCY

The TSA's Turn to Behavior Detection

Established alongside those layers of airport security that invite reflex-ive governance, involuntary transparency operates as a covert layer of airport security, which goes by the name behavior detection. The TSA's program in behavior detection began as a pilot study initiated at Boston's Logan International Airport in 2002.[1] After the terrorist attacks of 9/11, Massachusetts state police wondered if the techniques they'd been using to spot drug runners in airports might work to identify terrorists. They enlisted the help of Rafi Ron, former director of security at Ben-Gurion International Airport in Tel Aviv, and behavioral psychologist Paul Ekman, best known for his research on the facial cues of deception.

Two points must be made at the outset. First, modeling transportation security in the United States on Israeli security practices is far from politi-cally neutral. The quickness and ease with which the United States models its transportation security practices on Israel's is an index of the extent of Islamophobia in terrorism studies.[2] Second, the TSA's exclusive reliance on the work of Paul Ekman and his colleagues is astounding, given how contested his theories are within and beyond the social sciences. It is as if the TSA were willing to ignore forty years' worth of cultural critiques of scientific universalism simply because Ekman's theories promised an efficient means of reading passengers' intentions from the surfaces of their bodies.[3]

The resultant trial run, Behavior Pattern Recognition Program, was a hybrid of observation and questioning with emphasis placed on the former. It trained behavior detection officers (BDOS) to look for signs of stress in passengers' facial expressions, body and eye movements, changes in voice, and other indicators such as sweating or blanching. If a particular passenger's nonverbal behaviors aroused suspicion, officers would begin a conversation with that person. As with the brief conversations between border protection officers and passengers, what interested the BDOS was not so much the answers but the manner in which they were delivered. More specifically, they looked for suspicious persons or signs that the passenger was trying to hide something.[4] Based on favorable internal analyses at the TSA, the pilot program was expanded to twelve airports in December 2005 under its new name, Screening Passengers by Observation Techniques, or SPOT. In each of the initial twelve airports, the TSA chose six screeners for an additional four days of classroom training in observation and questioning techniques. The behavior detection trainees then underwent three days of field training.[5]

Consultant Rafi Ron faulted the TSA for placing too much emphasis on a remote behavior-scoring system and not enough on follow-up interviews. By comparison to the Israeli system, the SPOT program relies more on visual observation of passengers from a short distance away and eliminates the mandatory one-on-one interview. Paul Ekman developed the remote scoring system to which Ron refers. Ekman's research on lie detection proved more amenable to the TSA's demands for efficient, noninvasive passenger screening than the methods advocated by Ron. The incentives driving the TSA to avoid lengthy passenger interviews were both economic and legal. The agency was under immense pressure to screen passengers quickly, and as of yet the American legal and cultural context has proven less hospitable to generalized interrogation of its traveling public than the Israeli context. The difference in implementation also comes down to the practical inability of the TSA to interview every air traveler given the high volume of passengers moving through US airports. The TSA's observation-based approach to screening is indeed faster than the Israeli process, which begins with observation and then, based on suspicions raised, proceeds to short progressive interviews in which additional questioning strives to confirm or deny initial answers and may progress to the point of a full-scale interrogation.

While Ron faulted the SPOT program for being a minimalist version of the behavioral profiling practiced at Ben-Gurion, the TSA celebrated its differences from the Israeli system as assets.[6] When asked about the short follow-up interviews conducted by American BDOS, TSA spokesperson Ann Davis said: "I would not describe the questions as probing."[7] Her use of the adjective *probing* is telling. It marks behavior detection as a hands-off approach and therefore less invasive. Davis's word choice raises the specter of the probing question and by association the anal probe as the more severe and therefore less desirable security choice. Her wording reflects the basic assumption of American behavior detection: emotional information thought to reside in the interior of passengers becomes momentarily visible on the surfaces of their bodies, rendering it unnecessary to verbally or physically probe suspects in an attempt to access the contents of their interiors from without. This framing of the SPOT program as minimally invasive to passengers resonates with the TSA's framing of its technological solutions to transportation security (chapter 3). Significantly, verbal questioning and physical inspection are aligned and presented as more invasive of privacy than visual means of inspection.

Securitainment and the Popularity of the SPOT Program

The notion that there is a way to know for sure whether a person's intentions are good or bad is seductive. In an era of increased mobility and economic ruthlessness, it is undoubtedly the best superpower one could possess. In "Reading the Surface: Body Language and Surveillance," Mark Andrejevic identifies an emergent genre of "securitainment" that "instructs viewers in monitoring techniques as it entertains and informs them."[8] In the essay, Andrejevic explores the cultural range of what he calls "savvy skepticism" in an era of generalized risk: "The promise that viewers can learn to read the hidden truths revealed by the materiality of the body links together a constellation of cultural developments ranging from the proliferation of self-help body language books in the past decade or so, the emergence of the forensics-oriented police procedural as well as TV shows like *Lie to Me* and *The Mentalist*, the use of body language in news analysis, and new forms of marketing and deception-detection technologies."[9] While these programs celebrate the possibility of a scientific system for reading nonverbal communication, the proposed applications of such a universal reading method reveal the cultural values and assumptions informing savvy skepticism in an era of generalized risk. Rachel Dubrofsky's work on reality television has shown that the most valued trait within the genre is "authenticity," where authenticity is defined as performing a consistent self across different contexts. Authenticity is validated (or not) via the monitoring gaze of surveillance cameras.[10] Overall, the trendy applications of behavior detection in American popular culture breed suspicion; encourage social conformity; endorse peer-to-peer surveillance; model the competition and ruthlessness of the marketplace in all manner of social interaction; and promote the reader's or viewer's belief that she will somehow be the exception to the rule (i.e., the one who cannot be lied to and will get ahead of the others because she has mastered the art of strategic interaction).

In twentieth- and twenty-first-century versions of popular and behavioral psychology transparency expresses modern and postmodern anxieties produced by mobility, which renders one accessible and therefore vulnerable to strangers. At least since the rise of major urban centers in the United States and Europe, city dwellers have longed for, imagined, and invested in a variety of pseudo-scientific means for knowing the true intentions of strangers and intimates alike. Body language analysis is not unlike the art of personal detection popular in the nineteenth century.[11] It addresses the problem of the public body or how to make a private/interior life available for public scrutiny. Here transparency references the notion that one can read the interior dimensions of a person based on clues appearing on the surface of her face and body. In this tradition, the desire for transparency in others exposes the urban dweller or traveler's lack of humility in the face of cultural, racial, class, and religious difference. Rather than admit ignorance and confusion, one demands that others become self-evident. The demand for transparent strangers expresses fear of and hostility toward persons, objects, or situations, that defy immediate understanding and a generalized mistrust of anything unfamiliar or out of the ordinary.

Given the widespread fascination with behavior detection evident in American television and pop psychology, it is not surprising that behavior detection was largely well received in the United States. Many citizens greeted behavior detection as a welcome corrective to the TSA's blanket prohibitions and perturbing travel regulations. For example, Anna Quindlen pokes fun at the TSA for its ridiculous ban on liquids and gels and advocates behavioral profiling as a more cost-effective and surefire way to stop attacks: "In the airports themselves, security experts swear by carefully trained behavioral screeners, professionals who trawl the terminals perusing passports and passenger behavior and conducting interviews accordingly. Use of those screeners has made El Al the recognized leader in airline security—and so disdainful of American methods that the airline conducts its own additional checks at some US airports." The title of Quindlen's column says it all: "Taking Off Your Shoes; Osama bin Laden could get through the line if the name on his license was the same as that on his ticket and he wasn't packing Oil of Olay." By comparison to the blanket ban on liquids, gels, and aerosols, behavior detection promises to quell various public frustrations with airport security including inefficiency, inconvenience, property seizure, and hassling innocent passengers.

Behavior detection spares innocent passengers, so the logic goes, because a person with bad intentions will act differently from those without such intentions.[12] If passenger intention had proven irrelevant to the material regulations initiated and tightly enforced by the TSA, under the pressure of the behavior detectives' gaze, it has become the central focus of a new security regime. In addition to literally looking through passengers' bodies and belongings, the TSA claims the ability to metaphorically see through passengers' feigned innocence. In other words, the turn to profiling attempts to do away with the problem of interiority altogether by reading passengers' intentions from the surfaces of their bodies. The new technique deciphers the emotional truth and intentions of passengers, thought to reside within the body's interior, based on a body's surface appearance and by reference to a purportedly universal code of human behavior.

Spokespersons for the TSA frame behavior detection as a superior layer of security that concerns itself directly with terrorists rather than getting caught up in comically off-the-mark attempts to regulate any and all objects and matter moving through US airports. By way of explaining the program's focus, Kip Hawley, former head of the TSA, said: "There are infinite ways to find things to use as a weapon and infinite ways to hide them. But if you can identify the individual, it is by far the better way to find the threat."[13] Whereas the TSA's material regulations were designed to address the threat of ordinary objects with the potential to become instruments of terror, the program in behavior detection addresses the threatening possibility that once on board an airplane, a passenger will become a terrorist.

Behavior Detection and Its Discontents

The SPOT program's choice to rely on the visual observations and snap judgments of minimally trained BDOs raised flags with some members of the public, the press, and some in the national security community. The ACLU disputed the trial program at Boston Logan, charging that behavioral profiling was just a euphemism for racial, ethnic, and religious profiling. On November 10, 2004, the ACLU filed a lawsuit charging that the pilot program at Boston Logan was unconstitutional.[14] John Ramstein, the ACLU lawyer who handled the case, said: "There is a significant prospect this security method is going to be applied in a discriminatory manner. . . . It introduces into the screening system a number of highly subjective elements left to the discretion of the individual officer."[15] Caroline Fredrickson, director of the Washington legislative office for the ACLU, said the program sets "a very dangerous precedent." "Singling people out who seem to be different" may lead to racial profiling or stereotyping.[16] If that is the case, then there was nothing particularly new or special about the SPOT program. Rather, its BDOs were reminiscent of racist police officers free to exercise their subjective visual filters and detain those passengers found guilty of "flying while Muslim."

In response to continued charges that the SPOT program was merely the latest version of racial profiling, the TSA insisted that the ACLU and like-minded critics of the agency had it all wrong: SPOT was an "antidote to racial profiling."[17] Hawley appealed to the universal approach of behavior detection as the SPOT program's built-in protection against abuse: "It doesn't matter what race, ethnicity, age or whatever a person is. It's got to do with the human condition, that humans express certain emotions unknown to them that you can detect."[18] Hawley's language of equal opportunity suspicion provides tacit support for the TSA's claim that SPOT inoculated the agency against racial profiling.

Despite public criticism from the ACLU and considerable disagreement within the social scientific community, the TSA steadily increased its financial and labor investments in behavior detection, annually doubling the number of behavior detection officers in its employ from 2006 to 2009.[19] As of September 2011, the SPOT program employed three thousand BDOs at 161 airports at an annual cost of $212 million.[20] The dramatic expansion of the SPOT program from 2006 to 2009 was due to the leadership of Kip Hawley, who took over as head of the TSA in July 2005.[21] Hawley's decision to grow the TSA's behavior detection program was in part a managerial response to internal organizational and economic issues that had plagued the agency since its inception. In an article titled "Career Track for TSA Employees," *Washington Post* reporter Stephen Barr notes that high turnover rates were costing the agency the time and money necessary to constantly train replacements. Gale Rossides, the TSA's associate administrator for business transformation and culture, cited TSA studies which found that level of work performance was positively correlated with length of time spent with the agency. Morale was low because employees quickly realized that they could not advance and could not hope to make more money than the low base pay rates of entry-level screeners. Once it discovered this problem, the agency rolled out a new and more competitive organizational model, which would provide employees with opportunities for advancement and pay raises. "The career opportunities, announced this week," Barr writes, "will permit screeners to compete for jobs as supervisors and technical experts, such as behavior detection officers, who look for high-risk individuals, and bomb appraisal officers, who spot improvised explosive devices." In part, then, the turn to behavioral profiling was about the creation of an expert culture at the TSA, which would offer an incentive structure for professional and economic advancement. Other institutional incentives have encouraged the practice of racial or ethnic profiling. In late 2011, accusations of ethnic profiling at Honolulu and Newark Liberty International Airports were filed against the TSA. Employees of the agency reportedly nicknamed some of their coworkers "Mexicutioners" (at Honolulu Airport) and "Mexican hunters" (at Newark Liberty International) because these employees were known to regularly target passengers of Latino decent "as an easy way" to "drive up their productivity numbers."[22]

As the TSA pushed ahead, the Department of Homeland Security (DHS) expressed some reservations, but labored behind the scenes to bring the research up to speed with agency practice. Larry Willis, project manager of the Science and Technology Directorate Human Factors/Behavioral Sciences Division Hostile Intent Detection Validation Project, publicly expressed his skepticism in 2007 regarding the effectiveness of behavior detection: "The research in this area is fairly immature. We're trying to establish whether there is something to detect."[23] The expressed goal of Willis's validation project was to provide "cross-cultural validation of behavioral indicators employed by the Department of Homeland Security's operational components to screen passengers at air, land, and maritime ports."[24]

Interpersonal Deception Theory

The unstated premise in Hawley's argument that there is a universal code of human behavior derives from a contested school of American behavioral psychology called Interpersonal Deception Theory (IDT).[25] More specifically, the claim that deceivers are transparent, or display universal nonverbal "tells," is based on the research findings of Paul Ekman and his colleagues. Ekman began studying the universality of nonverbal behavior in the mid-1960s at the request of someone at the Department of Defense.[26] At the time, the culturalist school reigned. Ekman consulted with Margaret Mead, Gregory Bateson, Edward Hall, and Ray Birdwhitsell—all of whom were convinced that Charles Darwin had been wrong; facial expressions and bodily gestures were like languages, specific to one's culture rather than a product of evolutionary development. Only Sylvan Tomkins opposed this view, arguing that facial expressions were innate, rather than learned, and therefore universal to the human species.[27] Ekman began a cross-cultural study of facial expression in which he found evidence for the universal thesis.[28] Ekman tempered his universal claim regarding facial expression with the concept of "display rules," or the idea that there is cultural variance in norms regarding the appropriate expression of emotion in various public contexts.[29] Ekman conducted studies in order to prove that in private all people use the same innate emotional expressions, but they have learned from their cultures to manage those expressions differently when in public.[30]

In the 1970s, Ekman began work on what he refers to as the first "atlas of the face." He wanted to isolate and measure the facial movements that constitute expressions. In a departure from his predecessor, Guillaume-Benjamin Duchenne, Ekman electrically stimulated his own facial muscles rather than subjecting research subjects to that experience. In 1978, he published the Facial Action Coding System (FACS)—a "catalogue of every conceivable facial expression."[31] In her thorough analysis of the attempt to automate FACS, Kelly Gates demonstrates how the system's accuracy is constructed: "The accuracy of the system is defined not in terms of a correspondence between the system and a person whose face is being analyzed (or the full range of ways a facial expression might be interpreted), but in terms of the system's internal agreement—that is, whether the classification system consistently agrees with itself."[32] Gates argues that, far from neutral, classification systems are sites of political and ethical work. "The real power of FACS comes into play," she writes, "when this form of 'accuracy'—deriving from the process of standardization—in turn gets pushed back out onto faces, as the standardized coding system comes to define what facial expressions mean and how they work."[33] While the FACS system temporarily brackets interpretation, its purpose is not only to measure facial movement but also to enable a variety of researchers from various disciplines to "make new *meaning* of the face—to examine and map out the surface movements, temporal dimensions, and intensities of the face with the aim of interpreting the interior state of the person, claiming that those surface movements can provide direct, unmediated access to embodied, felt emotion."[34]

Indeed, Ekman and his colleagues Maureen O'Sullivan of the University of San Francisco and Mark Frank of the State University of New York at Buffalo used the coding system to begin research on the visual evidence of deception.[35] "In our studies," Ekman explains, "we recorded interviews set up in such a way that we knew when a person was lying. Afterward we replayed the tapes over and over in slow motion to identify the expressions and behaviors that distinguish lying from truth telling. We spent hours identifying the precise moment-to-moment movements of the facial muscles based on my Facial Action Coding System . . . to get comprehensive evidence of the kinds of facial looks that accompany spoken lies. Once such expressions are identified, people can be quickly trained to recognize them as they occur." As a result of the group's deception studies, Ekman and his colleagues claimed to have identified "the facial signs that betray a lie."[36] The research group has since been in demand by judges, police, lawyers, the FBI, the CIA, the Bureau of Alcohol, Tobacco, Firearms and Explosives, and comparable agencies in other countries to provide expert testimony or training workshops in lie detection. Like these other professional groups, the TSA operationalized Ekman's findings for the SPOT program to be used as a means of quickly coding the nonverbal behavior of air passengers from a distance.[37]

According to IDT, the real is located in the interior of the individual: the neurological, skeletal, and muscular processes of the human body. Gates argues that this type of research affects "the *biologization* of honesty and deception: defining these culturally variable and historically changing practices of the self, which take shape in humans' interaction with one another, as physiological processes that can be located and coded in individual bodies."[38] As proponents of IDT see it, what is happening inside the body may temporarily surface, thereby providing revealing glimpses of the truth.[39] Over time Ekman and his colleagues have become particularly interested in bodily changes that are involuntary and therefore extremely difficult for passengers/performers to inhibit. For Ekman, the fundamental feature of emotional experience is that we do not choose to start or stop feeling a particular emotion. This gives the behavior detection officer a slight advantage, Ekman argues, particularly if she is familiar with those signals least under the suspect's control. To this end, Ekman and his colleagues have identified what they call "reliable" facial muscles, or those that cannot be deliberately engaged by most people.[40] Building on Sigmund Freud's notion of slips of the tongue, Ekman also identified slips in body movement detectable to the trained eye.[41] "The body leaks," he argues, "because it is ignored."[42] By this he means that liars concentrate on their verbal and facial performance (at the expense of their bodily performance) because they know these are the elements that will get the most attention from their audience. Additionally, Ekman and his colleagues have conducted studies to discover the involuntary tells of deception produced by the autonomic nervous system including pattern of breathing, frequency of swallowing, amount of sweating, rate of blinking, pupil dilation, blushing, and blanching. Ekman and other researchers have speculated about the possibility of taking remote readings of a suspect's heart rate, blood pressure, and other physiological measures of emotional stress.

The New Normal

The behavior detective looks for individuals who stick out in the airport environment while calmer or more normal-acting passengers fade into the background. In 2007, former TSA Head Kip Hawley told Joe Sharkey of the *New York Times*: "We started thinking, what is it that we do better than anybody else? What's the advantage we have? And it's that we see two million people every day. We know what normal is."[43] Hawley explained that behavior detection officers have "developed the skills to separate normal airport anxieties from fundamental signs of 'hostile intent.'"[44] He offered some examples to illustrate his point: "We know what a hassled business traveler looks like. We know what somebody who's just had a fight with their girlfriend or boyfriend or whatever looks like. We know what the normal experience is. So you build on top of that."[45]

In the parlance of makeover television, the suspect is the passenger who "pops"—affectively and, therefore (by the logic of the program), visually—for the behavior detectives. Writing about a scenario at Dulles in which a SPOT agent decided to stop a passenger for questioning, reporter Thomas Frank observes: "The man had caught Kinsey's eye not just because he acted nervously, but because he acted differently. Other travelers shuffling blankly along the security line that quiet afternoon showed all the emotion of cattle. This passenger's contrasting anxiety showed, in TSA parlance, 'deviations from baseline behavior.'"[46] The SPOT agent's comment suggests that even if a passenger looks different (i.e., racially or ethnically), their acts reveal whether or not they are deviant according to a normal distribution of human behavior. His concept of "acting differently" fails to acknowledge the full range of cultural norms regarding public presentation and behavior.

Behavior detection works like a polygraph test: involuntary signs of stress are read as evidence of deceit. The problem with this model is that the public practice of behavior detection, like other techniques of risk management, produces and extends stress and fear among travelers. When it comes to the emotional life of airports in the post-9/11 era, passengers do not function as discrete containers. The TSA admits as much when its SPOT program claims to be perfectly calibrated to the new normal or perpetually high-anxiety level that corresponds to a system that tells passengers they are supposed to be ever vigilant, always on high alert. The security experts in charge of the SPOT program emphasize their training in and facility with the new affective and behavioral norms for airports in the post-9/11 context. The TSA claims that its program takes the affective temperature of the airport, sets a baseline reading of what's normal, and then sends its BDOs into the field to look for anomalous behavior. But the TSA's interest in affect does not stop there. The agency strives to manipulate the affective charge of the airport. It is in the interest of the behavior detectives to manage as well as monitor affect because if the affective norm of the checkpoint is "really stressed out," then it will be difficult to detect stress in a terrorist concealing his group's plans.

Whereas the generalized anxiety and fear periodically triggered by the color-coded threat advisory scale proved politically expedient for the Bush administration, generalized anxiety has proven with time to be counterproductive at the airport. Once fear becomes autonomous, writes Brian Massumi, "it wraps the time-slip so compellingly around experience that it becomes experience's affective surround."[47] Therefore the TSA assumes a generalized level of anxiety appropriate to individuals jacked into the threat advisory system *and* it attempts to manipulate the level of anxiety at the checkpoint.[48] Writing about the threat advisory scale, Massumi correctly describes the program as an unprecedented attempt at the mass coordination of affect through a state-sponsored practice of vague warnings or, as he puts it, "signaling without signification." In response to the threat advisory system, he writes, "each body's individuality performed itself, reflexively (that is to say, nonreflectively) in an immediate nervous response."[49] There is an inverse dynamic at work in behavior detection—an intentionally vague observational program of which passengers may or may not be aware. If the threat advisory scale mobilizes passengers to keep an eye out and act as informants, behavior detection treats them as objects of the behavior detective officer's monitoring gaze.

From the TSA's perspective, the traveling public is both that mobile mass, which may be hiding or obscuring those with terrorist leanings, and the collective of innocents from which the would-be terrorists must be visually filtered. Consequently, the TSA wants innocent passengers to show "all the emotion of cattle." In response to the question: "How do you tell an irate customer from a terrorist?" Hawley told the editors at *Aviation Week*: "We need to calm down the checkpoint. If we can calm down the process so the baseline data is lower, then it makes it easier for the other to pop out."[50] The calming effect desired by the TSA is being designed into checkpoints at new or refurbished airports. At the Indianapolis Airport's new terminal, which opened November 11, 2008, the security areas are intentionally more spacious. According to Robert Spitler, the Indianapolis airport's director of security, special blue lighting was installed at the checkpoint to produce "a calming effect."[51] In the process of calming the checkpoint, the TSA constructs the traveling public's collective innocence as reliant on, whether or not it conforms to, an observable physiological standard of nothing-to-hide.

The Terror of Suspicion

By appealing to a distribution of normal behavior, the SPOT program goes some way toward demystifying the figure of the terrorist. Former director of security at Ben-Gurion Rafi Ron told NPR: "Terrorists are far from being perfect. They are people, they are human beings, just like us," and they make mistakes. As he explained to *US News and World Report*, "Passengers with illegitimate, violent agendas don't act normally."[52] Behavior detection brings the terrorist back from beyond the pale, if you will, and inserts him into a universal distribution of human behavior ranging from normal to deviant. The problem with this move is that it inevitably raises the question: How does one tell the difference between an innocent passenger who is stressed out by airport security and a passenger trying to conceal the intent to do harm? In print at least, Ekman admits the difficulty and preaches extreme caution, but the TSA has consistently claimed that its behavior detectives can tell the difference just by looking.

When a behavior detective observes a passenger who is visibly addled but whose behavior does not comport with the TSA's visual stereotype of "the hassled business traveler" or "the woman whose just had a fight with her boyfriend," it is time to approach that passenger and start a casual conversation. Monitoring nonverbal behavior for involuntary signs of bad intentions requires the production of a set of visual stereotypes, which correspond to points along the continuum of normal human behavior. Carl Maccario, a program analyst for SPOT, says that in training behavior detection officers, "we teach that everybody's been in an airport long enough to know what the norm is. . . . There's an expected norm or an expected baseline environment. We teach the BDOs, in a simplified form, to look for anomalous behavior in that environment."[53] It is unclear from Hawley and Maccario's comments whether visual stereotypes of normal airport behavior are standardized and imparted to BDOs in training or whether they are the sum total of individual officers' incoming impressions of what's normal based on their cumulative experience as social creatures and airport employees.

What if one passenger's typical emotional state when flying is not considered within the normal range? Ekman admits this challenge. In fact, he has a name for it: the "Brokaw hazard."[54] Ekman named it the Brokaw hazard because during his tenure at the *Today Show*, Tom Brokaw stated that most clues of deception are verbal rather than physical, as in the case of a convoluted or evasive reply to a direct question. Ekman argues that Brokaw is wrong. The possibility of misjudging people is at work even in cases of indirect, confused, or evasive responses because that may be evidence merely of the particular individual's speech style. Detection errors are likely to be made, he argues, if the lie detector has no base for comparison—no reference point to know whether the suspect's behaviors are normal for her even if they appear somehow abnormal or otherwise suspicious. *"There is no sign of deceit itself,"* Ekman stresses, "no gestures, facial expression, or muscle twitch that in and of itself means that a person is poorly prepared and clues of emotions that don't fit the person's line."[55] Is it not the case that in the cosmopolitan space of the airport, the Brokaw hazard is always in effect?[56]

While Ekman admits that ideally the lie detector would have some familiarity with the individual he's profiling, he does not acknowledge the influence of cultural differences in nonverbal behavior. The SPOT program uniformly denies the fundamental opacity of cross-cultural encounter. Ekman defends the universal applicability of his system, hence its usefulness in the cosmopolitan space of the airport, where culturally specific nonverbal cues would be unintelligible to the majority of US behavior detectives. The Department of Homeland Security is working hard to establish the cultural neutrality of the SPOT program once and for all because otherwise, the TSA is still vulnerable to charges of racial, ethnic, and religious profiling. Even if the DHS is able to furnish additional proof of the universal applicability of Ekman's system, it does not mean the SPOT program affects all passengers equally. Neither the TSA nor the DHS acknowledges that in the eyes of some behavior detectives people displaying non-Western styles of grooming and dress may read as less transparent than those sporting culturally familiar hairstyles and fashions. Even if non-Western styles of facial hair and practices of veiling do not stimulate practices of racial or ethnic profiling per se within Ekman's system of lie detection, they may nonetheless be read as subtle deception clues or examples of what Ekman calls "masking" in reference to various attempts to cover or obscure the face. He argues that the best way to conceal a strong emotion is to mask it by covering the face, turning away, or the best mask of all: putting on another emotion to hide what's actually felt.[57]

From what we have learned about behavior detection thus far, performing innocence requires one to avoid the appearance of strange or unusual behavior and to trust and/or hope that one is not showing the involuntary signs of stress produced when trying to conceal emotions. The TSA demands conformity to the universal behavior norms of innocence recognized by a contested school of American behavioral psychology. It is reasonable to assume that under such circumstances, passengers who know they are being observed for nonverbal deception cues are likely to act in a self-conscious manner—even and especially if they have no idea what the behavior detectives identify as suspicious behavior.

This scenario potentially unleashes what I refer to as the terror of suspicion or a passenger's fear at her lack of control over how routine screeners and behavior detectives interpret her body's signs (voluntary and involuntary). A passenger's fear of being perceived as suspicious arguably produces some of the very same stress effects produced in the body of a passenger with the intent to do harm. Again, Ekman admits this problem and has a name for it. The "Othello error" refers to the fact that someone experiencing fear of being disbelieved will show the same signs of fear as the person experiencing detection apprehension.[58] This is particularly true, Ekman writes, in the case of individuals with strong generalized feelings of guilt. Persons who tend to feel guilty are likely to have those feelings aroused in situations where they may be suspected of wrongdoing.[59] What neither Ekman nor the TSA acknowledges is that members of some social and cultural groups have reason to fear they will be disbelieved. African Americans have expressed their fear of lacking credibility with police officers in terms of a broader critique of institutionalized racism in the United States. Muslims and Sikhs living in and traveling through the United States likely experience similar anxiety regarding the racial, ethnic, or religious biases of the behavior detectives and routine screeners working at US airports.

The same can be said for both documented and undocumented immigrants. A Government Accountability Office (GAO) report issued in 2011 found that 39 percent of arrests made on the basis of SPOT referrals were for immigration issues. In response to the report, TSA Chief John Pistole said:

> There are several reasons why a large percentage of arrests resulting from SPOT screening are due to an individual's immigration status. . . . A person in the US illegally is aware that they will be subjected to . . . [thorough] screening and may have a fear of discovery due to the potential consequences, including arrest and/or deportation from the country. Similarly a passenger who may intend to harm an aircraft may also have a fear of discovery. . . . BDOs have no way of knowing if an individual they are referring is carrying an explosive device or attempting to conceal their immigration status due to the strong correlation between criminal and terrorist behaviors.[60]

Pistole's comment contradicts former claims, made on behalf of the TSA, that behavior detection officers can tell the difference. His remarks exemplify what Rachel Ida Buff refers to as the preemptive criminalization of immigrants in the post-9/11 era. She writes: "The signal concern of the homeland security moment announces itself as being about transparency: the more we know about who comes to this country, the better off we will be. The USA PATRIOT Act extended the ability of the federal government to gather information from arenas previously considered private and protected, such as phone calls, voicemails, email, library records and criminal investigations."[61] While it is true that US citizens face greater scrutiny than they did prior to the PATRIOT Act, immigrants are preemptively criminalized and therefore face the harshest scrutiny. This is true even though "the only crimes the detention of hundreds of non-citizen, predominantly Muslim men after 9/11 has turned up have been immigration violations."[62] Buff is concerned, in particular, about migrant subjectivity in the homeland security moment because preemptive criminalization "narrows migrant access to political rights, like driver's licenses and other benefits, most notably, currently, health care. Migrants cannot have full political subjectivity, because they might be criminals, and criminals might be terrorists."[63] The information gathering performed in the name of Homeland Security is consonant, she argues, with bureaucratic practices during Chinese exclusion: "To exclude undesirables, it is necessary to have a vast state apparatus to carefully scrutinize all entrants for potential undesirability."[64]

A Government Accountability Office study found that from May 2004 to August 2008, SPOT detentions resulted in zero charges of terrorism and included 427 arrests of undocumented immigrants, 209 for outstanding warrants, 166 for fraudulent documents, and 125 for drug possession. The same study tracked sixteen people who had been charged in six terrorist plots during the same period only to discover that they had passed undetected a minimum of twenty-three times through eight airports with behavior detection officers.[65] When confronted with such evidence, TSA Chief John Pistole cites the SPOT Validation Study, completed in April 2011, which found that the SPOT program "was more effective than random screening to varying degrees." A separate report made by the GAO notes that problems with data-gathering methods used in the SPOT Validation Study render "meaningful analyses" of the results difficult to produce.[66] Finally, a 2011 hearing held in the House of Representatives before a Science, Space, and Technology subcommittee concluded that scientific support for connections between behavioral and physiological markers and mental state is "strongest for elementary states (simple emotions, attentional processes, states of arousal, and cognitive processes), weak for more complex states (deception), and nonexistent for highly complex states (terrorist intent and beliefs)."[67] Despite these findings, the recommendation was to continue use of behavior detection in the initial stages of the screening process.

Ekman argues that of all the things that can go wrong in lie detection, the Othello error poses the most difficult challenge. He implores aspiring behavior detectives to proceed with caution: "The lie catcher must make an effort to *consider the possibility that a sign of an emotion is not a clue to deceit but a clue to how a truthful person feels about being suspected of lying.*"[68] This involves ruling out the possibility that the signs in question are produced by an innocent person's fear of being wrongly judged.[69] Such challenges to the work of behavior detection have not deterred the TSA. As Chief John Pistole considers moving the agency toward more of a risk-based approach to airport security, he envisions expanding the SPOT program. An experiment is already under way at Boston Logan International Airport, where behavior detection officers "chat-down" passengers as they check their proof of identification and boarding pass. A play on the word *pat-down* used to describe the physical inspection of passengers, chat-downs are part of an attempt to move away from a one-size-fits-all approach to airport security, Pistole says. It is also part of an effort to shift away from a technology-focused approach to more investment in human interaction. Questioning is brief, lasting about forty seconds per passenger. Israeli security expert Rafi Ron approves. He has long argued that interviews are the most vital component of the airport screening process in Israel. Ron admits that in the Israeli security system, risk profiling relies on age-based and religious stereotypes. The system overtly labels "a twenty-five-year-old Palestinian from Gaza" as high-risk and "an elderly Holocaust survivor" as low-risk. He notes that this sort of system would not be acceptable in the United States. Ron then makes a 180-degree turn, noting: "They come in all colors, shapes, and ethnic backgrounds." Then he justifies the expansion of behavioral profiling by raising the specter of the "home-grown" terrorist, citing John Walker Lindh, an American convicted of working with the Taliban; Jose Padilla, a Hispanic American convicted of providing aid to terrorists; and attempted shoe-bomber Richard Reid, a British citizen of Jamaican descent.[70]

Indeed, passenger self-sorting (chapter 4) may soon be replaced by a system that segregates passengers based on their risk profile, dividing them into three groups: "Known Traveler," "Regular," and "Enhanced."[71] Profiles would be generated using some combination of the following: mining the data that is already being collected by airlines; reviewing the intelligence gathered by the government; checking passengers against watch lists; conducting short interviews or chat-downs; and flagging suspicious behavior. At present, the Air Line Pilots Association advocates a move to risk-based airport security queues and the International Civil Aviation Organization, a UN body that establishes policy for its member states, is considering the possibility. If adopted, the new system would potentially revamp the Global Entry system, offering passengers the option to buy trusted or known traveler status for a fee if they submit to an interview, a background check, and fingerprint scanning.[72] In addition to the aforementioned elements of risk profiling, passengers may also be subject to on-site physiological monitoring by remote sensing devices. Project Hostile Intent has been renamed Future Attribute Screening Technology (FAST). Funded by the DHS's Science and Technology Directorate, FAST is working to improve the techniques of behavior detection and develop technologies capable of covertly collecting and recording information on individual passengers, "including video images, audio recordings, cardiovascular signals, pheromones, electrodermal activity, and respiratory measurements."[73] That is to say, the DHS is presently trying to actualize Ekman's (and others') cultural fantasies of high-tech behavior detection.[74]

Monitoring Public Feelings

Within the post-9/11 era, the US security state has attempted to manage public feelings domestically with a "bad cop / good cop" routine, oscillating between fear mongering (e.g., the color-coded threat advisory system) and pacification (e.g., adopting new rules in the image of the last attack; mandatory customer-service training in small talk and nonthreatening demeanor for TSA employees; use of industrial engineers, urban planners, and efficiency experts to redesign the space of the checkpoint so as to produce a calming effect). Regardless of how particular passengers feel on given days at specific airports, many US citizens and international visitors have performed *as if* the security state's threat construction and corresponding risk management techniques are valid.

In the post-9/11 era, the passenger's feelings about the new security apparatuses (or rather the appearance of her feelings) become a crucial part of the performance of her innocence. The performance of innocence requires that one "get with the program," which means both embodying concern about the prospect of another terrorist attack and complying with security procedures. The performance of nothing-to-hide takes the form of performing affective compliance with the security apparatus (i.e., none of this bothers me in the least because *I* understand the threat "we" are facing, and *I* have nothing to hide). What is more, a particular passenger need not believe in the threat construction of another terrorist attack to fear the TSA official's power as what Judith Butler has called a "petty sovereign."[75]

Does it matter whether or not this performance of transparency is genuine on the part of passengers? Is it possible that performing "This doesn't bother me," even in those cases where it is a strategic or cynical performance, still has the effect (over time) of habituating those performers and the passengers who witness their performances to the new conditions on their mobility within the security culture of terrorism prevention? Passenger performances of affective compliance with the security apparatus preempt dissent. Because innocence tests are performance-based and instituted without a formal and publicly transparent process, public deliberation and opportunities for dissent are short-circuited.

The TSA's monitoring of public feelings involves the subtle calibration of bodily and affective norms within the public spaces of airports. The public feelings of passengers (or rather the appearance of passengers' feelings) are processed by the security state, which modulates the anxiety of the environment with the aim of making nonconformists stand out. Consequently, "publicness" no longer operates according to an expressive model of the presentation of the self to others. Rather, it is a condition of mobility that passengers achieve the collective appearance of a pacified public. Passenger performances of affective transparency within the space of the airport potentially pose a threat to public participation beyond, insofar as such performances simultaneously isolate members of the public, each of whom is caught in a private experience of the terror of suspicion, and breed conformity via the pressure to embody inconspicuousness according to the TSA's purportedly universal standard.

Writing about automated facial expression analysis, Kelly Gates offers the following observation: "The very possibility of automating the imperfect—and culturally and historically variably—human capacity to read the faces of others suggests that certain assumptions about facial expressions and their relationship to human affective relations are already in circulation, assumptions that posit affect as a physiological process capable of being not only coded and analyzed but also *engineered*."[76] While the SPOT program has not managed to automate the behavioral analysis of passengers (although this is in the works), the program assumes that affect is a physiological process "capable of being not only coded and analyzed but also *engineered*." Indeed, the SPOT program constitutes an unprecedented attempt by the security state to monitor and manage public feelings in airport settings. Many routine TSA screeners have been conscripted into the service of this mission in the name of providing better customer service to passengers (chapter 4). Within the airport context, public feelings threaten to distract security officials from the unwanted event that has yet to occur. According to the logic of the SPOT program, the terrorist's potential for violent action becomes visible only after the traveling public has been sufficiently pacified or, better yet, turned down. In other words, the terrorist's apparent status as a potential agent of violence requires the public's affective disappearance or the careful modulation of public feeling downward to the point that it reaches a level of irrelevance. More specifically, the appearance of the traveling public's collective innocence demands that individual passengers avoid activating the behavior detectives' racial, ethnic, or religious stereotypes, learn to keep their cool while moving through the airport, or, failing that, approximate the visual stereotype of the "harried but harmless" passenger.

Grounded as it is in a contested school of behavioral psychology, the SPOT program approaches passengers/suspects as individuals characterized by neurological, muscular, and skeletal processes, understood as bound by discrete bodies. The body-as-container model has particular legal implications within and beyond the space of the airport. At the same time, the TSA has at least partially embraced what could be characterized as a more fluid understanding of affect as something that circulates between and among bodies, objects, the airport environment, and the event of flying or of getting through security. Along these lines, the TSA has hired industrial engineers, urban planners, and efficiency experts to redesign the space of the checkpoint so as to produce a calming effect. According to the affective environment model, suspected terrorists continue to be treated as individuals who visually pop for the behavior detectives while innocent passengers fade into the background, becoming undifferentiated from one another and the environment. This approach carries potentially problematic legal implications for suspected passengers whose innocence is collectively constructed. Given these contradictory approaches to passengers, it behooves us to pay close attention to the SPOT program's legal implications—both for suspects whose observed interiority may become a screen for the projections of security experts and for innocents whose manipulated exteriority may serve as a visual filter for sorting out those passengers who fail to get with the program.

The Power of Performance

The *Washington Post* published Paul Ekman's letter to the editor on October 29, 2006, in which he defends the scientific validity of the SPOT program:

> Critics of the controversial new security program I was taking stock of [at Boston Logan]—known as SPOT, for Screening Passengers by Observational Techniques—have said that it is an unnecessary invasion of privacy, based on an untested method of observation, that is unlikely to yield much in the way of red-handed terrorists set on blowing up a plane or flying it into a building, but would violate fliers' civil rights.
>
> I disagree. I've participated in four decades' worth of research into deception and demeanor, and I know that researchers have amassed enough knowledge about how someone who is lying looks and behaves that it would be negligent not to use it in the search for terrorists. Along with luggage checks, radar screening, bomb-sniffing dogs and the rest of our security arsenal, observational techniques can help reduce risks— and potentially prevent another deadly assault like the attacks of Sept. 11, 2001.

Here the specter of 9/11 invoked by Ekman functions as a conversation stopper—a still-looming threat that squelches criticism of airport security programs and procedures. Ekman does not stop there but milks the attacks of 9/11 further. In order to marshal additional support for behavior detection, Ekman goes on to make the case that the technique would have prevented the attacks of 9/11. He notes that several of the hijackers were stopped and questioned but ultimately allowed to board their flights. Then he offers an anecdote about an airport screener who was suspicious of one of the hijackers that day but cleared the hijacker for takeoff nevertheless because he "had no training that would have given him the confidence to act on his suspicions":

> The hijackers' lies—to visa interviewers and airport check-in workers— succeeded largely because airport personnel weren't taught how to spot

liars. They had to rely on their hunches. The people who might have saved the lives of many Americans were needlessly handicapped.

Imagine if that screener had been taught to discern the signs of deception in a person's facial expressions, voice, body language and gestures. With such training, he could have been confident enough to report the hijacker's behavior.

In effect, Ekman admits that behavior detection legitimates the subjective assessments of screeners. In his words, it gives them the confidence to act on their "suspicions."[77] Note Ekman does not say behavior detection training gives screeners the confidence to act on their "hunches." By sleight of hand, Ekman moves from describing behavior detection training as empowering screeners to act on their suspicions to claiming that the screeners working on 9/11 failed to detect the hijackers' true intentions because they lacked the proper training. Behavior detection training would have allowed them to recognize the scientifically proven nonverbal cues of deception, thus freeing them from the amateur's reliance on intuition and wild hunches.

The imaginative exercise proposed by Ekman—what if there had been expert screeners working the airports that day, who were capable of exercising appropriate suspicion and acting on it—disavows the liar's or in this case the terrorist's ability to train for the behavior detectives. To put it another way, popular faith in the expertise of the behavior detectives refuses the possibility that a passenger could master the performance of involuntary, and therefore "genuine" calm. The term *involuntary* used to describe the nervous and behavioral tics of liars becomes important here. It is an appeal to the ground of nature, biology, physiology, the central nervous system—that which is beyond the purview of an individual's control. The SPOT program arrogantly assumes that the behavior detectives can control for the normal anxiety of innocent passengers but passengers cannot prepare for and play to the normative assumptions of the behavior detectives. In other words, the airport environment can be tweaked to recalibrate the affective charge of the place, thereby subtly influencing the autonomic nervous systems of innocent passengers. But it does not work the other way around. Nervous passengers may not intentionally calm themselves down such that their bodies genuinely produce the appearance of calm or, more precisely, the absence of signs of stress.

The security state's assumption on this score is rooted in the Western conception of performance as mimesis and therefore distinct from reality.

By parsing through Ekman's definition of deceit, we can see how this assumption informs his model of deception detection. In 1985, Ekman published *Telling Lies: Clues to Deceit in the Marketplace, Politics, and Marriage*. In this popular guide to lie detection, Ekman defines lies as willful acts of deception: "A liar can *choose* not to lie," he writes. But, Ekman notes, the liar is not the only agent one must consider when determining whether or not a deception has taken place. One must also consider the liar's "target" or audience: "In a lie the target has not asked to be misled, nor has the liar given any *prior notification* of an intention to do so. It would be bizarre to call actors liars," Ekman writes. "Their audience agrees to be misled, for a time; that is why they are there."[78] In Ekman's understanding of deception, there is a stable reality distinct from appearances—a ground of truth, which appearances may accurately reflect or partially conceal.

Experts in Interpersonal Deception Theory have developed a universal system for decoding the signs or nonverbal tells of deception. They have not, therefore, altogether escaped semiotics, which means that, in turn, they leave the door open for skilled performers to train for and rehearse unwitting performances of transparency. Because Ekman's model concentrates on the suspect's energy and its leakage, non-Western performance traditions, which do not subscribe to the same distinction between performance and reality characteristic of Western theater, are particularly well suited to the task of intentionally calming oneself down before and during one's time at the airport.

The TSA's rather naive operational assumption that individual passengers cannot master the performance of involuntary transparency is challenged by research at the intersections of performance studies, religious studies, and anthropology. Non-Western understandings of performance do not adhere to the mimetic model of performance as faking it or putting on false appearances. Performance is not separate from reality in this way. Performance is a means of altering reality, consciousness, physical, and spiritual well-being. Performance is efficacious. It has the power to change reality. Within these traditions, intentional practices can cultivate, if not directly cause, what Western science characterizes as involuntary emotional and physical effects. For example, Ekman defines an individual's pattern of breathing as an involuntary function of the autonomic nervous system. But in Buddhist meditation and Hindu yoga practice, performers intentionally slow their pattern of breathing as a means of inducing genuine physical, mental, and emotional states of calm detachment. In these performances, there is no distinguishing between performance and reality as one finds in Western understandings of theater as pretend, play-acting, or make-believe. Rather, the actions performed induce the reality experienced by participants. In the practice of "smile yoga," intentionally assuming a slight smile produces feelings of genuine calm. Within non-Western traditions of the performance of healing, one also finds room for collective affective engagement and experience. The Korean shaman, who is skilled in the arts of spirit possession, will guide a group performance with real healing effects for the mourning family members of the deceased. That said, the aforementioned techniques begin with individual or small group training and practice and are therefore distinct from the mass surveillance of affect practiced by the TSA.

Behavior detection also assumes that the relationship between reality and appearances—or feelings and the human containers in which they are kept—remain relatively stable over short periods of time. The SPOT program does not admit wild fluctuations of mood. Nor is there much room for suddenly changing one's mind. Ekman's origin story for his theory of deception detection begins with the film footage of a suicidal 1950s housewife, who no longer felt that she had any purpose in life after her children grew up and left home. Ekman studied tapes in which Mary told her doctors that she was well enough to leave the hospital for the weekend. She later confessed that she had lied and should not be granted a weekend pass because she would use the unsupervised time to kill herself. Ekman first developed his theory of micro-expressions and gestures by slowing down and repeatedly viewing and analyzing film footage of Mary assuring her doctors that she was okay. His reading of the tape as a scenario of deception is based on his acceptance of Mary's later word against her earlier word. This shows little understanding of the range of intensity, frequency, and duration of people's experiences with depression and suicidal thoughts.

The Mary origin story also raises another, perhaps obvious, challenge to behavior detection in nonclinical settings like airports. If Mary had been a depressive housewife of the 1960s, rather than the 1950s, perhaps her doctors would have given her a "mother's little helper" to alleviate her suffering. In an era when doctors and patients routinely use prescription drugs to manage and control a wide range of emotional problems—many of them anxiety disorders, which are often difficult to separate from depressive disorders—it is quite possible for passengers to intentionally produce the involuntary signs of calm collectedness by taking the appropriate drugs in advance of their arrival at the airport.

Ekman's model of deception also assumes that signs of stress observed correspond to the situations in which they arise. In other words, Ekman assumes that the liar is stressed out during the process of perpetrating the lie or concealing the truth from his or her audience. This assumption is contradicted by the research on and experience of people suffering from a wide range of anxiety disorders, which are defined by a set of symptoms with no conceivable connection to environmental cues, events, or stimuli. Like posttraumatic stress disorder, anxiety disorders are characterized by symptoms that have become disarticulated from their initial, external causes—free-floating assemblages of misery and panic that nevertheless feel like they are washing over the individual at that very moment and with little to no warning in acute cases. To the extent that the SPOT program assumes a normal range of human emotional experience and affective performance in public life, it discounts the experiences of passengers with mental, emotional, and cognitive disabilities.

Finally, and perhaps most important to the central argument of this book, screening passengers by observational techniques demands that passengers perform the affective labor of embodying and managing the appearance of the terrorist threat. This type of labor is new to some populations and all-too-familiar to other populations. Brent Staples's essay "Black Men and Public Space" comes to mind. In the essay, the author describes his discovery that if he whistled classical tunes when in the presence of white people on the street at night, it eased tensions and reduced the chances he would be mistaken for a mugger simply because he was black.[79] As anyone who has ever been mistaken for a criminal or a terrorist (or merely feared being mistaken for one) can attest, there are subtle and not-so-subtle ways of intentionally performing and stylizing the body against stereotype and/or cultural expectation.

By resorting to behavioral profiling, the TSA undercuts its own faith in its ability to see literally through bodies and belongings and falls back on codes for deciphering the surfaces of bodies and behaviors as clues to truths that reside within the interiors of those bodies. More important from a political and ethical standpoint, the SPOT program shows little respect for the polysemic character of social performance and refuses to acknowledge the irreducible opacity of cross-cultural encounters. Not incidentally, the majority of those detained and arrested under the SPOT program thus far have been undocumented immigrants.[80]

The biopolitical project of terrorism prevention is not only concerned with reflexive governance, or a suspect's capacity to perform voluntary transparency up to the TSA's standards. Terrorism prevention increasingly involves policing involuntary behavior, or the expert's ability to read a suspect's incapacity to control the communicative signals emitted by her body and face. If reflexive governance empowers citizens to police themselves, then involuntary policing takes some measure of that power away, reserving authority for a new class of experts schooled in the pseudoscience of behavior detection. The popular applications of this pseudoscience are unselfconsciously and unapologetically cynical. Popular books on behavior detection read like contemporary versions of *How to Win Friends and Influence People*. The animating tension in these performances is between the power of cynical performances in everyday life, which promise to earn the opaque performers money, status, power, sex, and the good life, and the weakness of involuntary performances of self in everyday life, which betray the performers, who prove vulnerably transparent to trained eyes. In official and popular practices, behavior detection is a mode of arrogant perception.[81] Cynical or strategic performances of self in everyday life are closely connected to what Mark Andrejevic calls "savvy skepticism." Obeying the laws of the market, these everyday performance and reading practices are enacted at the expense of others. Within the frameworks of cynical performance and savvy skepticism, non-Western modes of performance designed to attune interior and exterior worlds by intentionally inducing states of calm within and without are unthinkable. Likewise, self-consciously naive performances of self (e.g., the estranged traveler) and sensitive or humble readings of others (the empathic observer) remain unimaginable and therefore untapped resources for human interaction.

TRANSPARENCY BEYOND US AIRPORTS

International Airports, "Flying" Checkpoints, Controlled-Tone Zones, and Lateral Behavior Detection

The aesthetics of transparency is at work in security cultures ranging from US-controlled airports to those not under US control, from war zones to occupied territories, from professional police work to neighborhood watch programs, and from No-Joking Zones in airports to analogous controlled-tone zones beyond airports. What unites each of these geographically, culturally, and politically diverse security cultures is a paranoid orientation (introduction) toward local and mobile populations on the part of security officials, occupying forces, police, and vigilantes. In these contexts, paranoia manifests itself as the assumption that some unwanted event is about to occur and, based on this assumption, the practice of preemptive law and order. But the ways in which preemptive law and order are practiced vary drastically across security cultures. It is for this reason that I advocate a new conceptualization of *asymmetrical transparency*, which attends to the uneven application of the aesthetics of transparency across bodies and contexts.

Beyond US Airports

This book has provided a sustained critical analysis of airport security policies and practices in the United States during the post-9/11 era. Since its formation in 2001, the DHS has tried to influence global aviation security policy in two major ways: first, the DHS issues authoritative security directives to foreign airports, which serve as the last point of departure for flights to the United States; second, the DHS works diplomatically through the International Civil Aviation Organization and the European Union (EU) to encourage stricter security standards in international civil aviation. In the first case, lessons learned from the investigations of specific terrorist plots are applied not only to the US traveling public but also to international airports with flights to the United States. Typically, the DHS authoritatively communicates new security directives to all foreign airports immediately following a terrorist attack, close call, or other security breach.[1] According to Kip Hawley, head of the TSA from 2005 to 2009, the goal is to create an international network of airports, "beginning with Europe," that have the same full-body imaging technologies and regulations regarding liquids and gels, and share information about threats.[2] Acting as a global manager of aviation security, the TSA sets and communicates standards, provides training, and performs periodic assessments of all US and foreign carriers that serve as last points of departure to the United States. Technically, the US government has authority over airlines that fly here. In practice, the United States must rely on the willingness of airports and governments to implement changes, which requires not only the political will to carry out those changes but also the capital to invest in expensive new security technologies.[3]

The diplomatic approach did not emerge until one year into Janet Napolitano's term as the secretary of the DHS. From the perspective of the US government, the narrowly averted sabotage of Northwest Flight 253 from Amsterdam to Detroit on December 25, 2009, highlighted the shortcomings of the international aspect of the national security program. Analysts agreed that the failure of governments to efficiently share passenger information on the would-be bomber before he boarded his flight in Amsterdam had made the attempt possible. The case is instructive in terms of the international political dynamics of aviation security in the post-9/11 era. Foreign governments and regulatory agencies do not uniformly comply with security directives issued by the TSA. To date, those most likely to be enthusiastic in their cooperation are those governments implicated in the security breach that inspired the proposed security reforms. After a terrorist attack or close call, officials representing such agencies publicly perform political gestures meant to demonstrate their concern for the lives lost or nearly lost. After the attempted sabotage of Northwest Flight 253, Nigerian and Dutch officials were the first to publicly promise to purchase and install body scanners for use on passengers traveling to the United States. On December 30, Director of Homeland Security Janet Napolitano called the Dutch interior minister, Guusje ter Horst, to urge that the full body–imaging machines be used to screen passengers wishing to enter the United States.[4] Dutch officials agreed to employ the technology "immediately," but said it would take three weeks to get all of their machines up and running. Ter Horst explained that the machines had not been in use on the day of the attack because the United States had expressed privacy concerns about using the technology to look through the clothing of passengers headed to the United States. While the Dutch had been using the machines on a test basis since 2007, the European Union had not approved their routine use.[5] Harold Demuren, chief of the Nigerian Civil Aviation Authority, said he hoped to have the scanners in place by early 2010.[6] Not incidentally, attempted bomber Farouk Abdulmutallab had arrived in Amsterdam from Lagos, Nigeria, where he passed without notice through a metal detector carrying eighty grams of explosives sewn into his underwear.[7]

When presented with security suggestions from the DHS, some governments must balance attempts to comply with US standards and regulations, while managing citizens' impressions of how their leaders respond to political pressure from the United States. In the immediate aftermath of the attack on Flight 253, the *Toronto Star* reported that Transport Canada was actively researching ways to implement full-body scanners at its airports. Because the Canadian government faces pressure from its own citizens not to bow too swiftly to the Department of Homeland Security's wishes, the article quotes a spokesperson for Transport Canada stating, "Canada will make its own decision," and assures readers that the agency will not be hurried by "other governments."[8] Germany and Israel both declined to state publicly whether they would step up aviation security in response to the TSA directive. A spokeswoman for Israel's Civil Aviation Authority emphasized that "security is always tight on flights between the United States and Israel," while a spokeswoman for Germany's Interior

Ministry reminded reporters that Germany's security standards were already "among the strictest in the world."[9] Despite public assurances to the contrary, Canada was among a small number of nations that also included the United States, Britain, and the Netherlands, which accelerated the deployment of the body scanners in response to the attack on Northwest Flight 253.[10]

Security directives issued by the DHS or TSA to former imperial powers may move from there along old colonial routes of power and influence. For example, the Civil Aviation Authority, which is based in London and regulates civil aviation throughout the United Kingdom, "instructs" the Airports Company of South Africa (ACSA) on aviation security. Of course, private security firms and government regulatory agencies choose whether or not to comply with the urging of former imperial powers, which receive their marching orders from the DHS and TSA in the United States. Shortly after the attempted bombing of Northwest Flight 253, a spokeswoman for the ACSA told the BBC: "We are not considering full-body scanners at this stage. Full stop."[11]

Tensions over greater information sharing between countries and the implementation of full-body scanners ran highest in the EU, where privacy concerns had already created obstacles from the perspective of aggressive security officials operating from the United States. In 2008, the EU had suspended work regulating the use of body scanner because the European Parliament demanded an in-depth study of their impact on health and privacy. Consequently, the EU was allowing its member states to decide whether to use scanners at checkpoints. Following the attack on Northwest Flight 253, Italy joined the United States, Britain, Canada, and the Netherlands in their plan to install scanners immediately. But Belgium's secretary of state for transport described such measures as "excessive." Spain doubted the necessity of such measures, and Germany and France remained uncommitted.[12]

The United States met resistance to its global security agenda with a renewed commitment to pursue international compliance with US standards diplomatically. In his remarks about the intelligence failures that enabled the narrowly averted sabotage of Northwest Flight 253, President Obama emphasized the importance of expanding international aviation security partnerships. Secretary Napolitano followed up by saying that the US government would move to ensure "training and capacity is built in continents around the globe." She also noted that the DHS would urge foreign authorities to use the same new technologies for scanning passengers and their belongings at all airports with flights to the United States. At the time she made these remarks, Secretary Napolitano had already dispatched senior aides to South America, Europe, Asia, Africa, and the Middle East to discuss with government and airport officials how they might best collect and share passenger data.[13]

The language used by members of the international press to describe these international meetings highlights the tensions characteristic of global aviation security in the post-9/11 era. Were these genuine discussions of the security options between two officials of equal stature within the international security community? Or were these security briefings, during which time DHS officials informed foreign security officials of the department's wishes and urged them to comply, while diplomatically performing some of the conventions of a conversation? For example, the *Sydney Morning Herald* reported that Secretary Napolitano dispatched Janet Holl Lute, deputy head of the DHS, to meet with Australia's federal transport minister, Anthony Albanese, on January 10, 2010. During a one-hour briefing at Sydney International Airport, Lute and Albanese reportedly "discussed a combined response, including the prospect of using body scanners at Australian airports."[14] The article reports that the trip was the seventh stop in a two-week whirlwind tour aimed at garnering political support for stricter security measures for US-bound flights. Lute had already been to England and was also due to visit Singapore and the United Arab Emirates.[15]

Over the next nine months, Secretary Napolitano participated in regional international aviation security summits in Europe, Africa, Asia, the Middle East, and Western Hemisphere, where with the cooperation of security officials and administrators worldwide she developed a joint Declaration on Aviation Security. The declaration outlines an international framework of rules designed to support information sharing between countries, best practices in threat detection and screening, and upgrading screening technologies.[16] On September 28, 2010, Napolitano presented the Declaration to the Triennial Assembly of the International Civil Aviation Organization (ICAO) in Montreal. The ICAO is the international regulatory regime charged with setting global standards for aviation security. By its own description, the organization "sets standards and regulations necessary for aviation safety, security, efficiency and regularity, as well as for aviation environmental protection" and "serves as the forum for cooperation in all fields of civil aviation among its 191 Member States."[17] As the chief governing body of an international regulatory regime, the ICAO Council's major duties include the adoption of international Standards and Recommended Practices.[18] Consequently, the ICAO Council is the body that drafted and subsequently amended the primary international legal instrument for dealing with acts of unlawful interference with civil aviation: Annex 17 (also known as the Security Annex) to the Chicago Convention, which established the ICAO in 1944.[19] The Security Annex dates to the early 1970s and was initially developed in response to the dramatic increase of hijackings on commercial flights during the late 1960s. The document, which sets minimum standards for aviation security worldwide, endeavors to coordinate security programs around the world. Since its publication in 1974, the governing council of the ICAO continues to amend the document. On December 7, 2001, the ICAO adopted Amendment 10 in order to address the challenges to civil aviation authority posed by the events of September 11, 2001.

Amendment 10 obliges each member state to designate an official to manage a national civil aviation program. It further requires that every airport operating flights in or through a member state create a written security program document consistent with its national security program. The amendment also calls for the creation of a national regulatory mechanism for ensuring quality control by conducting surveys, performing audits, and making recommendations for security upgrades. Finally, by removing the adjective "international" from the Security Annex, the amendment imposes global standards applicable not only to international flights but also domestic air travel within member states.[20] Amendment 10 encourages member states to share threat information that applies to the aviation security of other states "as far as practicable." It also lays the groundwork for the implementation of new screening technologies at the checkpoint by requiring the human screeners working there not only to find but also identify dangerous objects that might be used to commit unlawful acts of interference. Other key aspects of the amendment include those provisions designed to respond to the possibility that passengers will become terrorists and transform airplanes into weapons of mass destruction. These include the routine inspection of any aircraft to which passengers may have had access; new in-flight security measures such as bullet-proof cockpits and the authorization of air security officers; the expansion of security-restricted areas at airports; and stricter background checks on airport employees empowered to access security-restricted areas without an escort.[21]

Unlike an additional amendment to Annex 17, Napolitano's joint Declaration on Aviation Security does not officially establish new security standards and practices. More of a political document than a policy document, the declaration brings considerable international political pressure to bear on the ICAO and its member states to comply with an expanded, and arguably more robust, interpretation of Amendment 10. The declaration opens diplomatically with a reference to Annex 17 and a suggestion that a new amendment may be needed. It "urges" member states to "strengthen and promote the effective application of ICAO Standards and Recommended Practices, with particular focus on Annex 17—*Security*, and develop strategies to address current and emerging threats."[22] The declaration devotes much of its limited space to the enhancement and implementation of screening technologies. When one considers that each body-scanning machine costs between US$100,000 and $200,000, this is not a minor request.[23] There is a provision for providing financial support to member states in the form of donor funds for the adoption of new screening technologies. Additionally, the declaration calls for member states to: harmonize approaches for air cargo security; adopt enhanced travel document security using biometrics; improve member states' ability to correct deficiencies discovered through the Universal Security Audit Programme; and share best practices. The declaration's call to share best practices is indicative of the United States' influence on the document and the processes by which best practices are determined. Among the range of areas recommended for sharing best practices it lists "screening and inspection techniques, including assessments of advanced screening technology for the detection of weapons and explosives; document security and fraud detection; behavior detection and threat-based risk analysis; screening of airport employees; the privacy and dignity of persons; and aircraft security."[24] The declaration was adopted with unanimous support at the Triennial Assembly of the ICAO on September 28, 2010.

A report filed by the GAO roughly one year after the attempted sabotage of Flight 253 confirms that the main lesson the US government took from the security event is that it was due to a failure of international cooperation regarding passenger information sharing and to a lack of proper technology for screening passengers on US-bound flights. The GAO report found that the DHS and TSA were making progress toward "enhancing international aviation security" and "facilitating foreign compliance with international aviation standards." The report uses the metaphor of harmonization in reference to efforts by the DHS and TSA to influence aviation security worldwide.[25] While the musical metaphor suggests a bilateral or multilateral collaborative process of making sure various national aviation security programs are playing in the same key, other language used in the report reflects a goal orientation more accurately described as the exportation of the US model. For example, the GAO report notes that despite efforts at harmonization by the DHS and TSA and related assessments of foreign security programs, "harmonization depends on the willingness of sovereign nations to voluntarily coordinate their aviation security standards and practices. In addition, foreign governments may view aviation security threats differently, and therefore may not consider international aviation security a high priority." It goes on to note additional challenges such as limited resources in developing countries, as well as legal and cultural factors, which may "affect nations' security enhancement and harmonization efforts." The report cites host governments' concerns about being assessed by the TSA as an additional example of the dissonance the DHS and TSA may encounter as they attempt to harmonize international aviation security.[26] One gets the sense that what the US government actually means by harmonization is that the United States will choose the key and take the melody line and the rest of the world will harmonize with it.

To date, the European Union has posed the most formidable public challenge to US attempts to leverage the moral authority of terrorist attacks to expand state and international surveillance capabilities unchecked and often without public debate. This is due, in part, to a robust public discourse on the right to personal data protection in Europe in contrast to the United States. Due to considerable public skepticism regarding the expansion of state surveillance via information networks, the EU is ahead of the United States in terms of its official public acknowledgment of the need for legal protections for data privacy and passenger dignity.[27] When the EU considers the adoption and regulation of new security measures and technologies, it evaluates them in terms of whether or not they are compatible with the Charter on Fundamental Rights. And yet, despite a more robust institutional culture of debate, over time the EU has adopted procedures, technologies, and guidelines that are largely consistent with those implemented without institutional debate in the United States.

To the extent that the United States has succeeded in influencing aviation security policy worldwide in the post-9/11 era, it has effectively exported aspects of the performance and culture of risk management as it is practiced in the United States to other countries. Consequently, the securitized international airport currently functions as a transnational stage for rehearsing a model of global citizenship, which treats performances of voluntary transparency—or willing submission to comprehensive, close surveillance—as a precondition of mobility.

Deterritorialized Checkpoints

The term *deterritorialized checkpoint* is useful for grouping together otherwise geographically dispersed and politically diverse contexts in which security officials and vigilantes employ what I am calling the aesthetics of transparency. It is also an important linguistic reminder that the aesthetics of transparency predates the security cultures formed in the United States and beyond in response to the terrorist attacks of 9/11. More accurately described as post–Cold War, rather than post-9/11, deterritorialized checkpoints are networked liminal zones of risk management within territories, which serve a preemptive legal framework embraced by the United States and other paranoid empires in the name of preventing terrorism and crime within the territory and, in some cases, immigration into the territory. At the deterritorialized checkpoint what is being checked is no longer exclusively, or even primarily, one's citizenship status; rather, it turns on the demonstration of one's innocence in terms of the aesthetics of transparency, where varying degrees of transparency and opacity are asymmetrically ascribed to different populations, based on the anti-immigration and counterterrorism policies of paranoid empires and occupying forces.

The checkpoints of security cultures formed in the post–Cold War era function differently than historical checkpoints once did in places like "Checkpoint Charlie." A powerful symbol of the Cold War, the primary function of a territorialized checkpoint like Checkpoint Charlie was to physically separate and thereby render concrete the significant ideological differences between the East and the West in a manner that functionally prevented westward emigration from the Eastern bloc. In contrast to this, post–Cold War checkpoints are powerful symbols of legitimacy, belonging, and mobility for some at the expense of others. The primary function of post–Cold War checkpoints (of which the post-9/11 airport security checkpoint is merely one example) is to monitor and control the mobility of populations that have been flagged as threatening or otherwise suspicious by the security experts and vigilant citizens of paranoid empires or occupying forces. Post–Cold War checkpoints are not designed to police the borders of well-defined geographic and political territories; rather, they exist to make particular mobile populations submit to rituals of surveillance in the name of preventing future acts of violence or crimes against property.

The post–Cold War checkpoint corresponds to the paradigm shift, described by Michael Hardt and Antonio Negri, from national defense to national security in the post–Cold War era: "The notion of 'security' signals a lack of distinction between inside and outside, between the military and the police. Whereas 'defense' involves a protective barrier against external threats, 'security' justifies a constant martial activity equally in the homeland and abroad."[28] As Claudio Lomnitz argues, frontiers and borders have given way to checkpoints, where anyone can be asked for identification at any time and in any place. While the ostensible reason for stopping someone may be to check their documents, the inspection includes not only identity verification but also analysis and interrogation of the suspect's performance of transparency or opacity. As such, post–Cold War checkpoints primarily serve the interests of paranoid empires, occupying forces, border and neighborhood vigilantes, and those who identify with the aforementioned institutions and individuals. In the Cold War checkpoint, you were assumed to be either Eastern or Western, and the checkpoint was there to maintain those differences as stable and meaningful. By contrast, in the post–Cold War checkpoint, anyone could be a terrorist, a criminal, or an illegal immigrant, therefore each person may be subject to rituals of surveillance and interrogation.

Post–Cold War checkpoints take the form of relatively permanent installations, as is the case with airport security checkpoints, or they may materialize as impromptu searches, seizures, and interrogations initiated anywhere and anytime by petty security officials authorized to detain members of flagged populations or neighborhood vigilantes operating in a manner consistent with laws like Florida's Stand Your Ground. Near the end of his cultural history of automobility, Jeremy Packer observes in dystopic science fiction movies, biometrics and other implements of control still operate at designated sites or checkpoints: "In simple terms it is still the space that is the site of control, not the very mobility of any given individual or population. For this second possibility to come into being, all of space would be a perpetual checkpoint."[29] This eventuality has already been realized in low-tech security cultures operative along the

Israeli-Palestinian border and, more recently in the United States. Consider the "flying" or impromptu checkpoints set up between permanent checkpoints, which materialize wherever the Palestinian attempts to move within the occupied territories. Ariella Azoulay writes: "In the absence of an official territorial divide between the state of Israel's citizens and its subjects . . . and in a situation where the Palestinian has not been acknowledged as a citizen with equal rights but only as an enemy of the state, the border shifts to the place where the Palestinian stands."[30] Security practices along the Israeli-Palestinian border and within the occupied territories provide a good comparative case of asymmetrical transparency across US airports and Israeli security cultures. Terrorism prevention is the reason cited in both contexts for the installation of checkpoints as a key component of the preemptive legal apparatus established to prevent terrorist attacks within Israeli and United States territories. The key difference between security overreaches happening in these two contexts is that the Palestinians monitored and frequently abused at these checkpoints are noncitizens living under a system of apartheid established and enforced by the state of Israel. As noncitizens they have no recourse to justice through a system that refuses to recognize them as anything other than permanent residents and potential terrorists.[31] Along the Israeli-Palestinian border, there is no attempt whatsoever to codify the criteria and filters used by Israeli security officers. In other words, the security checks within the occupied territories establish a security culture in which it is impossible for Palestinians to perform transparency because the innocence tests are subject to change and unpredictable. There is not even the pretense of institutional transparency within the security culture. The Palestinian has virtually no rights and is therefore uniquely vulnerable to abuses by petty officials, which in most cases go undocumented and are never formally redressed.

Flying checkpoints can be found in the United States as well as in the Occupied Territories. The TSA now has Visible Intermodal Prevention and Response squads (VIPRs), which perform random security sweeps to prevent terrorist attacks at transportation hubs and entertainment venues across the United States.[32] Other important examples of flying checkpoints within the United States include stop-and-frisk policies in New York City and Arizona Senate Bill 1070 (also known as the Support Our Law Enforcement and Safe Neighborhoods Act). Like the flying checkpoints operative within the occupied territories, these new security policies promote highly flexible and impromptu checkpoints, which rise up wherever the categorically excluded, unwanted, or otherwise "unworthy" person attempts to move. The voluntary checkpoints established by the Minute Men along the US-Mexican border and the recent upholding of the Stand Your Ground law in the Trayvon Martin case in Florida are other important examples of the kind of body for whom it is impossible to perform transparency within post–Cold War security cultures. The preemptive pursuit of terrorists, criminals, and illegal aliens (and all of those individuals misrecognized as belonging to these categories—often due to the racist filters of their monitors) is coercive and pulls the suspected person into a performance of himself as suspicious, opaque, or otherwise not transparent. Also relevant in this regard are the failures of grand juries to indict US police officers that committed acts of police brutality and murder against Michael Brown and Eric Garner in 2014. These cases attest to the continuation of older forms of institutionalized racial violence in the United States even as the aesthetics of transparency is in ascendancy. Even in the United States, where citizens have the opportunity to seek legal recourse in response to vigilante violence and police brutality, there is a well-established pattern of a failure to hold the agents running deterritorialized checkpoints accountable for actions committed against bodies presumed to be irredeemably opaque. The ensuing debate in US public culture about which human lives are presumed to matter (or not) is consistent with my description of the aesthetics of transparency as activating a racial norm that divides populations according to their perceived ability to participate in the asymmetrical and coercive project of risk management.[33]

The aesthetics of transparency thrives in the empty present of prevention, where history is narrowly conceived through the paranoid monitor's attempts to prevent the unwanted historical event from happening again. For example, the State of Israel sponsors group tours of Auschwitz for Israeli youth. Palestinian, nonviolent activist Sami Awad describes the tenor of these trips.[34] The youth arrive singing patriotic songs, literally wrapped in the flag. Most of them are thoroughly unprepared for what they are about to experience. After leading the youth through the camp, the guides have them sit in circles. They tell the youth what happened there and impart the relevant historical facts. Then the story rises to a moral:

> You see what happened to us years ago, 60 years ago, by the Nazis, you know what (and in your mind you are praying this should never happen

again to anyone, but of course), this should never happen again to *us*. And you know what, if given the opportunity, the Arabs, the Muslims, the Palestinians will do the same thing to us as what happened to our grandparents. So this thirteen-year-old child, who has just gone through the shock of his experience, does not see this as his history, his past, they see this as their present and their future.

Awad's point is that these trips function as rites of passage, which indoctrinate Palestinian youth into a culture of fear. The fear shapes the men who will one day man the checkpoints, what they see when they look at Palestinians, and produces populations that unconditionally support the State of Israel and its policies.

Controlled-Tone Zones

The TSA established a precedent for the establishment of what I call controlled-tone zones. In reaction to an incident in which a twenty-one-year-old British woman joked with a TSA agent about the "bombs" in her luggage, the TSA declared airport security checkpoints No-Joking Zones in February 2004.[35] A student visiting the United States, the joker was arrested at Miami International airport prior to boarding a British Airways flight back to London. According to newspaper reports, as Samantha Marson placed her rucksack on the conveyor belt, she told the TSA agent manning the X-ray machine: "Hey, be careful, I have three bombs in here." The TSA agent asked her to repeat herself, which she did twice. She was subsequently arrested for making a false bomb report and taken to Miami–Dade County jail. The screener who reported Marson said: "After what happened on September 11, you just cannot come on flights and make these types of jokes." "If it was a joke," he added, "it wasn't a very good joke."[36]

In fairness to the TSA employee involved in the incident, screeners are under strict orders not to have a sense of humor when it comes to passengers' comments about security, weapons, or terrorism. Unlike behavior detectives, who are charged to consider the affective and social context of the airport, routine screeners are instructed to ignore the contextual cues, tone of voice, and gestures accompanying threatening topics. Passengers who even utter the word *bomb* are to be taken deadly seriously. It is not the screener's job to interpret what a passenger says or attribute harmlessness to her words based on social cues. Perhaps what is funniest and saddest about the TSA's no-joking policy is that it reveals the agency's lack of faith in the ability of its screeners to read the contextual and nonverbal cues that would enable them to tell the difference. It is akin to the way in which the material regulations (chapter 1) attempt to reduce the interpretive work of monitoring to a simple, straightforward process of sorting objects into the yes or no pile. Screeners are to act like dumb word processors. They are to pay attention to the content of what is said and to take it at face value. The No-Joking Zone makes the routine TSA screener conform to a well-worn but always funny comedic role: the character who takes everything a bit too literally.

Irony works like deception. In both cases you say something you do not mean. In the first case, you want and expect your audience to know you do not mean what you are saying. In the second case, you hope to pull one over on them.[37] The establishment of a No-Joking Zone expresses a hygienic dream that it would be possible to create a safe linguistic environment in which language would operate in a perfectly transparent manner. Miami International Airport police sergeant Joe Wyche explains: "After 9/11 there's no room for kidding or joking, if that's the person's intention, so it's taken in a serious manner."[38]

In the United States, dissent has been criminalized through the creation of free-speech or protest zones at major political events such as the Republican and Democratic National Conventions. Rowdy and subdued protestors alike are herded into containment areas, from which they are "allowed" to express political dissent apparently to one another, since their physical confinement cuts off access to the institutions and representatives of government to which they wish to speak. The United States has also witnessed the use of Taser guns to subdue rabble-rousers and silence protestors at public events, and/or the interpretation of such individual and small group protests as an inadmissible sign of disrespect for those in office and an intolerable disruption of civil discourse.

In a creative protest of controlled-tone zones, a Kansas City improvisational theater group called the KC Improv Company performed a "guerrilla improv" piece titled *No Joking Zone* at a popular outdoor shopping area in the city called the Country Club Plaza on April 1, 2006.[39] The group used Augusto Boal's invisible theater technique, in which performers take their show into public spaces not designated as theatrical spaces and perform for audiences who have not been previously informed that what is taking place is mere theater. Boal recommends using the technique to stage various forms of social injustice *as if they were actually taking place* in order to give unwitting members of the public a chance to get involved and the performers a chance to improvise solutions to existing social and political problems. Within invisible theater, the lines between performers and audience members quickly become blurred.

No Joking Zone takes its inspiration from the TSA's antijoking policy. A sign stationed near an airport security checkpoint at LAX in February 2004 attracted the attention of one of the group's members. It read: "ATTENTION! Making any jokes or statements during the screening process may be grounds for both criminal and civil penalties. All such matters will be taken seriously. We thank you for your restraint in this matter." Group member Scott Connerly writes: "This was just too much to pass up. From there, we came up with the idea of having a no-joking area in some other place than an airport." Here is how the members of KC Improv Company describe the conceit and execution of *No Joking Zone*:

> With materials and costumes prepared and location scouted out, we descended on our target. The Plaza has a great parking garage system, so we were able to park inconspicuously and make a quick arrival at the site.
>
> Agents Curtis and Carlson drove up and dropped off our signs and split. There were two signs with text on each side.
>
> On the sides facing the outside of the NJZ, they simply said "No Joking Zone." On the sides people would see as they left the NJZ, they said "Thank you for Not Laughing." They were placed a good 25 feet apart. They were in an area where there would be plenty of pedestrian traffic, but unless we were REALLY successful, wouldn't cause any problems for the nearby stores. Agent Marks and I walked calmly out of the stairwell and right over to our signs where we quietly stood guard. Our premise, if anybody asked, was that we were guarding this future site of a Federal mailbox. Think like this:
>
> With all the threatening things that can be sent through the mail and all, you know, we didn't want any funny business. Mail isn't funny, ma'am. We improvised from there. During the scene we discovered the NJZ extended 50 ft. in every direction from the future site of the mailbox, not just to our signs. More and more details came out through the day, of course.

During the performance, which lasted two hours, members of the KC Improv Company observed four types of "civilian responses" to *No Joking*

Zone. These included: "unquestioningly obedient; quietly amused; amazingly offended; and confused, curious, then playful." Of these, they note that the first was the most disappointing and the last was the most generative.

Community Behavior Detection

Through a program initially developed by New York City's Metropolitan Transportation Authority, with a $13 million grant from the DHS's Transit Security Grant Program, the DHS has deputized members of the public to engage in behavior detection in select public spaces. In December 2010, DHS Secretary Janet Napolitano announced that the agency would expand its "If You See Something, Say Something" campaign to Walmart stores across the country. At total of 588 Walmart stores are projected to participate in the campaign. A short video message from DHS Secretary Napolitano plays at some checkout locations:

> Hi, I'm Janet Napolitano, secretary of the Department of Homeland Security. Homeland security begins with hometown security. That's why I am pleased that Walmart is helping to make our communities more safe and secure. If you see something suspicious in the parking lot or in the store, say something immediately. Report suspicious activity to your local police or sheriff. If you need help, ask a Walmart manager for assistance. Thank you for doing your part to help keep our hometowns safe.

The DHS is also working with federal, state, local, and private sector partners, as well as the Department of Justice, to further expand the program. Since the program's beginning in late 2010, the DHS has partnered with states, cities, universities and transportation organizations, sports leagues and teams, private sector corporations, special sporting events, and others.[40]

Whereas the TSA's SPOT program trains behavior detectives to identify involuntary performances of transparency, the "If You See Something, Say Something" program teaches lay persons how to recognize and report what the program refers to as "precursor activities," or the behaviors that terrorists typically perform before an attack. As Joshua Reeves has observed, the pedagogical video available on the program's website "features seemingly average Americans acting out the 'suspicious' activities of potential terrorists, such as leaving one's backpack unattended, talking nervously on a cell phone, using cash, or repeatedly checking one's wristwatch."[41] The video's teachable moments are reminiscent of the low-budget reenactments of true-crime shows like *America's Most Wanted*. Costumed in dark, hooded sweatshirts, the video's cast of suspicious persons bear an ironic resemblance to images generated during the "I am Trayvon Martin" social media protest.

An Alternative Politics of Mobility

It is my hope that the critical analysis of the aesthetics of transparency offered here helps air passengers, members of neighborhood associations, residents of gated communities, people who work in gated communities, and others to think in more complex and nuanced ways about the global privilege of securitized mobility. What is needed right now is an alternative politics of mobility. As a way to begin to construct this alternative vision, I suggest that scholars of mobility and surveillance studies engage more with work by scholars of carceral and disability studies. When the discussion remains within the analytic frameworks of mobility and surveillance technologies, the global traveling classes tend to see themselves as the victims of Big Brother. The interdisciplinary critical project I am calling for under a new conceptualization of asymmetrical transparency would document patterns of privilege and discrimination across populations that uncritically aspire to transparency chic as a security ideal, those for whom it is physically, mentally, or emotionally impossible to approximate that ideal, and those who have been discounted from the project of risk management altogether.

The reconceptualization of asymmetrical transparency would enable critiques of the moralizing function of the aesthetics of transparency, which ascribes the capacity to risk to populations understood to be capable of reflexive governance and the status of being high-risk and therefore in need of management via risk-control measures to those populations presumed incapable of reflexive governance. The capacity to risk is also extended to a third category of criminalized or otherwise uncontrolled populations, for whom risk-control measures are thought to be no match. Consequently, those populations are separated and contained via incarceration. In a neoliberal age, it has become increasingly important to ask: Which risks are considered necessary and which are portrayed as optional? Who benefits from risk taking, and who deals with the consequences?

Risk management treats some risks as detestable and others as utterly necessary, some bodies as appropriate bearers of risk and others as appropriately risk free. In select contexts, citizens are encouraged to revere the risk-taking behaviors of exceptional neoliberal subjects, as for instance with respect to the financial sector. The United States recently witnessed the financial meltdown created by the deregulation of markets over the last thirty years. And yet, despite what appears to be incontrovertible evidence that the laissez-faire approach has not benefited the majority of US citizens, the financial industry continues to argue against regulation. It claims that if government sets limits on its ability to take risks, then we the people won't get the rewards it can bring (e.g., economic growth, buying power, etc.). So in this case, ordinary US citizens are supposed to continue to live with the risks generated by elites, which have a much greater chance of adversely affecting them than, for example, another terrorist attack on a commercial airplane.

Conversely, some populations are understood to be inherently risky insofar as they symbolize the threat of death. Within the biopolitical regime of risk management, those who are ill, disabled, poor, dependent, or otherwise visibly vulnerable inspire fear and dread in cultures where people are under pressure to repeatedly perform their capacity for life and futurity . . . or else. As Mary Russo writes, "'High-risk' groups elicit 'risk-control' measures which treat risk as almost entirely negative, seeking to out-regulate (or make invisible) those performances and groups which embody such double riskiness."[42] Writing in 1994, Russo offers up the moralizing of AIDS as an example of the most visible high-risk group of the day. Today, one could argue that vulnerable, mobile populations such as refugees from oppressive political regimes and natural disasters serve as highly visible high-risk groups, who are perceived to be in need of risk-control measures. Members of these populations embody the double riskiness of pressing, present needs and massive, future threats to human beings and the planet as a whole.

Insofar as the aesthetics of transparency is about blending in, it is about belonging, not necessarily to the nation-state but rather to the category of the good, or better yet exceptional, neoliberal subject. In this regard, the aesthetics of transparency organizes relations of privilege and practices of discrimination like race has historically done and continues to do. It is an ambient, affective surround that produces a comforting sense of belonging for some while alienating others at every turn: "We all understand each other here, don't we?" For example, when mobility is considered the engine of global capitalism, physically disabled people, in particular, risk the invisibility of exclusion from public life and those forms of worth that are derived from participation in reflexive governance or the hypervisibility of stigma, registered visually as slow movement, awkwardness, or stillness against the blur or bouquet effect (as it is called in photography) of the rest of the world in fast motion.

The aesthetics of transparency supports a global politics of mobility in which global, docile suspects support and celebrate their mobility via "voluntary" transparency and globally disenfranchised communities are incarcerated or subject to institutionalized abuse for reasons that have more to do with their perceived embodiment or general condition of riskiness than punishment for a particular crime—a sort of riskiness that is not celebrated as an affirmation of life but carries the threat of death and must therefore be confined or extinguished. Unlike docile suspects, who retain their mobility and are managed as immanent threats, high-risk groups are increasingly managed via enclosure in what Michelle Brown has called neoliberal carceral regimes for reasons that far exceed punishment and penalty.[43] Influenced by the work of feminist geographer Allison Mountz, she calls for criminologists to broaden their concept of the carceral beyond prisons to include refugee camps, detention camps and island detention centers, border cities and special economic zones, encampments of the poor and homeless within cities, and gated trailer parks and/or camps for refugees from natural disasters.[44] Our reliance on aerial photography to picture such sites, Brown argues, makes them "look like carceral spaces." Brown wants us to take this visual metaphor seriously. Aerial photographs picture neoliberal carceral regimes from the perspective of the privileged, securitized mobility of the photojournalist, government official, or curious tourist being flown over the site. Indeed, the photojournalistic genre of the aerial shot of these neoliberal encampments could be analyzed in terms of what I have described as the use of photography to produce opacity effects. More broadly, scholars of surveillance and criminology might engage in focused case studies and comparative analyses that explore asymmetrical transparency within and across particular neoliberal carceral regimes.

An alternative politics of mobility requires calling out the rhetorical use of the aesthetics of transparency as a means of clear-coating unpopular and undemocratic policies. Concerned citizens might begin to think of the security cultures that facilitate mobility and those that suspend mobility as networked, asymmetrical sites for controlling flows of people. Protestors might begin to imagine compelling ways of symbolizing and distilling these relations for diverse publics. Rather than accepting the rhetoric of transparency as a guarantee of democratic participation, people would exercise democratic participation by asking: What symbolic work is the aesthetics of transparency doing in this situation? What does transparency achieve here, for whose benefit, and at whose expense?

An alternative politics of mobility thinks in terms of journeys rather than destinations. It requires Westerners and especially US citizens to stop pretending that where "we" go and what "we" do and how fast "we" get there have no consequences. In other words, it rejects a video-game aesthetic/politics of mobility, where individual players access and move through space virtually unchanged and perceive threats as enfolded in racial, religious, and cultural others. The spatial logic of transparency views geography in terms of frontiers asking to be transcended. Consequently it denigrates the process of getting there, as well as the geographic and cultural specificity of that which is perceived as a frontier region. Likewise, transparency denigrates human experience or the traveler's privilege to be changed by travel to new places and encounters with different people.

An alternative politics of mobility would mean organizing politically not on behalf of the privacy rights of the world's most privileged but instead asserting the right of all people to be presumed innocent until proven guilty. It might begin with a serious discussion of the potential political, social, and cultural effects of the post-9/11 shift, led by the United States, toward preemptive warfare abroad and preemptive law in domestic security contexts. Treating all human beings as potential terrorists is not a sustainable model. Using a racial norm to treat some of those suspects as subhuman and others as worthy of obscenely expensive high-tech security apparatuses is tragically off the mark in the first case and grossly unjust in the second. In the context of this conversation, it would be necessary to account for the differential application of low- and high-tech security techniques, technologies, and procedures across bodies differently marked by citizenship and immigration status, race, ethnicity, religion, health, and ability. What is more, it would be crucial to acknowledge that submission to high-tech surveillance has become a means of symbolically marking the distinction of mobile citizens from incarcerated populations. In turn, this admission ought to shift public discourse about airport security within the United States and in other domestic contexts away from sophomoric attacks on TSA employees to a more substantive critique of a global politics of mobility in which passengers and TSA employees are mutually implicated.

An alternative politics of mobility would refuse to inhabit securitized spaces and spaces of distraction as suspects and consumers are intended to inhabit them. It would require a revolt against design and engineering— the performance of a refusal by individuals to be opened up to the wishes of hyperdesigned spaces. Instead, what if individuals risked being open to fellow inhabitants of those spaces? While transparency looks like an opening, in practice, it is often a shutting down. The pressure to perform voluntary transparency may drastically reduce our opportunities to be changed by different spaces and the social encounters that happen within them. Over the long term, the aesthetics of transparency may curtail people's willingness to be "genuinely confused, curious, and playful." It may cause them to miss out on the thrilling challenge—not to mention the fun—of not knowing where or how things will go this time.

Contrary to the demand that members of the public achieve transparency by making themselves inconspicuous, an alternative politics of mobility involves making a spectacle of one's failure to perform transparency. If transparency is the new white, an alternative politics of mobility devalues with good humor and repeatedly, if necessary, the aesthetics of transparency as hopelessly generic and therefore not worthy of one's aspirations and efforts. A more humane politics of mobility would publicly affirm the opacity of intercultural encounters and the affective complexity of social encounters in public spaces. This would require giving up the popular fantasy that an individual or state can gain positional advantage over others by reading the surface for signs of that person's interior, while failing to be seen and/or accurately read by others. It would balk at, rather than facilitate, social conformity. It would practice reasonable trust in people, rather than absolute faith in technical or technological procedures. It would attempt to shrug off and perhaps even interrupt misguided scenarios of peer-to-peer surveillance. It would reject the market model of social relations as an endless and ruthless competition. And it would humbly reject the notion that one is going to be the exception to the rule (i.e., the one who cannot be taken, fooled, lied to, or manipulated).

The politics of mobility that I have in mind is closer to what Maria Lugones has theorized as the playful, humble, and loving attitude appropriate to the work of "world"-traveling.[45] While I am advocating an alternative to transparency chic, I want to be clear that I am not calling for a return to the naive, optimistic cosmopolitanism of the 1990s. Rather, I am calling for a politics of mobility that does not bend to the persistent pressure to perform the capacity for life and futurity . . . or else. It strikes me as cruelly ironic that many members of the global traveling classes have embraced an aesthetics of openness (understood in the narrowly material and psycho-physiological sense of openness-to-inspection) in the spirit of sealing privileged securitized mobility off from the threats that attend genuine openness to the world, to the other, to the unexpected, to that which is out of the ordinary, and ultimately to death. An alternative politics of mobility does not cherish life for its own sake and above all else. It cherishes the rich heterogeneity of the full present—so full it cannot be neatly contained, zipped, monitored, inspected, read, or otherwise managed into securitized emptiness. There are no guarantees. There are no assurances. There is no preapproval. There is no fast lane. There is no special pass. There is no escape hatch. There is only the possibility of inhabiting a moment together.

NOTES

Introduction. Rethinking Asymmetrical Transparency

1. Brian Massumi writes that the work of managing threat to ensure security is never done because "there is no objective measure" of security, "any more than there is of a mood" ("The Future Birth of the Affective Fact," 7).
2. See Agamben, *Means without End*.
3. I adopt Nikolas Rose's historical understanding of risk management as a neoliberal mode of social administration that displaced the welfare state. In place of the welfare state's pastoral approach (care of the population), we have the new logics of risk management: "a multitude of diverse pockets, zones, folds of riskiness each comprising a linking of specific current activities and conducts and general probabilities of their consequences" (strategies for managing riskiness). Rose, *Powers of Freedom*, 160.
4. Laird, "Airport Screening Rules Changed December 22."
5. Quindlen, "Taking Off Your Shoes."
6. Nicole Woo, letter to the editor, *New York Times*, September 29, 2006.
7. My approach is indebted to anthropologist Victor Turner's assertion that cultural performance makes, rather than fakes, reality.
8. Beck, *World at Risk*, 10.
9. Beck, *World at Risk*, 10.
10. Gordon, "Governmental Rationality: An Introduction," 4–5.

11. Monhan, *Surveillance in the Time of Insecurity*, 24.

12. Puar, *Terrorist Assemblages*, 200.

13. Schechner, *Between Theater and Anthropology*, 36.

14. Puar, *Terrorist Assemblages*, 200.

15. My understanding of risk management as a never-ending, compulsory performance of capacity for futurity is indebted to performance scholar Jon McKenzie's formidable theoretical treatise, *Perform or Else: From Discipline to Performance*, in which he "rehearses" a general theory of performance. As promised, McKenzie's theory of performance moves us from the disciplinary society theorized by Michel Foucault to the performance reviews characteristic of American corporate culture and high-tech industries. In these arenas, workers and technologies "perform . . . or else" they get fired, defunded, or discontinued. In other words, workers and technologies perform profitability and innovation in order to ward off the looming threat of obsolescence. McKenzie's theory of performance articulates the perpetual conditional status of having to prove economic viability and technological innovation, even at the risk of death and catastrophe, as in the case of his brilliant analysis of the events that led up to the explosion of the *Challenger* space shuttle.

McKenzie's theory of performance is inspired by attempts in recent years to theorize the ways in which performances serve to reinforce the status quo. McKenzie argues that performance scholars inspired by Victor Turner's work on ritual have been guilty of celebrating the liberatory aspects of cultural performance (via Turner's concept of liminality) at the expense of theorizing the ways in which performances serve to reinforce existing power relations. This tendency is a product of the intellectual moment in which Turner was writing. Turner's theory of liminality resonated with the countercultural movements of the period. But times have changed. In recent years, McKenzie notes, theorists like Judith Butler, Eve Sedgwick, and Andrew Parker have recovered J. L. Austin's concept of performative utterances as a foundation for theories of performativity that explore the more oppressive aspects of performance in everyday life. In his book *Perform or Else*, McKenzie participates in this move by recovering early uses of the concept of performativity by Herbert Marcuse and Jean-François Lyotard to develop his notion of "the power of performance."

16. Fuller, "Life in Transit," 5.

17. The phrase is a play on Brian Massumi's use of the French tense, *futur antérieur*, to theorize the degradation of deliberation and persuasion in matters of war and governance since 9/11: "The traditional tense of threat, the indefinite future of the what-may-come, has been translated into the future perfect: the 'will have' of the always-will-have-been-already. The French term, 'futur antérieur,' says it well. The future anterior is the time of certainty. It is the temporal equivalent of a tautology—which is precisely the form of governmental logic that expresses it: the foregone conclusion. A time-slip evacuates the suspended present, and with it deliberative reason. Analysis, decision, and

debate are shortcircuited. . . . What replaces persuasion is the presumption of allegiance" ("The Future Birth of the Affective Fact," 6).

18. Massumi, *The Politics of Everyday Fear*, 22. In the post-9/11 context, Massumi argues that security is dominated by preemption, which is not the same thing as prevention: "Prevention corresponds to neoliberal Cold War politics. Preemption does not prevent, it effects. It induces the event, *in effect*. Rather than acting in the present to avoid an occurrence in the future, preemption brings the future into the present. It makes present the future consequences of an eventuality that may or may not occur, indifferent to its actual occurrence. The event's consequences precede it, as if it had already occurred" (Massumi, "The Future Birth of the Affective Fact," 8). Preemption cues off of risk indicators. For example, a financial expert or cable TV host expresses some anxiety about the economy and this indication of trouble on the horizon produces widespread panic, which dramatically effects the direction of global markets. In the context of airport security, preemption is the domain of the failed terrorist attack, close call, near miss, or harmless stunt, which produces real elaborations of the security apparatus (see Massumi's discussion of the "toxic substance alert" initiated at the Montreal airport in May 2005). The TSA responds in the same manner to historical attacks and failed attempts. For this reason, I retain the term *prevention* to describe the work of airport security.

19. Nikolas Rose also uses the spatial metaphor of folding to describe the risk management mind-set. See *Powers of Freedom*, 160.

20. Deleuze, "Postscript on Societies of Control," 3–4.

21. He defines nonplace in contrast to what he understands as anthropological place: "'Anthropological place' is formed by individual identities, through complicities of language, local references, the unformulated rules of living knowhow; non-place creates the shared identity of passengers, customers or Sunday drivers. No doubt the relative anonymity that goes with this temporary identity can even be felt as a liberation, by people who, for a time, have only to keep in line, go where they are told, check their appearance." Augé, *Non-places*, 81.

22. Parks, "Points of Departure," 197.

23. Anne McClintock analyzes the nexus of photography, torture, and death since 9/11 in terms of a broader theoretical understanding of the post-9/11 United States as a "paranoid empire." In her essay by that name, McClintock writes: "By now it is fair to say that the United States has come to be dominated by two grand and dangerous hallucinations: the promise of benign US globalization and the permanent threat of the 'war on terror'" ("Paranoid Empire," 51). She conceives of paranoia as "an inherent contradiction with respect to power: a double-sided phantasm that oscillates precariously between deliriums of grandeur and nightmares of perpetual threat" (53).

24. McClintock argues that we cannot understand the extravagance of the US response to 9/11 unless we come to grips with "a deep and disturbing doubleness with respect to power" ("Paranoid Empire," 51). She names this double-

ness paranoia. McClintock cautions her readers not to interpret her use of the term *paranoia* as an attempt to offer "a *psychological diagnosis* of the imperial nation-state. Nations do not have 'psyches' or an 'unconscious'; only people do. Rather a social entity such as an organization, state, or empire can be spoken of as 'paranoid' if the dominant powers governing that entity cohere as a collective community around contradictory cultural narratives, self-mythologies, practices, and identities that oscillate between delusions of inherent superiority and omnipotence, and phantasms of threat and engulfment" (53).

25. Fuller, "Life in Transit," 6.

26. Mark Salter observes that both public and private authorities exploit the liminal character of the airport: "to conduct policing and border functions, which take place inside the state but at the margins of the law" ("Introduction: Airport Assemblage," xi). According to Gallya Lahav, "the creation of transnational spaces, such as airports, airspace, seas, and cyberspace, challenge traditional border control and national sovereignty. They also represent areas where rights may be circumvented. According to some human rights groups, these types of spaces have been known to 'create a corporate equivalent of Guantanamo Bay'—a virtual, rules-free zone in which perpetrators are not likely to be held accountable for breaking the laws" ("Mobility and Border Security," 80).

27. That is not to say that the threat of force is entirely absent from airport security checkpoints. In 2007, Royal Canadian Mounted Police tasered immigrant Robert Dziekanski at a Vancouver airport checkpoint. He died of a heart attack. A British Columbia coroner later ruled his death a homicide ("Dziekanski Death at Hands of RCMP a Homicide, B.C. Coroner Rules"). In the context of airport security, this case represents an anomaly, whereas brutal violence and accidental (or not) deaths are built in to the patterned interrogation and torture techniques employed in the prisons established and used in the name of the war on terror.

28. I understand voluntary transparency as an example of what Nikolas Rose, Mitchell Dean, and Mark Andrejevic, among others, call "reflexive governance." The term *reflexive* denotes not cultural or political self-awareness but self-governance, or the ways in which neoliberal strategies of governance "offload" the duties of risk management and homeland defense onto citizens (Andrejevic, "Interactive (In)security," 442).

29. Taylor, "Afterword: War Play," 1893.

30. Lyon, *Surveillance Studies*, 181.

31. Lyon, *Surveillance Studies*, 181.

32. Lyon, *Surveillance Studies*, 181–82.

33. Lyon, *Surveillance Studies*, 125.

34. McGrath, *Loving Big Brother*, 218. In addition to regulating surveillance along the lines discussed by Lyon, McGrath recommends that we practice politicized countersurveillance (219). He defines countersurveillance as a matter of taking up the master's tools: "Counter-surveillance involves using surveillance equip-

ment in a way that reverses the usual vectors of power" (198). McGrath expands this initial definition of countersurveillance to include methods of resistance beyond the act of seizing the means of surveillance: "Counter-surveillance then becomes not only about reversing the gaze but about opening a space for all sorts of reversals in relation to how the gaze and its imagery may be experienced" (201). The operation he describes is, in large part, a matter of critical and artistic practice. Throughout his book, McGrath celebrates visual and performance artists whose work challenges the surveillance status quo.

35. Kumar, *Passport Photos*.

36. McGrath, *Loving Big Brother*, 218.

37. According to Foucault, the Panopticon drew its inspiration from the Enlightenment dream of "a transparent society, visible and legible in each of its parts, the dream of there no longer existing zones of darkness, zones established by the privilege of royal power or prerogatives of a corporation, zones of disorder" ("The Eye of Power," 152). Defined as a clean field of vision, order is presumed to foster, if not guarantee, justice. "The seeing machine," writes Foucault, "was once a sort of dark room into which individuals spied; it has become a transparent building in which the exercise of power may be supervised by society as a whole" (*Discipline and Punish,* 207). In a conversation with Jean-Pierre Barou and Michelle Perrot, published in *Power/Knowledge*, Foucault traces the panoptic model of disciplinary power to Rousseau's vision of a truly democratic society: one in which the opinion of all should reign over each (Foucault, *Power/ Knowledge*, 152).

38. Foucault, "The Eye of Power," 159.

39. Foucault, *Discipline and Punish*, 200.

40. Clive Thompson, "The Visible Man."

41. Curlee, "The Perfect Alibi."

42. Clive Thompson, "The Visible Man."

43. Curlee, "The Perfect Alibi."

44. Clive Thompson, "The Visible Man."

45. Clive Thompson, "The Visible Man."

46. Curlee, "The Perfect Alibi."

47. Exemplary in this regard is a new volume, *Feminist Surveillance Studies*, edited by Rachel Dubrofsky and Shoshana Magnet. See also Gates, *Our Biometric Future*, and Magnet, *When Biometrics Fail*. The feminist critique of privacy insists that defending the privacy rights of individuals is an insufficient and problematic goal of surveillance studies as a field, given that welfare recipients, people living in poverty, and queers have never been entitled to privacy, as well as the fact that "privacy" has not always kept women safer (i.e., violence against women and children often occurs in the "private" space of the home). For a critique of the use of biometric technologies on welfare recipients, see Magnet, *When Biometrics Fail*. For a critique of the privacy debate from the perspective of low-income mothers, see Gilliom, *Overseers of the Poor*. For a critique of the

heterosexism of the privacy critique of surveillance, see McGrath, *Loving Big Brother.*

1. The Art of Performing Consumer and Suspect

1. Sturken, *Tourists of History*, 85.
2. Transparency chic participates in what Mark Andrejevic has described in another context as the festishization of mediation. In *Reality TV: The Work of Being Watched*, Andrejevic argues that reality television produces its cast members as "translucent commodities," which, in turn, demands the development of new methods of media criticism. The point, he writes, is that this new translucency calls not for the familiar critical operation of Marxian demystification. Rather, the new translucency ought to be read as "a fetishization of mediation itself—the savvy reduction of reality to mediation with no remainder." In other words, the promise of reality television is not unmediated access to reality but access to the reality of mediation. Transparency chic functions as shorthand for access to the reality of mediation. It translates this process into an aesthetic, giving the impression that one can glimpse the reality of mediation all at once.
3. Sturken reads the work of some of the artists included in the Museum of Modern Art's 2005 show *Safe: Design Takes on Risk* as critical commentaries on risk culture as a form of "privileged paranoia" (*Tourists of History*, 82).
4. Transparency chic, understood as an embodiment of a brand of neocosmopolitanism, connects my analysis and critique of the aesthetics of transparency and its politics of mobility to work by scholars who have recently attempted to rethink cosmopolitanism, including Gilroy, *Postcolonial Melancholia*; Cheah and Robbins, *Cosmopolitics*; and Calhoun, "The Class Consciousness of Frequent Travelers."
5. Ahmed, *The Cultural Politics of Emotion*, 69.
6. Fuller, "Welcome to Windows 2.1," 162.
7. Peter Adey argues that the purpose of windows within airports is to "arrest movement, by drawing people's gaze and capturing their attention." "'May I Have Your Attention,'" 526.
8. Friedberg, *The Virtual Window*, 121.
9. Friedberg, *The Virtual Window*, 122.
10. Fuller cites Paul Scheerbart's 1914 technical manifesto *Glass Architecture* (163).
11. Fuller, "Welcome to Windows 2.1," 162–63.
12. Friedberg, *The Virtual Window*, 117.
13. Friedberg, *The Virtual Window*, 119.
14. See Jahn and Blaser, *Airports.*
15. See Adey's discussion of the airport as an architecture of spectatorship, "'May I Have Your Attention,'" 523.
16. Fuller, "Welcome to Windows 2.1," 162.
17. Adey, "Mobilities and Modulations," xx.
18. Reagan National is an exception to this rule. Ambient light floods the restrooms due to the incorporation of large windows of heavily frosted glass.

19. Gates, *Our Biometric Future*, 126.
20. In her discussion of cultural memory and performance, Diana Taylor references Sigmund Freud's mystic writing pad metaphor and notes that today the computer "serves as a better analogy, though it too fails to generate memories and its exterior body—a see-through shell in the recent Macintosh model—serves only to protect and highlight the marvelous internal apparatus. Neither the mystic writing pad nor the computer allows for a body" (Taylor, *The Archive and the Repertoire*, 25).
21. Nakamura, "'Where Do You Want To Go Today?,'" 256.
22. Fuller, "Welcome to Windows 2.1," 166.
23. Fuller, "Welcome to Windows 2.1," 167.
24. In critical surveillance studies literature, "surveillance space" refers to the mise-en-scène of surveillance video or close-captioned television as, for example, in the work of John McGrath (*Loving Big Brother*), who understands surveillance space as theatrical or performed space. Or it refers to global positioning systems and tracking devices used to monitor an individual's movement through space. Finally, surveillance space refers to the collection and tracking of geo-demographic data and trends. In the context of post-9/11 performances of border and airport security, surveillance is concentrated on the passenger's space or her body and belongings.
25. Fuller, "Welcome to Windows 2.1," 166.
26. Adey, "Mobilities and Modulations," 151.
27. Adey, "Mobilities and Modulations," 156–57.
28. Lyon, *Surveillance Studies*, 103.
29. In an earlier essay, I refer to the "citizen-suspect" (Hall, "Of Ziploc Bags," 320). Gillian Fuller references the "consumer-suspect" (Fuller, "Welcome to Windows 2.1," 170).
30. Salter, "Introduction: Airport Assemblage," ix.
31. Foucault, "Of Othering Spaces," 235.
32. McKee, "Suspicious Packages," 105.
33. Parks, "Points of Departure," 195.
34. Bell, *Ritual*, 108.
35. Bell, *Ritual*, 108.
36. Gopnick, "The Fifth Blade," 50.
37. Massumi, "Everywhere You Want to Be," 9.
38. Parks, "Points of Departure," 194.
39. Calder, "Passengers Face Chaos as Cabin Baggage Rules Are Changed Yet Again."
40. Anderson and DeYoung, "Plot to Bomb US-Bound Jets Is Foiled."
41. Calder, "Passengers Face Chaos as Cabin Baggage Rules Are Changed Yet Again."
42. Wilber, "US Eases Carry-on Liquid Ban; Some Drinks, Small Toiletries Allowed."
43. Millward, "US Eases Rules on Flight Cabin Baggage but British Ban Stays."

44. Millward, "US Eases Rules on Flight Cabin Baggage but British Ban Stays."
45. Thompson, "Liquid Ban for Glasgow Airport Passengers Lifted."
46. Weeks, "When Flying, Small Is Beautiful."
47. Weeks, "9/11 5 Years Later: Safer Skies Just Beyond Our Reach."
48. Creedy, "Tougher Baggage Rules Are in the Air."
49. Kaur, "Australia Bans Liquids on Aircraft."
50. "Liquid Gel Watch."
51. Sharkey, "Will Cost Prematurely Doom Security-Check Fast Lanes?"
52. See Patton, *Fatal Advice*.
53. In the words and imagery of Gillian Fuller and Ross Harley, the checkpoint delineates between the "sterile" and "non-sterile" sections of the airport. See their photo-essay, *Aviopolis*, 19.
54. Augé, *Non-places*, 72. Later Augé connects this to Foucault's heterotopia, which is also about ships. Not surprisingly, Augé draws a connection between the traveler's mobile gaze and distinctly modern practices of looking described by Baudelaire and theorized by Walter Benjamin (74–76).
55. Lloyd, "Dwelltime," 94.
56. Lloyd, "Dwelltime," 94.
57. See also Adey, "'May I Have Your Attention,'" 356.
58. Once a mere afterthought in airport design, concessions and other sites of consumption became integral to airport architecture beginning in the 1980s (Adey, "Mobilities and Modulations," 148).
59. Remizowski, "Airport Security Lines Help Food Biz Takeoff."
60. Thorstein Veblen developed a theory of cultural consumption as a form of social competition. Georg Simmel argued that fashion is the product of a social cycle of imitation and differentiation. Mary Douglas and Baron Isherwood observe that consumer goods always possess a double value: use and expression. Pierre Bourdieu writes that what people consume does not simply reflect distinctions and differences embedded elsewhere and made visible by practices of consumption, but that cultural consumption is the means by which such differences are produced, maintained, and reproduced. See "Cultural Consumption as Communication," in Storey and Turner, *Cultural Consumption and Everyday Life*.
61. Writing about the American response to 9/11, Marita Sturken notes: "The marketing of security has produced not only a new array of products but a new set of design challenges and design style. It has thus helped to create an aesthetic of security that not only integrates security measures into daily life but also gives defensiveness and militarism a kind of aesthetic coolness" (*Tourists of History*, 80).
62. Transportation Security Administration, "Laptop Bags: Industry Process and Guidelines," July 29, 2008 (www.tsa.gov).
63. Transportation Security Administration, "Laptop Bags: Industry Process and Guidelines," July 29, 2008 (www.tsa.gov).

64. Richtel, "The Mystery of the Flying Laptop."
65. "What's in My Bag: Bebel Gilberto."
66. "Exposed Bag."
67. The ads were uploaded to YouTube in November 2008. As of August 12, 2009, they were still available as the new line of watch ads on Dolce & Gabbana's official website.
68. Huettel, "Ads Land on Bottom of the Bins."
69. Sontag, "Fascinating Fascism."
70. Eilan and McGlaughlin, "Translator's Foreword," in Benjamin, *The Arcades Project*, xii.

2. Opacity Effects

1. McClintock, "Paranoid Empire," 56–57.
2. I borrow the phrase *diabolical opacity* from Diana Taylor, who uses it to describe the antipathy that Spanish colonizers expressed toward the stubborn survival of Mexica religious and cultural practices under the guise of adherence to Catholic doctrine (Taylor, *The Archive and the Repertoire*, 40).
3. Mirzoeff, *The Visual Culture Reader*, 5.
4. Nakamura, "'Where Do You Want to Go Today?,'" 256.
5. Shohat and Stam, *Unthinking Eurocentrism*, 19.
6. This form of military-technological spectatorship was first offered to US citizen-consumers during the Gulf War. Marita Sturken argues that the two most iconic images of the Gulf War: bombs in the night sky over Baghdad and the POV approach of the "smart" bomb to its target signified the myth of the war as one of clean technology (*Tangled Memories*, 129).
7. Walter Benjamin distinguishes between two modern forms of visual subjectivity: "Let us not, however confuse the *flâneur* with the rubberneck: there is a subtle difference. . . . The average *flâneur* is always in full possession of his individuality, while that of the rubberneck disappears, absorbed by the external world, . . . which moves him to the point of intoxication and ecstasy. Under the influence of the spectacle, the rubberneck becomes an impersonal being. He is no longer a man—he is the public; he is the crowd" (*The Arcades Project*, 429).
8. My concept of clear-coating is a play on the term *whitewashing* and is inspired by recent critical riffs on that term by environmentalists (e.g., "green-washing") and, in particular, rhetorician Phaedra Pezzullo's spin on the term: "pinkwashing, by which I mean talk about women that does not necessarily correlate with empowering women" (*Toxic Tourism*, 113).
9. Joint Task Force Guantanamo Command Video, accessed February 17, 2015, http://www.jtfgtmo.southcom.mil/command-video/index.html.
10. Esposito and Ross, "Exclusive: Photos of the Northwest Airlines Flight 253 Bomb."
11. Ferran, "Stink Bomb: Underwear Bomber Wore Explosive Undies for Weeks, FBI Says." According to the article, two FBI agents stated that Abdulmutallab

had worn the underwear for three weeks so that he could make his way through security without attracting notice. FBI agent Ted Pressig, who interrogated Abdulmutallab, said: "We think ultimately, that probably is what caused a little bit of separation in the sequence of events in the explosion."

12. Russo, *The Female Grotesque*, 1–2.

13. Puar, *Terrorist Assemblages*, xxiii.

14. Packer, *Mobility without Mayhem*, 381.

15. Security officials relied on myths of nonintervention and total transparency borrowed from the visual culture of medicine. José van Dijk identifies the assumptions underlying these rationales: "The myth of total transparency generally rests on two underlying assumptions: the idea that seeing is curing and the idea that peering into the body is an innocent activity, which has no consequences." The author cites Ian Hacking's influential critique of the innocence of looking into the body: every act of peering into the body is also a transformation or intervention (*The Transparent Body*, 7–8).

16. Shoshana Magnet's book *When Biometrics Fail* demonstrates how surveillance technologies play a role in managing incarcerated populations.

17. In the visual strategy of "haptic vision," writes Lisa Parks, technological mediation serves as a precursor to and justification for human contact: "What distinguishes close sensing from other forms of surveillance," she writes, "is the authority the state has granted to supplement vision with touch" ("Points of Departure," 190).

18. Parks, "Points of Departure," 190.

3. Transparency Effects

1. The claim that the new body scanners would have stopped the underwear bomber before he boarded the plane is an example of what Pat Gill has called "technostalgia" ("Technostalgia: Making the Future Past Perfect"). Kelly Gates opens her study of biometrics by reference to a similar moment in the history of facial recognition technology, which was hailed as *the* technological solution that would have allowed security officials to prevent the events of 9/11. Gates describes technostalgia as "the desire to revise the past to redetermine the present by harnessing technology toward human ends, all the while recognizing the impossibility of the endeavor" (*Our Biometric Future*, 2).

2. Lipton, "U.S. Struggles Anew to Ensure Safety as Gaps Are Revealed."

3. At that time, Thomas Frank reported for *USA Today* that the scanners aim to "close a loophole by finding non-metallic weapons such as plastic and liquid explosives, which the TSA considers a major threat" ("Body Scanners Replace Metal Detectors").

4. Zeleny and Cooper, "Obama Details New Policies in Response to Terror Threat."

5. As early as March 2010, security experts noted that the new machines might not have prevented the "Christmas Day attack" by Farouk Abdulmutallab. Hsu, "Scanners May Not Have Detected Alleged Explosive in Detroit Jet Case,

GAO Experts Report." A study of the backscatter machines conducted by two physicists at the University of California San Francisco found that the machines could easily miss objects of shapes and sizes that resemble human organs, as well as items taped to the side of the body. Kaufman and Carlson, "An Evaluation of Airport X-ray Backscatter Units Based on Image Characteristics." In a congressional hearing in May 2012, a report released by the House Transportation and Infrastructure Committee and the Oversight and Government Reform Committee characterized the technology as "ineffective" and a waste of taxpayers' money. Stellin, "Foiled Bombing Plot Sets Off Debate about Body Scanners in Congress." On March 5, 2012, twenty-seven-year-old engineer Jonathan Corbett posted a video clip explaining how he fooled both types of scanners by sewing a pocket to the side of a shirt, which allowed him to smuggle a metallic carrying case that would have set off the old metal detectors in use prior to the scanners. Christopher Elliott, "What the TSA's Body Scanners Can't See," *Washington Post*, March 25, 2012.

6. Lisa Cartwright first described an "aesthetic of flatness" in her work on microscopy in the early twentieth century. She understands microscopy's aversion to depth, its attempts to "manage depth," to "clean up" and "correct" for it within the context of related developments in photography and painting during the first two decades of the twentieth century. Cartwright argues that a cubist visual culture spanning art and science developed "as a cultural response to the epistemological instability of human observation and to the site of the human body." She makes the case that "the reverence for the flat and the abhorrence of the dimensional form and the corporeal cannot be overlooked as operative forces in the formation of a pervasively cubist culture—a culture that reconfigures the bodily interior as an endlessly divisible series of flat surfaces and mobile networks" (*Screening the Body*, 91).

7. Other scholars have forcefully articulated the racial dimension of biopolitics. Citing Rey Chow's assertion that biopolitics is implicitly about the ascendancy of whiteness, Jasbir Puar writes: "The terms of whiteness cannot remain solely in the realm of racial identification or phenotype but extend out to the capacity for capacity: that is, the capacity to give life, sustain life, promote life—the registers of fertility, health, environmental sustainability, and the capacity to risk" (Puar, *Terrorist Assemblages*, 200).

8. See "Technology That Might Have Helped."

9. Sachs, "A Reporter Faces the Naked Truth about Full-Body Scanners."

10. Rosemarie Garland-Thomson, *Freakery*.

11. In *"The Hunger Games"* Dubrofsky and Ryalls demonstrate how the character Katniss performs not-performing, which situates her as authentic and true. In contrast, altered bodies (marked by surgery, adorned with makeup or ornate clothing) are portrayed as deviant. Unexamined notions of certain performances of white femininity as "authentic" shut down possibilities by privileging certain racialized and gendered behaviors over others (2).

12. Dubrofsky and Wood, "Gender, Race, and Authenticity," xx.

13. Dubrofsky and Wood, "Gender, Race, and Authenticity," xx.
14. Magnet and Rodgers, "Stripping for the State," 13.
15. Magnet and Rodgers, "Stripping for the State," 14.
16. Magnet, *When Biometrics Fail*, 17.
17. Halsey, "TSA Debuts System for More Modest Scans."
18. Dvorak, "No Pat-Downs for Little Sally."
19. Kravitz, "Protestors' Body Scanner Opt-Out Day Could Bring Nationwide Delays at Airports."
20. More information about the We Won't Fly Campaign can be found on the group's website (http://wewontfly.com).
21. One year earlier, as Germans debated whether to fast-track full-body scanners in response to Farouk Abdulmutallab's attempt to bomb Northwest Flight 253, members of the Pirate Party demonstrated at several German airports by stripping down to their underwear and carrying signs that read: "No need to scan us—we're already naked" ("Pirate Party Protests 'Naked' Scanners in Their Underpants").
22. Kravitz, "Protestors' Body Scanner Opt-Out Day Could Bring Nationwide Delays at Airports."
23. The machines are being moved from major metropolitan airports like New York's LaGuardia and Kennedy Airports, Chicago's O'Hare, Los Angeles International, Boston Logan, and airports in Charlotte, NC, and Orlando, FL. The machines are not being retired. Rather, they are being transferred to smaller, regional airports in places like Mesa, AZ; Key West, FL; and San Juan, Puerto Rico. "TSA Quietly Removing Some Full Body Scanners."
24. This was true even though the new technologies also raised concerns about radiation exposure from the backscatter machines. See Marshall, "Bear Any Burden . . . (Don't Touch My Junk Edition)." Electronic Privacy Information Center (EPIC) filed a Freedom of Information Act request and obtained documents from the Department of Homeland Security, which provide evidence that the government failed to conduct proper safety tests on the X-ray scanners before installing them in exports and dismissed TSA employees concerns about excessive exposure to radiation. EPIC argues that the documents indicate the DHS mischaracterized safety findings by the National Institute of Standards and Technology (NIST). More specifically, a NIST official stated in an e-mail that the agency had not tested the scanners for safety over time. The TSA has yet to respond to requests by TSA union representatives at Boston Logan Airport for the TSA to allow its screeners to wear radiation-monitoring devices or dosimeters. Romero, "Did Airport Scanners Give Boston TSA Agents Cancer?"
25. Ott, "TSA Chief Endorses Body Imagers, Defines Role of Intelligence."
26. Jokes about the "bush" (i.e., pubic hair worn as-is rather than meticulously groomed) as retrograde (i.e., prior to the normalization of carefully waxed or shaved genitals) are ubiquitous in American popular culture today. When these jokes surface, "bush" is shorthand for the female grotesque. If the joke is made

in reference to a particular woman or female character, it often functions to shame her as not only grotesque but also dysfunctional or derelict in her duties of maintaining her body as a sexual spectacle.

27. For example, a passenger could wear a merkin, or pubic hairpiece, or engage in the practice of vajazzling, which refers to "the act of applying glitter and jewels to a woman's bikini area for aesthetic purposes" (www.vajazzling.com). Indeed, some protestors of the new technologies have created metallic-laden, scanner-proof underwear featuring a strategically placed "fig leaf." Kravitz, "Protestors' Body Scanner Opt-Out Day Could Bring Nationwide Delays at Airports."

28. Halsey, "TSA Debuts System for More Modest Scans."

29. With 250 backscatter machines in airports and warehouses, the TSA canceled its contract with the security company, which was responsible for removing the machines by May 31, 2013, at the company's expense. The TSA continues to use millimeter-wave body scanners. Halsey, "TSA to Pull Revealing Scanners from Airports."

30. Kelly Gates makes the case that "biometric systems are being designed primarily to invest institutional users with the enhanced capacity to control networks and information, to increase the scale and effectiveness of surveillance systems, and to secure forms of differential access to the resources of value in late capitalist societies" (*Our Biometric Future*, 127–28).

31. Shoshana Magnet takes on the presumed objectivity of biometrics by analyzing the technology's failures: "In examining those instances in which biometrics break down, we see that the real-world deployment of biometric technologies depends upon practices of inscription, reading, and interpretation that are assumed to be transparent and self-evident and yet remain complex, ambiguous, and, as a result, inherently problematic" (*When Biometrics Fail*, 3).

32. Magnet, *When Biometrics Fail*, 8.

33. While the new biometric technologies used at US airports and ports of entry purport to be technologies of individualization, in practice they often serve a classificatory logic. As Kelly Gates has argued with respect to facial recognition technology, "Although facial recognition algorithms were *not* designed to classify faces according to particular identity typologies, the deployment of large-scale, database-driven identification systems very much depended upon, and promised to facilitate, a set of 'biopolitical' security strategies that aimed to differentiate the population according to racially inflected criteria for determining who belonged and who did not, who was entitled to security and who posed a threat to that security" (*Our Biometric Future*, 21). More recently, Shoshana Magnet has thoroughly demonstrated that "biometric technologies, which claim to eliminate racial profiling through mechanical objectivity, simultaneously are explicitly based upon assumptions that categorize individuals into groups based on phenotypical markers of racialization and used in the implementation of programs specifically aimed at racial profiling" (*When Biometrics Fail*, 47).

34. As, for instance, under the Western Hemisphere Travel Initiative, all Canadians

will be subject to biometric identification by US customs officials (Magnet, *When Biometrics Fail*, 111).

35. The TSA's spatial strategies do not acknowledge poststructuralist approaches to geography. If anything, they attempt to bracket relational aspects of space and place. According to Jonathan Murdoch, for poststructuralist geographers, spaces and places are not understood as closed and contained but rather as open and engaged with other places and spaces. As a result, places and spaces are not unary but characterized by multiple practices, identifications, and forms of belonging. The practice of reading a particular place or space is contested. The meaning of a place or space is not predetermined by structural appeals to an economic or geographical base. "The performance of social practice and the performance of space go hand in hand. Space is therefore not fixed but mutable. Moreover, the notion that the 'performer' and the context of performance are distinct from one another should be abandoned: both are entangled in the heterogeneous processes of spatial 'becoming'" (*Post-structuralist Geography*, 18).

36. As Magnet puts it: "Biometric discourse thus produces individual bodies as publicly available human inventory" (*When Biometrics Fail*, 11).

37. O'Harrow and Higham, "2-Fingerprint Border ID System Called Inadequate."

38. See Braiker, "Very, Very Accurate."

39. http://www.dhs.gov/obim.

40. IBIS is a database managed by Customs Border Patrol of "lookouts, wants, warrants, arrests, and convictions consolidated from over 20 agencies. A complete IBIS query also includes a concurrent check of selected files in the Federal Bureau of Investigation's (FBI) National Criminal Information Center." Department of Homeland Security Office of Inspector General, "A Review of US Citizenship and Immigration Services' Alien Security Checks" (www.oig .dhs.gov, accessed February 17, 2015).

41. Magnet, *When Biometrics Fail*, 12.

42. Lyon, *Surveillance Studies*, 125.

43. Agamben, "Italian Professor Resigns NYU, Refuses Fingerprinting at US Border."

44. See the US Customs and Border Protection website (www.globalentry.gov).

45. See the US Customs and Border Protection website (www.globalentry.gov).

46. See the US Customs and Border Protection website (www.globalentry.gov).

47. Hoversten, "Legislation to Reform TSA Would Encourage Airports to Invest in Advanced Technologies."

48. ICAO Doc 9303, Machine Readable Travel Documents Part 3 (www.icao.int, accessed February 17, 2015).

49. Packer, *Mobility without Mayhem*, 276.

50. Lyon, *Surveillance Studies*, 43. For an extensive discussion of biometric data capture at the border see Lyon, "Filtering Flows, Friends, and Foes," 29–49.

51. Agamben, *Means without End*, 6.

52. Magnet, *When Biometrics Fail*, 4–5.

53. First produced in 2004, the video was later revised. The DHS uploaded the revised version to YouTube on May 5, 2009.

54. An important scene was edited out of the revised version of the US-VISIT video. In the original version, the narrator informs the viewer: "This does not apply to United States citizens or its legal permanent residents. Using biometrics, US-VISIT enhances security while facilitating legitimate travel and trade." As the narrator says, "using biometrics," the video cuts to an overhead shot of two queues, as they might appear to a third official who monitors the action from a remote location via a surveillance camera. The next line is: "This does not apply to US citizens." The corresponding shot shows the queue in which the visitor is standing still and then pans over to a separate line where a second official waves the US citizens past. In the time that has elapsed between the original and revised versions of the video, biometric capture has been extended to US citizens via TSA precheck, which expedites screening for US citizens who are members of one of several trusted traveler programs.

55. Braiker, "Very, Very Accurate."

56. Hsu and Johnson, "TSA Accidentally Reveals Airport Security Secrets."

57. Ann Cvetkovich used the term *low punctum* in a talk she gave at the Feeling Photography Conference at the University of Toronto in October 2009.

58. Muller, "Travelers, Borders, Dangers," 135.

59. O'Harrow and Higham, "US Border Security at Crossroads."

60. "Report: U.S. Border Vulnerable."

61. O'Harrow and Higham, "US Border Security at Crossroads."

62. Gathright, Coile, and Hua, "Photos, Fingerprints Taken at U.S. Borders."

63. Lipton, "U.S. Turns to Science to Protect Its Borders."

64. Privacy International (PI) reports that the personal information collected under the program will be retained for seventy-five to one hundred years and the system could encompass 1 billion people within fifteen years ("PI Raises Alarm as U.S. Starts Mass Fingerprinting" (www.privacyinternational.org, accessed September 27, 2004). As the system grows, PI argues, the opportunity for error will rise exponentially (Willan, "Human Rights Group Blasts New U.S. Border Controls").

65. Magnet and Rodgers draw on Angela Davis's argument that body-cavity searches performed on prisoners is a form of state-sanctioned sexual assault to argue the same about the virtual strip search performed by body scanners (Magnet and Rodgers, "Stripping for the State," 13–14).

66. Parks, "Points of Departure," 191.

67. Because it triangulates desire for and fear of the penetrated male, a white-washed prison-rape joke—especially as it is reconfigured in representations of transportation security after 9/11—offers an important site for countering what Jasbir Puar identifies as the "heteronormative penetration paradigms," which "continue to inform feminist and progressive theorizing of globalization, conquest, and war" (Puar, *Terrorist Assemblages*, 47).

68. Volpp, "The Citizen and the Terrorist," 562.

4. How to Perform Voluntary Transparency More Efficiently

1. For a sophisticated discussion of discourses of identity and authenticity in reality television, see Rachel Dubrofsky, "Therapeutics of the Self."
2. Fuller, "Welcome to Windows 2.1," 169.
3. Andrejevic, *Reality TV*, 175.
4. Andrejevic, *Reality TV*, 2–3.
5. Nikolas Rose's concept of reflexive governance emerges from his critique of neoliberalism and is informed by Michel Foucault's concept of governmentality. According to Nikolas Rose, Foucault's concept of governmentality was an attempt to articulate thought and practice in the arts of government, as well to link the micro and macro levels of governance in a nonhierarchical fashion: "Government, here, refers to all endeavors to shape, guide, direct the conduct of others, whether these be the crew of a ship, the members of a household, the employees of a boss, the children of a family or the inhabitants of a territory. And it also embraces the ways in which one might be urged and educated to bridle one's own passions, to control one's own instincts, to govern oneself." Rose's genealogy of freedom in political thought demonstrates how citizens of late liberal or neoliberal governments are "responsibilized" to take care of themselves via appeals to their liberty and autonomy. "To govern," he writes, "is to presuppose the freedom of the governed." Rose tends to be most interested in the historical conditions from which governmental solutions to problems constructed as such emerge. His valuable critique of neoliberalism rightly accents the cost-benefit analyses informing reflexive governance as a cost-saving measure and as a means of refusing the responsibility of caring for citizens (*Powers of Freedom*, 3–4).
6. Salter, "Introduction: Airport Assemblage," xii.
7. Frank, "Holiday Airline Travelers Urged to Chuck Carry-on Clutter, Pack Neatly."
8. In March 2009, Salt Lake City airport sued the TSA for trademark infringement. Salt Lake City International Airport had been using the phrase since 2003 to publicize a toll-free service that answers questions travelers may have. Interestingly, the TSA had chosen the airport the previous year to be a test site for its new separate travel lanes approach to the security checkpoint. Frank, "TSA's SimpliFLY Motto Challenged."
9. Jacobs-Huey, "'The Arab Is the New Nigger,'" 64.
10. Over a period of fifteen months, Jacobs-Huey conducted an ethnographic study of African America/ "urban" stand-up comedy ("'The Arab Is the New Nigger'").
11. Frank, "Holiday Airline Travelers Urged to Chuck Carry-on Clutter, Pack Neatly."
12. Frank, "Travelers Stray from Categories."
13. Wilson, "TSA Reaches Out to Travelers with Help in Checkpoint Security."
14. Huettel, "Agency Working to Speed Security."

15. Huettel, "Agency Working to Speed Security."
16. Wong, "Logan Lanes Pave Way for Shorter Waits."
17. Huettel, "Beyond a Single-File Solution."
18. Frank, "Travelers Stray from Categories."
19. Dijck, *The Transparent Body*, 5.
20. From its inception the Smart Border Declaration, signed by key political figures in the United States and Canada three months after 9/11, envisioned border security as a twofold project. Biometric technologies would be used to "scrutinize bodies represented as high-risk at the same time as they facilitate the movements of business travelers" (Magnet, *When Biometrics Fail*, 114–16).
21. Marita Sturken argues that the Department of Homeland Security's public pedagogy campaigns "attempt to interpellate the citizen as a citizen-soldier-consumer" (*Tourists of History*, 74). See also Sturken, "Weather Media and Homeland Security."
22. Russo, *The Female Grotesque*, 29.
23. Huettel, "Beyond a Single-File Solution."
24. Wong, "Logan Lanes Pave Way for Shorter Waits."
25. Huettel, "Pick a Screening Lane."
26. Wilson, "Hartsfield Opens New Security Lanes to Cut PAX Wait Times."
27. Wilson, "TSA Expands Self-Serve Security Lines to Three More Airports."
28. Huettel, "Agency Working to Speed Security."
29. Huettel, "Pick a Screening Lane."
30. "TSA Introduces Black Diamond Self-Select Lanes at Norfolk International Airports."
31. "Air Travel: Queue for Change."
32. Kornblut and Bacon, "Airport Security Uproar Frustrates White House Advisers."
33. See "Health Information Privacy" (hhs.gov, accessed February 18, 2015).
34. "A Guide to Disability Rights Laws" (www.ada.gov, accessed February 18, 2015).
35. "Travelers with Disabilities and Medical Conditions" (www.tsa.gov, accessed February 18, 2015).
36. "Travelers with Disabilities and Medical Conditions" (www.tsa.gov, accessed February 18, 2015).
37. "Mobility Disabilities" (www.tsa.gov, accessed June 30, 2014).
38. "Travelers with Disabilities and Medical Conditions" (www.tsa.gov, accessed June 30, 2014).
39. Bailey and Peters, "The Long Wait for the Chance to Empty Pockets and Shed Shoes."
40. Bailey and Peters, "The Long Wait for the Chance to Empty Pockets and Shed Shoes."
41. Bailey and Peters, "The Long Wait for the Chance to Empty Pockets and Shed Shoes."
42. Huettel, "Agency Working to Speed Security."

43. "TSA and Ad Council Launch Public Education Campaign to Build Greater Awareness of Security Procedures at Airport Checkpoints."

5. Performing Involuntary Transparency

1. Lipton, "Faces, Too, Are Searched as U.S. Airports Try to Spot Terrorists."
2. As Jasbir Puar has pointed out before me, "The entrenchment of Islamophobia in terrorism studies is structural as well as ideological" (*Terrorist Assemblages*, 55).
3. It is not uncommon for security officials and even scientists to ignore years of critical cultural research when it proves expedient to do so. As Shoshana Magnet notes, biometric scientists have ignored thirty years of research disproving a biological basis for race (*When Biometrics Fail*, 46).
4. Lipton, "Faces, Too, Are Searched as U.S. Airports Try to Spot Terrorists." By the summer of 2005, state police at the Minneapolis airport were also participating in the pilot program (Croft, "Screening Hybrid," 64).
5. Lipton, "Faces, Too, Are Searched as U.S. Airports Try to Spot Terrorists."
6. Ron noted that Israeli security workers undergo more intensive screening and training than their American counterparts. At Ben Gurion, interviewers are most often university students, who've just finished their mandatory military service. They are screened for above average intelligence and a "strong sense of curiosity." The training process for interviewers at Ben Gurion is nine weeks long. Burnout is an issue so they try not to keep anyone on the job longer than three to five years at the maximum (Croft, "Screening Hybrid," 64).
7. Engle, "TSA Screeners Being Trained to Monitor People, Not Just Bags."
8. Andrejevic, "Reading the Surface," 15.
9. Andrejevic, "Reading the Surface," 18.
10. According to Dubrofsky, reality television positions itself as possessing therapeutic value for contestants and by extension home viewers. Within reality television, the therapeutic goal is not so much to improve the self as to remain the same. Remaining true to one's self no matter what demonstrates that one is coping with, if not attempting to alter, reality. Dubrofsky worries about the implications of what she calls "the therapeutics of the self" for public deliberation and political change ("Therapeutics of the Self," 276).
11. See Green-Lewis, *Framing the Victorians*.
12. Croft, "Screening Hybrid," 64.
13. Lipton, "Faces, Too, Are Searched as U.S. Airports Try to Spot Terrorists."
14. The lawsuit was based on an incident in which the national coordinator of ACLU's Campaign against Racial Profiling was asked to show ID and refused to show it without explanation from the officers. Four state police surrounded him and told him he would be arrested if he did not comply. After showing his ID and ticket, they let him go. At one point they threatened to bar him from the airport if he did not comply. "ACLU Sues Massport over Logan 'Profiling.'"
15. Lipton, "Faces, Too, Are Searched as U.S. Airports Try to Spot Terrorists."
16. Engle, "TSA Screeners Being Trained to Monitor People, Not Just Bags." The

TSA's claim that behavior detection offers a welcome antidote to racial, ethnic, or religious profiling was contradicted again in 2009, when a TSA operations manual was leaked and posted online, revealing that the DHS targets passengers from certain countries for special screening.

17. TSA workers trained in behavior detection undergo cultural awareness and sensitivity training. The agency stresses that individuals are selected for questioning based on behavior rather than race, ethnicity, nationality, or religion. "ACLU Sues Massport over Logan 'Profiling.'"

18. Sharkey, "Giving Human Intuition a Place in Airport Security."

19. Shortly after the liquid explosives threat of August 2006, the TSA announced it wanted to train hundreds of additional behavior detection officers by the end of 2007 and to have them working at most of the nation's biggest airports. Lipton, "Faces, Too, Are Searched as U.S. Airports Try to Spot Terrorists." In the summer of 2007, the TSA announced plans to double the number of behavior detection officers again in the next fiscal year and probably double it once more the following year. Sharkey, "Giving Human Intuition a Place in Airport Security." In November 2008, the TSA announced its plans to double its behavior detection officers yet again in 2009. The TSA promised to have twenty-four hundred behavior detection officers on the job by the end of 2008 and to double that number once more the following year. "TSA Plans to Double Behavior Detection Officers in 2009."

20. Jansen, "In Boston, Airport Security Now Begins with a Chat."

21. Hawley helped the George W. Bush administration set up the TSA following the attacks of September 11, 2001. Prior to that Hawley was a member of the National Commission on Intermodal Transportation in President George Herbert Walker Bush's administration and former deputy assistant and special assistant to President Reagan. He also boasted significant private sector experience, having served as a top executive at Union Pacific, Arzoon Inc., and Skyway. Hawley lasted longer as head of the TSA than any of his three predecessors, holding the office through the duration of the Bush administration's second term (Doyle, "Security Blanket," 50).

22. Davidson, "Ethnic Profiling Accusations Prompt Legislator to Again Question TSA Program's Legitimacy."

23. "House Hearing 112 before the Subcommittee on Investigations and Oversight Committee on Science, Space, and Technology," April 6, 2011 (gpo.gov, accessed February 18, 2015).

24. "House Hearing 112 before the Subcommittee on Investigations and Oversight Committee on Science, Space, and Technology," April 6, 2011 (gpo.gov, accessed February 18, 2015).

25. Tim Levine and his colleagues at Michigan State University (MSU) understand their research as a "counterpoint" to Interpersonal Deception Theory (IDT). For the last forty years, researchers working at the MSU lab have carefully studied and systematically disproven what they identify as the operative assumptions of IDT: the human body is a leaky container for the individual's thoughts and

emotions; nonverbal tells are more reliable than verbally communicated information; lies are detected in the moment the lie is being perpetrated or the truth is being concealed; there are universal nonverbal tells of deception; it is possible to train individuals in order to improve their rate of success at detecting deception via nonverbal cues (www.msu.edu/~levinet/deception.htm, accessed February 18, 2015).

26. Ekman, *Emotions Revealed*.

27. Ekman, *Emotions Revealed*.

28. He showed members of different cultures still photographs of facial expressions and asked them to describe the emotional state of the person in the photograph. He reported overwhelming evidence of cross-cultural agreement regarding which emotions were expressed in the photos (Ekman, *Emotions Revealed*, 3).

29. Ekman, *Emotions Revealed*, 4.

30. Ekman, *Emotions Revealed*, 4.

31. FACS has since been used by hundreds of scientists. Computer scientists are currently developing software to automate the coding system developed by Ekman and his colleagues (Ekman, *Emotions Revealed*, 14). See also Gates, *Our Biometric Future*, 151–90.

32. Gates, *Our Biometric Future*, 171.

33. Gates, *Our Biometric Future*, 171.

34. Gates, *Our Biometric Future*, 174.

35. Ekman, "How to Spot a Terrorist on the Fly."

36. Ekman, *Emotions Revealed*, 15.

37. The SPOT program uses a modified form of FACS in combination with other methods of reading and coding human behavior. Gates notes that it takes a human being over one hundred hours of training to achieve minimal competency in FACS. Gates, *Our Biometric Future*, 169.

38. Gates, *Our Biometric Future*, 183.

39. Ekman et al. argued that concealed emotions temporarily flit across the surface of the face, becoming momentarily visible to trained observers. These "microexpressions," so named by Ekman, appear on the liar's face for one twenty-fifth of a second. "They are so fast," he says, "that unless you've been trained you don't see them" (Gadher, "'SPOT' Teams to Spy on Passengers").

40. Ekman, *Emotions Revealed*, 132.

41. Ekman, *Emotions Revealed*, 102.

42. Ekman, *Emotions Revealed*, 85.

43. Sharkey, "Giving Human Intuition a Place in Airport Security."

44. Sharkey, "Giving Human Intuition a Place in Airport Security."

45. Sharkey, "Giving Human Intuition a Place in Airport Security."

46. Frank, "Security Arsenal Adds Behavior Detection."

47. Massumi, "Fear (The Spectrum Said)," 41.

48. As Peter Adey reminds us: "The management of how an airport *feels* is of course not new" ("Mobilities and Modulations," 151).

49. Massumi, "Fear (The Spectrum Said)," 33.

50. Doyle, "Security Blanket,"50.

51. Ott, "Security, Ease Come First at New Indianapolis International Airport," 1.

52. Last, "One Last Thing: Behavior Reveals All."

53. Duke, "The Picture of Conformity."

54. Ekman, *Telling Lies*, 90–91.

55. Ekman, *Telling Lies*, 80.

56. Presumably Ekman worked with the TSA to get the behavior detectives to focus on behavioral tells for which the detective needs no base of comparison. Ekman identifies four sources of leakage not vulnerable to the Brokaw hazard: slips of the tongue, emotional tirades, emblematic slips, and micro-expressions. According to him, any one of these necessarily breaks concealment. While some tells are more reliable than others, it is also true that in the live airport setting, it would be extremely difficult to completely avoid the Brokaw hazard (*Telling Lies*, 168).

57. Ekman, *Telling Lies*, 33.

58. Ekman, *Telling Lies*, 94.

59. Ekman, *Telling Lies*, 170.

60. Davidson, "Ethnic Profiling Accusations Prompt Legislator to Again Question TSA Program's Legitimacy."

61. Buff, "'We Don't Blow Things Up, We Build Things,'" 5–6.

62. Buff, "'We Don't Blow Things Up, We Build Things,'" 5.

63. Buff, "'We Don't Blow Things Up, We Build Things,'" 5.

64. Buff, "'We Don't Blow Things Up, We Build Things,'" 6.

65. Jansen, "In Boston, Airport Security Now Begins with a Chat."

66. Serwer, "How Effective Is the TSA's Behavior Detection Program?"

67. "House Hearing 112 before the Subcommittee on Investigations and Oversight Committee on Science, Space, and Technology," April 6, 2011 (gpo.gov, accessed February 18, 2015).

68. Ekman, *Telling Lies*, 174.

69. Ekman, *Telling Lies*, 142.

70. Jansen, "In Boston, Airport Security Now Begins with a Chat."

71. Biesecker, "Pistole Wants to Look at Risk-Based Approach to Passenger Screening."

72. Stellin, "U.S. Groups Seek Airport Security That Would Divide Fliers by Threat Level."

73. Electronic Privacy Information Center, "Future Attribute Screening Technology (FAST) Project FOIA Request" (epic.org, accessed February 18, 2015).

74. Kelly Gates's work on the cultural fantasies about and funded research programs in automated facial expression analysis is illuminating. Gates, *Our Biometric Future*, 151–90.

75. Butler, *Precarious Life*, 56.

76. Gates, *Our Biometric Future*, 155.

77. There is a similar slipperiness between science and intuition in popular psy-

chology versions of behavior detection as found in the work of someone like nonverbal communication consultant Tanya Reiman, perhaps best known for her guest appearances on *The O'Reilly Factor*. In her book *The Power of Body Language: How to Succeed in Every Business and Social Encounter*, Reiman argues that babies are skilled at reading nonverbal behavior and it is only when language takes over that people forget to listen to their bodies' hunches regarding "whether someone is lying to us or loves us" (18–19).

78. Ekman, *Telling Lies*, 26–27.

79. Staples, "Black Men and Public Space."

80. In the fall of 2007, Thomas Frank reported: "Of the 43,000 of the millions of travelers watched by crowd-scanning behavior-detection screeners have appeared suspicious enough to warrant a closer look, the TSA says. The closer looks generated 3,100 calls from the TSA to police for further questioning. The police arrested 278 of those people, none on terror charges. Among the charges described in TSA news releases about behavior-related arrests are immigration violations and possessing guns and illegal prescription drugs" ("Security Arsenal Adds Behavior Detection; Controversial Technique Targets 'Suspicious' People").

81. For a critique of arrogant perception and a thorough articulation of an alternative worldview, see Lugones, "Playfulness, 'World'-Travelling, and Loving Perception," 3–19.

Conclusion. Transparency beyond US Airports

1. For example, following Farouk Abdulmutallab's attempted bombing of Northwest Flight 253 from Amsterdam to Detroit on December 25, 2009, the DHS issued a Security Directive calling for the immediate worldwide implementation of extra security measures on all flights destined for the United States. Aviation Security Directives issued by the Department of Homeland Security are generally off limits to the public. This security measure was breached on December 27, 2009, when two bloggers posted the Security Directive issued in response to the attempted sabotage of Northwest Flight 253 in its entirety. For the complete contents of the directive, see Frischling, "TSA Security Directive SD-1544-09-06." Steven Frischling, author of the travel blog *Flying with Fish*, and Christopher Elliott, who writes a weekly column for the *Washington Post* and produces a weekly segment for MSNBC, posted the sensitive document. Within forty-eight hours, the DHS served both men with subpoenas and demanded to see their personal computing devices and to know who had sent them the sensitive document. See Grant, "TSA Agents Subpoena Bloggers to Find Out Who Leaked the New Security Document." Perhaps in an effort to quiet bad press, the DHS dropped the subpoena on December 31, 2009. See Elliott, "Your Subpoena Is 'No Longer Necessary.'"

2. Hsu and Adam, "International Cooperation a Challenge for Air Security."

3. Hsu and Adam, "International Cooperation a Challenge for Air Security."

4. Healy and Simons, "Full-Body Scans to Be Used for Flights from Amsterdam to U.S."

5. Healy and Simons, "Full-Body Scans to Be Used for Flights from Amsterdam to U.S."

6. Lelsey Ciarula Taylor, "Full-Body Scans Top Priority; Transport Canada Studies Ways to Tighten Airport Security Screening."

7. Lelsey Ciarula Taylor, "Full-Body Scans Top Priority; Transport Canada Studies Ways to Tighten Airport Security Screening."

8. Lelsey Ciarula Taylor, "Full-Body Scans Top Priority; Transport Canada Studies Ways to Tighten Airport Security Screening."

9. Max, "US Steps Up Global Travel Security after Bombing Attempt on Detroit-Bound Airplane."

10. Hsu and Adam, "International Cooperation a Challenge for Air Security."

11. "Use of Full-Body Scanners in South African Airports Not Likely 'at This Stage.'"

12. Lekic, "Full-Body Scan or Not? Europe Divided on Airport Security Steps."

13. In her remarks, DHS Secretary Janet Napolitano also mentioned that the DHS would work with the State Department to bolster international security measures and partner with the Energy Department national laboratories to research new screening technologies (Hsu, "U.S. to Push for Full-Body Scanners at Foreign Airports").

14. Welch, "US Raises Full Body Scanners in Fly-By Visit over Terrorism."

15. Welch, "US Raises Full Body Scanners in Fly-By Visit over Terrorism."

16. Rockwell, "Napolitano Promotes Joint Declaration at the ICAO Meeting."

17. See the website of the International Civil Aviation Organization (http://www .icao.int).

18. The council, the organization's chief governing body, is comprised of thirty-six member states elected by the assembly to serve three-year terms. According to the ICAO, the council comprises "States of chief importance in air transport, States not otherwise included but which make the largest contribution to the provision of facilities for international civil air navigation, and States not otherwise included whose designation will ensure that all major geographic areas of the world are represented on the Council." See the ICAO website's description of its governing bodies (http://www.icao.int, accessed February 18, 2015).

19. Stancu, "AVSEC Conventions: Beyond Chicago, until Beijing."

20. Office for Transportation Security of the Philippines, "ICAO Annex 17."

21. Office for Transportation Security of the Philippines, "ICAO Annex 17."

22. See "Annex 17 to the Convention on International Civil Aviation: Security: Safeguarding International Civil Aviation against Acts of Unlawful Interference," in the ICAO Collection, Industry Standards and Regulations (www.ihs.com).

23. Magnet and Rodgers, "Stripping for the State," 8.

24. See "Declaration on Aviation Security" on the International Civil Aviation Organization's website (http://www.icao.int).

25. The report cites the fact that Napolitano participated in five regional summits "aimed at developing an international consensus to enhance aviation security" during 2010. The reported mentions that in the wake of the attempted sabotage of Flight 253 in 2009, the DHS had encouraged other nations to consider using Advanced Imaging Technologies (AIT), otherwise known as body scanners. As a result of these efforts, several nations have committed to test and/or adopt AIT at present or in the near future. Finally, the report notes that the TSA assesses the security efforts of foreign airports to ensure their compliance with international aviation security standards. The report noted that the TSA could do a better job of following up at those airports where security upgrades have been recommended in order to ensure their effective implementation. See "Aviation Security: DHS Has Taken Steps to Enhance International Aviation Security and Facilitate Compliance with International Standards, but Challenges Remain."

26. "Aviation Security: DHS Has Taken Steps to Enhance International Aviation Security and Facilitate Compliance with International Standards, but Challenges Remain."

27. Consequently, the two US-led international aviation security measures that have faced the most criticism from the EU are the guidelines for the exchange and retention of Passenger Name Data Records (PNR) and the use of body scanners. PNR is "information provided by passengers, and collected by and held in the carriers' reservation and departure control systems." In 2011, the EU requested a modification of its PNR agreement with the United States to reduce the length of data storage and ensure that EU citizens have a right to appeal travel bans based on their PNR data. EU member states debate the necessity and proportionality of the collection, exchange and retention of PNR and whether such prosecurity measures violate the Charter on Fundamental Rights. The United Kingdom and France are pro-PNR. Austria is skeptical. Czechoslovakia is concerned about privacy violations, and Romania questions the proportionality of these measures. As a result of these debates, the EU has considered the risks of "indirect discrimination" made possible by the use of PNR data, particularly in relation to profiling. Concerned members of the EU stress the importance of monitoring the use of PNR data in order to detect patterns of indirect discrimination. European Union Agency for Fundamental Rights, "Information Society and Data Protection," in *Fundamental Rights: Challenges and Achievements in 2011* (http://fra.europa.eu, accessed February 18, 2015), 91–92.

28. Hardt and Negri, *Multitude*, 21.

29. Packer, *Mobility without Mayhem*, 276.

30. Azoulay, *The Civil Contract of Photography*, 72.

31. For an overview of the abuses happening at checkpoints in the Occupied Territories, see the report published by B'TSELEM: The Israeli Information Center for Human Rights in the Occupied Territories (www.btselem.org), entitled "Ground to a Halt: Denial of Palestinians' Freedom of Movement in the West Bank."

32. The VIPR teams were initially formed in 2005, in reaction to the Madrid train

bombing in 2004 that killed 191 people. The program currently has a $100 million annual budget. TSA records show that the teams ran eighty-eight hundred unannounced checkpoints and search operations outside of airports last year alone (Nixon, "T.S.A. Expands Duties beyond Airport Security").

33. George Yancy and Judith Butler, "What's Wrong With 'All Lives Matter'?" *New York Times*, January 12, 2015.

34. Farrell, "Overcoming the Fear in Israeli Society."

35. Prior to the Marson incident, an Air France pilot was arrested at Kennedy International on August 10, 2003, for balking at removing his shoes and then joking about having a bomb in them. Onlookers reported that the pilot appeared to be making a joke. The TSA responded to the incident by reinforcing the point that there is no joking at the checkpoint: "We have zero tolerance for those kinds of comments," said Lauren Stover, a spokesperson for the agency (McFadden, "Air France Co-Pilot Is Accused of Making Remark about Bomb"). The no-joking policy is not limited to US airports or to the American perspective, which narrates 9/11 as the origin of our terrified new world. In the summer of 2005, a Belfast man was fined five hundred pounds after a security screener at Heathrow International in London asked him if he had any firearms or explosives on his person. The man answered: "Yeah, I've loads." A writer for the *Belfast Telegraph* notes the culture-blind aspect of the policy. Writing about the incident, Linda McKee observed: "The black Northern Irish sense of humor is known worldwide but could backfire at the security check—resulting in prosecution" ("Heard the One about the Man Who Told a Joke and Was Fined?").

36. "British Student Faces Jail over Bomb Joke."

37. My thinking about irony and deception has been influenced by the work of Jeffrey Hancock, associate professor of communication at Cornell University.

38. "Bomb Joke Lands Briton in Miami Jail." The no-joking policy predated the terrorist attacks of 9/11. On March 9, 2000, a New Zealand businessman was arrested for making a joke about having a bomb in his bag and eventually charged under the Aviation Act for communicating false information. Under the Aviation Act, passengers could face a maximum penalty of twelve months in prison and a $10,000 fine (Morrison, "Passenger Charged over Bomb 'Joke'").

39. The KC Improv Company, *Guerilla Improv: No Joking Zone* (http://kansascity-comedy.com).

40. A complete list of their partnerships can be found on the Department of Homeland Security website.

41. Reeves, "If You See Something, Say Something," 235. You can access the video on the Department of Homeland Security website.

42. Russo, *The Female Grotesque*, 22.

43. Brown, "Violence, Vulnerability, and Visual Criminology."

44. Mountz, *Seeking Asylum*.

45. Lugones, "Playfulness, 'World'-Travelling, and Loving Perception."

BIBLIOGRAPHY

"311 Gains International Acceptance." www.tsa.gov.

"ACLU Says New Border Fingerprinting System Likely to Sow Confusion, Tracking of Arab and Muslims Based on National Origin Will Continue." www.aclu.org. Accessed January 5, 2005.

"ACLU Sues Massport over Logan 'Profiling.'" *Airports* 26, no. 1: 1 (2004).

Adey, Peter. "'May I Have Your Attention': Airport Geographies of Spectatorship, Position and (Im)Mobility." *Environment and Planning D: Society and Space* 25 (2007): 526.

———. "Mobilities and Modulations: The Airport as a Difference Machine." *Politics at the Airport*, edited by Mark B. Salter, 145–60. Minneapolis: University of Minnesota Press, 2008.

Agamben, Giorgio. "Italian Professor Resigns NYU, Refuses Fingerprinting at US Border." http://artists.refuseandresist.org. Accessed January 10, 2004.

———. *Means without End: Notes on Politics.* Minneapolis: University of Minnesota Press, 2000.

———. *State of Exception.* Chicago: University of Chicago Press, 2005.

Ahmed, Sara. *The Cultural Politics of Emotion.* New York: Routledge, 2004.

"Air Travel: Queue for Change." *Travel Trade Gazette* (UK and Ireland), September 8, 2011.

Anderson, John Ward, and Karen DeYoung. "Plot to Bomb US-Bound Jets Is Foiled." *Washington Post*, August 11, 2006.

Anderson, Patrick, and Jisha Menon. *Violence Performed: Local Roots and Global Routes of Conflict*. Studies in International Performance. New York: Palgrave Macmillan, 2009.

Andrejevic, Mark. "Interactive (In)security." *Cultural Studies* 20, nos. 4–5 (2006): 441–58.

———. "Reading the Surface: Body Language and Surveillance." *Culture Unbound* 2 (2010): 15–36.

———. *Reality TV: The Work of Being Watched*. Lanham, MD: Rowman and Little-field, 2004.

Antonelli, Paola. *Safe: Design Takes on Risk*. New York: Museum of Modern Art, 2005.

Arenson, Karen. "In Protest, Professor Cancels Visit to U.S." *New York Times*, January 17, 2004.

Augé, Marc. *Non-places: Introduction to an Anthropology of Supermodernity*. London: Verso, 2008.

"Aviation Security: DHS Has Taken Steps to Enhance International Aviation Security and Facilitate Compliance with International Standards, but Challenges Remain." *GAO Highlights*, December 2, 2010. www.gao.gov.

Azoulay, Ariella. *The Civil Contract of Photography*. Cambridge, MA: MIT Press, 2012.

Bailey, Jeff, and Jeremy W. Peters. "The Long Wait for the Chance to Empty Pockets and Shed Shoes." *New York Times*, November 24, 2005.

Baker, Peter, and Scott Shane. "Obama Seeks to Reassure U.S. after Bombing Attempt." *New York Times*, December 29, 2009.

Barr, Stephen. "A Career Track for Airport Screeners." *Washington Post*, July 20, 2006.

Baskas, Harriet. "Airport Check-In: Every Monday." *USA Today*, March 24, 2008.

Beck, Ulrich. *World at Risk*. Malden, MA: Polity, 2009.

Beckman, Karen. "Terrorism, Feminism: Sisters, and Twins: Building Relations in the Wake of the World Trade Center Attacks." *Grey Room* 7 (2002): 24–39.

Bell, Catherine M. *Ritual: Perspectives and Dimensions*. New York: Oxford University Press, 1997.

Benjamin, Walter. *The Arcades Project*. Cambridge, MA: Belknap Press, 2002.

Bennett, Jane. "The Force of Things: Steps toward an Ecology of Matter." *Political Theory* 32 (2002): 347–72.

Berlant, Lauren Gail. *The Female Complaint: The Unfinished Business of Sentimentality in American Culture*. Durham, NC: Duke University Press, 2008.

Bisecker, Calvin. "Health Risks from Full-Body X-Ray Security Systems 'Miniscule,' FDA, TSA Say." *Defense Daily*. http://www.defensedaily.com/health-risks-from-full-body-x-ray-security-systems-miniscule-fda-tsa-say/. Accessed November 12, 2010.

———. "Pistole Wants to Look at Risk-Based Approach to Passenger Screening." *Defense Daily*, February 11, 2011.

"Bomb Joke Lands Briton in Miami Jail." *Straits Times*, January 22, 2004.

"Border Patrol Fingerprint System Identifies 30,000 Criminal Suspects Attempting to Enter the U.S." *Government Technology*, February 22, 2005.

Braiker, B. "'Very, Very Accurate': A Biometrics Consultant Argues in Favor of the Technology Used to Fingerprint and Photograph Visitors to the United States." *Newsweek*, January 7, 2004.

"British Student Faces Jail over Bomb Joke." *Birmingham Post*, January 21, 2004.

Brown, Michelle. "Violence, Vulnerability, and Visual Criminology." International Crime, Media, and Popular Culture Studies Conference, Indiana State University, Terre Haute, September 24, 2013.

Buff, Rachel Ida. "'We Don't Blow Things Up, We Build Things': Migrant Subjectivity in the Homeland Security Moment." American Studies Association Conference, Washington, DC, November 5–8, 2009.

Butler, Judith. *Precarious Life: The Powers of Mourning and Violence*. London: Verso, 2006.

Calder, Simon. "Passengers Face Chaos as Cabin Baggage Rules Are Changed Yet Again." *The Independent* (London), October 30, 2006.

Calhoun, Craig. "The Class Consciousness of Frequent Travelers." *South Atlantic Quarterly* 101, no. 4 (2002): 869–97.

Cartwright, Lisa. *Screening the Body: Tracing Medicine's Visual Culture*. Minneapolis: University of Minnesota Press, 1995.

Catalanello, Rebecca. "Airport-Style Safety Measure in the Mix." *St. Petersburg Times*, January 24, 2009.

Cheah, Pheng, and Bruce Robbins, eds. *Cosmopolitics: Thinking and Feeling beyond the Nation*. Minneapolis: University of Minnesota Press, 1998.

Chertoff, Michael. "'We Must Remain Flexible': Layers of Security Ensure Safe Air Travel; 'Continued Patience' Critical." *USA Today*, August 16, 2006.

Cohen, Lizabeth. *A Consumers' Republic: The Politics of Mass Consumption in Postwar America*. New York: Knopf, 2003.

Copeland, Libby. "Full-Body Scanners: Exposing Issues of Privacy and Body Image." *Washington Post*, December 23, 2010.

Creedy, Steve. "Tougher Baggage Rules Are in the Air." *The Australian*, September 26, 2006.

Croft, John. "Screening Hybrid: Israeli Techniques Fill Technology Gaps, but Also Raise Some Privacy Concerns." *Aviation Week and Space Technology* 163, no. 8 (2005): 64.

Curlee, Elizabeth. "The Perfect Alibi: An Ankle Device Lets One Man Make the World—and Big Brother—His Witness." *CBS News*, June 18, 2007.

Davidson, Joe. "Ethnic Profiling Accusations Prompt Legislator to Again Question TSA Program's Legitimacy." *Washington Post*, November 29, 2011.

Davis, Tracy C. *Stages of Emergency: Cold War Nuclear Civil Defense*. Durham, NC: Duke University Press, 2007.

Deleuze, Gilles. "Postscript on Societies of Control." *October* 59 (1992): 3–7.

Dijk, José van. *The Transparent Body: A Cultural Analysis of Medical Imaging, In Vivo*. Seattle: University of Washington Press, 2005.

Doyle, John. "Security Blanket." *Aviation Week and Space Technology* 168, no. 1 (2008): 50.

Dubrofsky, Rachel. "Therapeutics of the Self: Television in the Service of the Therapeutic." *Television and New Media* 8 (2007): 263–84.

Dubrofsky, Rachel, and Shoshana Amielle Magnet, eds. *Feminist Surveillance Studies*. Durham, NC: Duke University Press, 2015.

Dubrofsky, Rachel, and Emily D. Ryalls. "*The Hunger Games*: Performing Not-Performing to Authenticate Femininity and Whiteness." *Critical Studies in Media Communication* 31 no. 5 (2014): 1–15.

Dubrofsky, Rachel, and Megan Wood. "Gender, Race, and Authenticity: Celebrity Women Tweeting for the Gaze." In *Feminist Surveillance Studies*, edited by Rachel Dubrofsky and Shoshana Amielle Magnet. Durham, NC: Duke University Press, 2015.

Duke, Lynne. "The Picture of Conformity: In a Watched Society, More Security Comes with Tempered Actions." *Washington Post*, November 16, 2007.

Durhams, Sharif. "Airport Draws Smiles with 'Recombobulation Area.'" *Journal Sentinel*, July 9, 2008.

Dvorak, Petula. "No Pat-Downs for Little Sally." *Washington Post*, December 26, 2010.

"Dziekanski Death at Hands of RCMP a Homicide, B.C. Coroner Rules." *Canadian Press*, April 8, 2013.

Ekman, Paul. *Emotions Revealed: Recognizing Faces and Feelings to Improve Communication and Emotional Life*. New York: Times Books, 2003.

———. "How to Spot a Terrorist on the Fly." *Washington Post*, October 29, 2006.

———. *Telling Lies: Clues to Deceit in the Marketplace, Politics, and Marriage*. New York: W. W. Norton, 1991.

Elliot, Christopher. "What the TSA's Body Scanners Can't See." *Washington Post*, March 25, 2012.

———. "Your Subpoena Is 'No Longer Necessary.'" *Christopher Elliott*, December 31, 2009. www.elliott.org.

Engle, Jane. "TSA Screeners Being Trained to Monitor People, Not Just Bags." *Los Angeles Times*, August 27, 2006.

Esposito, Richard, and Brian Ross. "Exclusive: Photos of the Northwest Airlines Flight 253 Bomb: Accused Bomber Abdulmutallab's Underwear, Explosive Packet and Detonator." *ABC News*, December 28, 2009.

"The Evolution of the Bag: Going 'Checkpoint Friendly.'" www.tsa.gov. Accessed July 7, 2008.

"Exposed Bag." *Better Living through Design*. www.betterlivingthroughdesign.com. Accessed October 26, 2007.

"FAA Takes Steps to Reduce Flight Delays during Summer Season." *Airline Industry Information*, May 27, 2002.

Farrell, Bryan. "Overcoming the Fear in Israeli Society." http://wagingnon-violence .org. Accessed June 3, 2010.

Ferran, Lee. "Stink Bomb: Underwear Bomber Wore Explosive Undies for Weeks, FBI Says." *ABC News*, September 28, 2012.

Foucault, Michel. *Discipline and Punish: The Birth of the Prison*. New York: Vintage, 1995.

———. "The Eye of Power." In *Power/Knowledge: Selected Interviews and Other Writings 1972–1977*, edited by Colin Gordon. New York: Pantheon, 1980.

———. "Of Othering Spaces." In *Visual Culture Reader*, edited by Nicholas Mirzoeff. New York: Routledge, 2002.

———. *Power/Knowledge: Selected Interviews and Other Writings 1972–1977*. Edited by Colin Gordon. New York: Pantheon, 1980.

Frank, Thomas. "Body Scanners Replace Metal Detectors in Tryout at Tulsa Airport." *USA Today*, February 17, 2009.

———. "Holiday Airline Travelers Urged to Chuck Carry-on Clutter, Pack Neatly: 'Simplifly' Campaign Aims to Speed Security." *USA Today*, November 19, 2007.

———. "Security Arsenal Adds Behavior Detection: Controversial Technique Targets 'Suspicious' People." *USA Today*, September 26, 2007.

———. "Travelers Stray from Categories: Airports Don't Force People into Lanes." *USA Today*, March 3, 2008.

———. "TSA's 'SimpliFLY' Motto Challenged: Salt Lake City Airport Alleges Trademark Infringement in Lawsuit against Feds." *USA Today*, March 27, 2009.

Friedberg, Anne. *The Virtual Window: From Alberti to Microsoft*. Cambridge, MA: MIT Press, 2006.

———. *Window Shopping: Cinema and the Postmodern*. Berkeley: University of California Press, 1993.

Frischling, Steven. "TSA Security Directive SD-1544-09-06: The Fallout from NW253." *Flying with Fish: The Blog for Those Who Fly and Those Who Want to Fly Smarter*, December 27, 2009. http://boardingarea.com.

Fuller, Gillian. "Life in Transit: Between Airport and Camp." *borderlands* 2, no. 1 (2003). http://www.borderlands.net.au/vol2no1_2003/fuller_transit.html. Accessed February 20, 2015.

———. "Welcome to Windows 2.1: Motions Aesthetics at the Airport." In *Politics at the Airport*, edited by Mark B. Salter, 161–73. Minneapolis: University of Minnesota Press, 2008.

Fuller, Gillian, and Ross Harley. *Aviopolis: A Book about Airports*. London: Black Dog, 2004.

Gadher, Dipesh. "'SPOT' Teams to Spy on Passengers." *Times* (United Kingdom), August 20, 2006.

Garland-Thomson, Rosmarie. *Freakery: Cultural Spectacles of the Extraordinary Body*. New York: New York University Press, 1996.

Gates, Kelly. *Our Biometric Future: Facial Recognition Technology and the Culture of Surveillance*. Critical Cultural Communication. New York: New York University Press, 2011.

Gathright, Alan, Zachary Coile, and Vanessa Hua. "Photos, Fingerprints Taken at U.S. Borders: Anti-Terror Program Screens Visitors at Airports." *San Francisco Chronicle*, January 6, 2004.

Gill, Pat. "Technostalgia: Making the Future Past Perfect." *Camera Obscura* 14 (1997): 161–79.

Gilliom, John. *Overseers of the Poor: Surveillance, Resistance, and the Limits of Privacy.* Chicago: University of Chicago Press, 2001.

Gilroy, Paul. *Postcolonial Melancholia.* New York: Columbia University Press, 2006.

Gopnick, Adam. "The Fifth Blade: Evolution and the Razor." *New Yorker,* May 11, 2009.

Gordon, Colin. "Governmental Rationality: An Introduction." In *Foucault Effect: Studies in Governmentality,* edited by Graham Burchell, Colin Gordon, and Peter Miller, 4–5. Chicago: University of Chicago Press, 1991.

Grant, Allison. "TSA Agents Subpoena Bloggers to Find Out Who Leaked the New Security Document." *Cleveland Plain Dealer,* December 31, 2009. http://www.cleveland.com.

Green-Lewis, Jennifer. *Framing the Victorians: Photography and the Culture of Realism.* Ithaca, NY: Cornell University Press, 1996.

"Ground to a Halt: Denial of Palestinians' Freedom of Movement in the West Bank." B'TSELEM: The Israeli Information Center for Human Rights in the Occupied Territories. www.btselem.org, August 2007. Accessed February 20, 2015.

Guarino, Mark. "Do Airport Full Body Scanners Violate Islam?" *Christian Science Monitor,* March 15, 2010.

"A Guide to Disability Rights Laws." US Department of Justice (Civil Rights Division), 2005. www.ada.gov. Accessed February 20, 2015.

Hall, Rachel. "Of Ziploc Bags and Black Holes: The Aesthetics of Transparency in the War on Terror. *The Communication Review* 10, no. 4 (2007): 319–46.

Halsey, Ashley, III. "Radiation Risk from Full-Body Airport Scanners 'Truly Trivial,' Study Says." *Washington Post,* March 31, 2010.

———. "TSA Debuts System for More Modest Scans." *Washington Post,* February 2, 2011.

———. "TSA to Pull Revealing Scanners from Airports." *Washington Post,* January 18, 2013.

Harcourt, Bernard. "Search and Defend." *New York Times,* August 25, 2006.

Hardt, Michael, and Antonio Negri. *Multitude: War and Democracy in the Age of Empire.* New York: Penguin, 2004.

"Health Information Privacy." Health and Human Services. www.hhs.gov. Accessed February 20, 2015.

Healy, Jack, and Marlise Simons. "Full-Body Scans to Be Used for Flights from Amsterdam to U.S." *New York Times,* December 31, 2009.

Higgins, Michelle. "What Can Be Carried On?" *New York Times,* August 15, 2006.

Hoversten, Paul. "Legislation to Reform TSA Would Encourage Airports to Invest in Advanced Technologies." *Aviation Week's Aerospace Daily and Defense Report* 216, no. 51 (December 14, 2005). http://awin.aviationweek.com/portals/awin/cms files/media/pdf/as_pdf/2005/12/14/asd_12_14_2005.txt.

Hsu, Spencer S. "Scanners May Not Have Detected Alleged Explosive in Detroit Jet Case, GAO Reports." *Washington Post,* March 17, 2010.

———. "U.S. to Push for Full-Body Scanners at Foreign Airports." *Washington Post*, January 8, 2010.

Hsu, Spencer, and Karla Adam. "International Cooperation a Challenge for Air Security: Foreign Governments May Lack Cash or Will to Meet U.S. Standards." *Washington Post*, January 9, 2010.

Hsu, Spencer, and Carrie Johnson. "TSA Accidentally Reveals Airport Security Secrets." *Washington Post*, December 9, 2009.

Huettel, Steve. "Ads Land on Bottom of the Bins." *St. Petersburg Times*, January 12, 2007.

———. "Agency Working to Speed Security." *St. Petersburg Times*, June 26, 2008.

———. "Beyond a Single-File Solution." *St. Petersburg Times*, March 19, 2008.

———. "Pick a Screening Lane: Fast or Slow." *Tampa Bay Times*, September 5, 2008.

Hughes, Kathryn. "Comment and Debate: Open Your Mind, Please: Forget Sharp Objects and Hair Gel; Our Private Emotions Are Now up for Grabs at Airport Check-Ins." *Guardian*, August 22, 2006.

ICAO Doc 9303, Machine Readable Travel Documents Part 3, Machine Readable Official Travel Documents Volume 1, MRtds with Machine Readable Data Stored in Optical Character Recognition Format, 3rd ed., 2008. www.icao.int. Accessed February 20, 2015.

Jacobs-Huey, Lanita. "'The Arab Is the New Nigger': African American Comics Confront the Irony and Tragedy of September 11." *Transforming Anthropology* 14, no. 1 (2006): 60–64.

Jahn, Helmut, and Werner Blaser. *Airports*. Basel: Birkhèauser, 1991.

Jansen, Bart. "In Boston, Airport Security Now Begins with a Chat." *USA Today*, October 14, 2011.

Kaufman, Leon, and Joseph W. Carlson. "An Evaluation of Airport X-ray Backscatter Units Based on Image Characteristics." *Journal of Transportation Security* 4, no. 1 (2011): 73–94.

Kaur, Karamjit. "Australia Bans Liquids on Aircraft." *Singapore Straits Times*, December 9, 2006.

Kornblatt, Sara. "Are Emerging Technologies in Airport Passenger Screening Reasonable under the Fourth Amendment?" *Loyola of Los Angeles Law Review* 41 (fall 2007): 385–412.

Kornblut, Anne E., and Perry Bacon Jr. "Airport Security Uproar Frustrates White House Advisers." *Washington Post*, November 22, 2010.

Kravitz, Derek. "Protestors' Body Scanner Opt-Out Day Could Bring Nationwide Delays at Airports." *Washington Post*, November 23, 2010.

Kumar, Amitava. *Passport Photos*. Berkeley: University of California Press, 2000.

Lahav, Gallya. "Mobility and Border Security." In *Politics at the Airport*, edited by Mark B. Salter. Minneapolis: University of Minnesota Press, 2008.

Laird, Doug. "Airport Screening Rules Changed December 22." *USA Today*, December 13, 2005.

"Laptop Bags: Industry Process and Guidelines." www.tsa.gov, July 29, 2008.

Last, Jonathan. "One Last Thing: Behavior Reveals All." *Philadelphia Inquirer*, August 27, 2006.

Lekic, Slobodan. "Full-Body Scan or Not? Europe Divided on Airport Security Steps." *Christian Science Monitor*, January 7, 2010.

Levin, Alan, and Thomas Frank. "TSA: Public 'Getting Better' about Knowing What Not to Bring." USA *Today*, April 27, 2006.

Levine, Timothy R. "A Few Transparent Liars: Explaining 54% Accuracy in Deception Detection Experiments." *Communication Yearbook* 34 (2010): 41–61.

Levine, Timothy R., T. Feeley, S. A. McCornack, C. Harms, and M. Hughes. "Testing the Effects of Nonverbal Training on Deception Detection Accuracy with the Inclusion of a Bogus Training Control Group." *Western Journal of Communication* 69 (2005): 203–18.

Lipton, Eric. "Faces, Too, Are Searched as U.S. Airports Try to Spot Terrorists." *New York Times*, August 17, 2006.

———. "Seeking to Control Borders, Bush Turns to Big Military Contractors." *New York Times*, May 18, 2006.

———. "U.S. Struggles Anew to Ensure Safety as Gaps Are Revealed." *New York Times*, December 29, 2009.

———. "U.S. Turns to Science to Protect Its Borders." *International Herald Tribune*, August 11, 2005.

Lipton, Eric, and Christine Hauser. "Screeners to Be Changed at U.S. Airports." *New York Times*, August 14, 2006.

"Liquid Gel Watch." ComingAndGoing section, *Washington Post*, November 5, 2006.

Lloyd, Justine. "Dwelltime: Airport Technology, Travel, and Consumption." *Space and Culture* 6, no. 2 (2003): 93–109.

Lloyd, Linda. "Philadelphia Airport Launches Kinder, Gentler Body Scanning." *Philadelphia Inquirer*, October 28, 2011.

Lowery, Annie. "A Very Close-Up View of One Manufacturer of Airport Scanners." *Washington Post*, November 28, 2010.

Lugones, Maria. "Playfulness, 'World'-Travelling, and Loving Perception." *Hypatia: A Journal of Feminist Philosophy* 2, no. 2 (1987): 3–19.

Lyon, David. "Filtering Flows, Friends, and Foes." In *Politics at the Airport*, edited by Mark Salter, 29–49. Minneapolis: University of Minnesota Press, 2008.

———. *Surveillance Studies: An Overview*. Cambridge: Polity, 2007.

Magnet, Shoshana. *When Biometrics Fail: Gender, Race, and the Technology of Identity*. Durham, NC: Duke University Press, 2011.

Magnet, Shoshana, and Tara Rodgers, "Stripping for the State: Whole Body Imaging Technologies and the Surveillance of Othered Bodies." *Feminist Media Studies* 12, no. 1 (2012): 1–18.

Marks, Alexandra. "Bomb Lot Spurs a 'New Normal' for Flying." *Christian Science Monitor*, August 18, 2006.

Marshall, Josh. "Bear Any Burden . . . (Don't Touch My Junk Edition)." *Talking Points Memo*, November 22, 2010. http://talkingpointsmemo.com.

Massumi, Brian. "Everywhere You Want to Be: Introduction to Fear." In Massumi, *The Politics of Everyday Fear*, 3–37.

———. "Fear (the Spectrum Said)." *Positions* 13, no. 1 (2005): 31–48.

———. "The Future Birth of the Affective Fact." Paper presented at the Genealogies of Biopolitics, October 2005. Sponsored by the Workshop in Radical Empiricism, Université de Montreal and the Sense Lab, Concordia University, May 7–8, 2005.

———, ed. *The Politics of Everyday Fear*. Minneapolis: University of Minnesota Press, 1993.

Max, Arthur. "US Steps Up Global Travel Security after Bombing Attempt on Detroit-Bound Airplane." *Jerusalem Post*, December 27, 2009.

Mayer, Jane. *Dark Side: The Inside Story of How the War on Terror Turned into a War on American Ideals*. New York: Doubleday, 2008.

Maynard, Micheline, and Eric Lipton. "More Pilot Discretion on Security Measures." *New York Times*, December 29, 2009.

McClintock, Anne. "Paranoid Empire: Specters from Guantanamo and Abu Ghraib." *Small Axe* 26 (March 2009): 50–74.

McFadden, Robert D. "Air France Co-Pilot Is Accused of Making Remark about Bomb." *New York Times*, August 10, 2003.

McGrath, John E. *Loving Big Brother: Performance, Privacy and Surveillance Space*. London: Routledge, 2004.

McKee, Linda. "Heard the One about the Man Who Told a Joke and Was Fined?" *Belfast Telegraph*, July 7, 2005.

McKee, Yates. "Suspicious Packages." *October* 117 (2006): 99–121.

McKenzie, Jon. "Abu Ghraib and the Society of the Spectacle of the Scaffold." In *Violence Performed: Local Roots and Global Routes of Conflict*, edited by Patrick Anderson and Jisha Menon, 338–56. New York: Palgrave Macmillan, 2009.

———. *Perform or Else: From Discipline to Performance*. London: Routledge, 2001.

Millward, David. "US Eases Rules on Flight Cabin Baggage but British Ban Stays." *Daily Telegraph*, September 27, 2006.

Mirzoeff, Nicholas. *The Visual Culture Reader*. 2nd ed. New York: Routledge, 2012.

Mitchell, W. J. T. *What Do Pictures Want? The Lives and Loves of Images*. Chicago: University of Chicago Press, 2005.

"Mobility Disabilities." www.tsa.gov, June 30, 2014.

Monhan, Torin. *Surveillance in the Time of Insecurity*. New Brunswick, NJ: Rutgers University Press, 2010.

Morrison, Tina-Marie. "Passenger Charged over Bomb 'Joke.'" *Wellington* (NZ) *Dominion*, March 9, 2000.

Mountz, Allison. *Seeking Asylum: Human Smuggling and Bureaucracy at the Border*. Minneapolis: University of Minnesota Press, 2010.

Muller, Benjamin. "Travelers, Borders, Dangers: Locating the Political at the Biometric Border." In *Politics at the Airport*, edited by Mark B. Salter. Minneapolis: University of Minnesota Press, 2008.

Murdoch, Jonathan. *Post-structuralist Geography: A Guide to Relational Space*. London: Sage, 2005.

Nakamura, Lisa. "'Where Do You Want to Go Today?' Cybernetic Tourism, the Internet, and Transnationality." In *The Visual Culture Reader*, edited by Nicholas Mirzoeff. New York: Routledge, 2002.

"National Strategy for Homeland Security." Department of Homeland Security, 2002. www.dhs.gov/sites/default/files/publications/nat-strat-hls-2002.pdf. Accessed February 20, 2015.

Nixon, Ron. "T.S.A. Expands Duties beyond Airport Security." *New York Times*, August 5, 2013.

O'Harrow, Robert, Jr., and Scott Higham. "2-Fingerprint Border ID System Called Inadequate." *Washington Post*, October 19, 2004.

———. "US Border Security at a Crossroads." *Washington Post*, May 22, 2005.

Ott, James. "Security, Ease Come First at New Indianapolis International Airport." *Airports* 26, no. 47 (2008): 1.

———. "TSA Chief Endorses Body Imagers, Defines Role of Intelligence." *Aviation Daily*.

Packer, Jeremy. *Mobility without Mayhem: Safety, Cars, and Citizenship*. Durham, NC: Duke University Press, 2008.

Park, H. S., T. R. Levine, S. A. McCornack, K. Morrison, and M. Ferrara. "How People Really Detect Lies." *Communication Monographs* 69, no. 2 (June 2002): 144–57.

Parks, Lisa. "Points of Departure: The Culture of U.S. Airport Screening." *Journal of Visual Culture* 6, no. 2 (2007): 183–200.

Patton, Cindy. *Fatal Advice: How Safe-Sex Education Went Wrong*. Series Q. Durham, NC: Duke University Press, 1996.

Pezzullo, Phaedra Carmen. *Toxic Tourism: Rhetorics of Pollution, Travel, and Environmental Justice*. Tuscaloosa: University of Alabama Press, 2007.

"PI Raises Alarm as U.S. Starts Mass Fingerprinting." www.privacyinternational .org, September 27, 2004.

"Pirate Party Protests 'Naked' Scanners in Their Underpants." *The Local: Germany's News in English*, January 11, 2010.

Puar, Jasbir K. *Terrorist Assemblages: Homonationalism in Queer Times*. Durham, NC: Duke University Press, 2007.

Quindlen, Anna. "Taking Off Your Shoes; Osama Bin Laden Could Get through the Line if the Name on His License Was the Same as That on His Ticket and He Wasn't Packing Oil of Olay." *Newsweek*, November 13, 2006.

Reeves, Joshua. "If You See Something, Say Something: Lateral Surveillance and the Uses of Responsibility." *Surveillance and Society* 10, nos. 3–4 (2012): 235–48.

Reiman, Tonya. *The Power of Body Language: How to Succeed in Every Business and Social Encounter*. New York: Pocket Books, 2007.

Remizowski, Leigh. "Airport Security Lines Help Food Biz Takeoff." *New York Daily News*, January 24, 2010.

"Report: US Border Vulnerable." www.cnn.com. Accessed May 29, 2006.

"A Review of US Citizenship and Immigration Services' Alien Security Checks." www.oig.dhs.gov. Accessed February 20, 2015.

Richtel, Matt. "The Mystery of the Flying Laptop." *New York Times*, April 4, 2012.

Rockwell, Mark. "Napolitano Promotes Joint Declaration at the ICAO Meeting." *Government Security News*, September 29, 2010. http://www.gsnmagazine.com.

Romero, Frances. "Did Airport Scanners Give Boston TSA Agents Cancer?" *Time .com*, June 30, 2011.

Rose, Nikolas S. *Powers of Freedom: Reframing Political Thought*. Cambridge: Cambridge University Press, 1999.

Rumerman, Judy. "Aviation Security." www.centennialofflight.net. Accessed February 20, 2015.

Russo, Mary J. *The Female Grotesque: Risk, Excess, and Modernity*. New York: Routledge, 1995.

Sachs, Andrea. "A Reporter Faces the Naked Truth about Full-Body Scanners." *Washington Post*, February 7, 2010.

Said, Edward, Homi K. Bhabha, and W. J. T. Mitchell. *Edward Said: Continuing the Conversation*. Chicago: University of Chicago Press, 2005.

Salter, Mark. "Introduction: Airport Assemblage." In *Politics at the Airport*, edited by Mark B. Salter. Minneapolis: University of Minnesota Press, 2008.

Schechner, Richard. *Between Theater and Anthropology*. Philadelphia: University of Pennsylvania Press, 1985.

Schneier, Bruce. "Life in the Fast Lane." *New York Times*, January 21, 2007.

Serwer, Adam. "How Effective Is the TSA's Behavior Detection Program?" *Mother Jones*, September 21, 2011.

Sharkey, Joe. "Airport Checkpoint Logic Still Defies Good Sense." *New York Times*, November 11, 2008.

———. "Giving Human Intuition a Place in Airport Security." *New York Times*, August 21, 2007.

———. "Memo Pad." *New York Times*, February 24, 2004.

———. "Will Cost Prematurely Doom Security-Check Fast Lanes?" *New York Times*, September 19, 2006.

Shepard, Willard, and Brian Hamacher. "Suspicious Package: TSA Worker Jailed after Junk Joke." www.nbcmiami.com, May 7, 2010.

Shohat, Ella, and Robert Stam. *Multiculturalism, Postcoloniality, and Transnational Media*. New Brunswick, NJ: Rutgers University Press, 2003.

———. *Unthinking Eurocentrism: Multiculturalism and the Media*. London: Routledge, 1994.

Son, Hugh, and Helen Kennedy. "Airports Check Out Stressed-Out Fliers." *New York Daily News*, May 19, 2006.

Sontag, Susan. "Fascinating Fascism." *New York Review of Books*, February 6, 1975.

Stabile, Carol. "Shooting the Mother: Fetal Photography and the Politics of Disappearance." In *The Visible Woman: Imagining Technologies, Gender, and Science*, edited by Lisa Cartwright, Paula A. Treichler, and Constance Penley, 171–97. New York: New York University Press, 1998.

Stancu, Diane M. "AVSEC Conventions: Beyond Chicago, until Beijing." *Aviation Security International: The Global Journal of Airport and Airline Security* 16, no. 5 (2010): 11–13.

Staples, Brent. "Black Men and Public Space." *Harper's*, December 1986.

Stellin, Susan. "U.S. Groups Seek Airport Security That Would Divide Fliers by Threat Level." *International Herald Tribune*, February 9, 2011.

———. "Failed Bombing Plot Sets Off Debate about Body Scanners in Congress." *International Herald Tribune*, May 16, 2012.

Stoller, Gary. "TSA: Airport Body Scans More 'Private': Critics Say New Software May Not Ease Fliers' Concerns." *USA Today*, July 21, 2011.

Storey, John, and Graeme Turner, eds. *Cultural Consumption and Everyday Life*. New York: Bloomsbury, 1999.

Sturken, Marita. *Tangled Memories: The Vietnam War, the AIDS Epidemic, and the Politics of Remembering*. Berkeley: University of California Press, 1997.

———. *Tourists of History: Memory, Kitsch, and Consumerism from Oklahoma City to Ground Zero*. Durham, NC: Duke University Press, 2007.

———. "Weather Media and Homeland Security: Selling Preparedness in a Volatile World." *Understanding Katrina: Perspectives from the Social Sciences,* June 11, 2006. http://understandingkatrina.ssrc.org.

Taylor, Diana. "Afterword: War Play." *PMLA* 124, no. 5 (2009): 1893.

———. *The Archive and the Repertoire: Performing Cultural Memory in the Americas*. Durham, NC: Duke University Press, 2003.

Taylor, Lelsey Ciarula. "Full-Body Scans Top Priority: Transport Canada Studies Ways to Tighten Airport Security Screening." *Toronto Star*, December 31, 2009.

"Technology That Might Have Helped." *New York Times*, December 27, 2009.

Thompson, Clive. "The Visible Man: An FBI Target Puts His Whole Life Online." *Wired*, May 22, 2007.

Thompson, Gordon. "Liquid Ban for Glasgow Airport Passengers Lifted." *Glasgow Evening Times*, November 2, 2006.

"Travelers with Disabilities and Medical Conditions." www.tsa.gov. Accessed February 20, 2015.

"TSA and Ad Council Launch Public Education Campaign to Build Greater Awareness of Security Procedures at Airport Checkpoints." November 19, 2008. http://multivu.prnewswire.com/mnr/adcouncil/35826/.

"TSA Introduces Black Diamond Self-Select Lanes at Norfolk International Airports." *Airline Industry Information*, December 5, 2008.

"TSA Plans to Double Behavior Detection Officers in 2009." *Aviation Daily* 374: 39.

"TSA Quietly Removing Some Full Body Scanners." *CBS News*, October 25, 2012. www.cbsnews.com.

Turner, Victor. "Images of Anti-Temporality: An Essay in the Anthropology of Experience." *Harvard Theological Review* 75, no. 2 (1982): 243–65.

———. "Social Dramas and Stories about Them." *Critical Inquiry* 7, no. 1 (1980): 141–68.

"Use of Full-Body Scanners in South African Airports Not Likely 'at This Stage.'" BBC *Monitoring Africa (Supplied by* BBC *Worldwide Monitoring),* January 5, 2010.

"US Fingerprints Foreign Visitors." www.news.bbc.co.uk, January 5, 2004.

Volpp, Leti. "The Citizen and the Terrorist." *Immigration and Nationality Law Review* 23 (2002): 561–86.

Weeks, Carly. "9/11 5 Years Later: Safer Skies Just Beyond Our Reach." *Montreal Gazette,* September 5, 2006.

———. "When Flying, Small Is Beautiful." *Montreal Gazette,* September 26, 2006.

Wegenstein, Bernadette. "Getting under the Skin, or, How Faces Have Become Obsolete." *Configurations* 10 (2002): 221–59.

Welch, Dylan. "US Raises Full Body Scanners in Fly-By Visit over Terrorism." *Sydney Morning Herald,* January 11, 2010.

"What's in My Bag: Bebel Gilberto, Brazilian Singer." *Delta Sky,* November 2009, 18.

"What's Missing in Airport Security?" Room for Debate section, *New York Times,* December 28, 2009.

Wilber, Del Quentin. "US Eases Carry-on Liquid Ban; Some Drinks, Small Toiletries Allowed." *Washington Post,* September 26, 2006.

Willan, Philip. "Human Rights Group Blasts New U.S. Border Controls." October 1, 2004. www.infoworld.com.

Wilson, Benet. "Hartsfield Opens New Security Lanes to Cut PAX Wait Times." *Aviation Daily,* October 31, 2008.

———. "TSA Expands Self-Serve Security Lines to Three More Airports." *Aviation Daily,* March 25, 2008.

———. "TSA Pilots Target Quicker Checkpoint Lines for Travelers." *Aviation Daily,* February 21, 2008.

———. "TSA Reaches out to Travelers with Help in Checkpoint Security." *Aviation Daily,* June 23, 2008.

Wong, Nicole C. "Logan Lanes Pave Way for Shorter Waits: Multiple Lines Aim to Ease Gridlock at Security Checkpoints." *Boston Globe,* March 19, 2008.

Woo, Nicole. Letter to the Editor, *New York Times,* September 29, 2006.

Yancy, George, and Judith Butler. "What's Wrong with 'All Lives Matter'?" *New York Times,* January 12, 2015.

Young, Dannagal Goldthwaite. "Sacrifice, Consumption, and the American Way of Life: Advertising and Domestic Propaganda during World War II." *Communication Review* 8 (2005): 27–52.

Yu, Roger. "Airport Check-In." *USA Today,* June 29, 2009.

———. "Elite Fliers Get Own Lines Back; Airlines Court Travelers Who Are Paying More." *USA Today,* October 28, 2008.

Zeleny, Jeff, and Helene Cooper. "Obama Details New Policies in Response to Terror Threat." *New York Times,* January 8, 2010.

INDEX

Note: Page numbers in italics indicate figures.

ABC News, 74
Abdulmutallab, Umar Farouk, 72–75, 77, 80, 159, 200n1
Abu Ghraib prison, 105
ACLU. *See* American Civil Liberties Union
ACSA. *See* Airports Company of South Africa
ADA. *See* Americans with Disabilities Act (ADA, 1990)
Ad Council, 127, 129
Ad Dwar, Iraq, *59*
Adey, Peter, 29, 30, 33
affect environment model, 150–51
Agamben, Giorgio, 8, 66, 92, 93
Ahmed, Sara, 28
Air Line Pilots Association, 148

airports: architecture of, 30–31; as controlled spaces, 32–34, 41–44; as cultural performance, 10–11; global security standards, 160–64; as heterotopia, 34; No-Joking Zones, 169–70, 203n35; as nonplaces, 41–42; as vital places, 6–10; wait times, 44. *See also* checkpoints
Airports Company of South Africa (ACSA), 160
Albanese, Anthony, 161
Ambrefe, Joe, Jr., 53
American Civil Liberties Union (ACLU), 100, 136
Americans with Disabilities Act (ADA, 1990), 124
Andrejevic, Mark, 109, 110, 133, 156, 184n1
Andreu, Paul, 30
Annex 17, 162, 163

Massumi, Brian, 5, 36, 142
McClintock, Anne, 57, 181–82nn23–24
McGlaughlin, Kevin, 55
McGowan, Mo, 117
McGrath, John, 15–16, 49, 185n24
McKee, Yates, 34
McKenzie, Jon, 180n15
Mead, Margaret, 138
media, US: on full-body scanners, 78–80, 83–86; opacity/transparency in, 61, 75–76; war on terror coverage, 57–59
Metropolis (Lang film), 80
Metropolitan Transportation Authority (NYC), 172
Microsoft slogan, 32
millimeter-wave machines, 80–81, 88, 89, 191n29
Mirzoeff, Nicholas, 58
Mitchell, Kevin, 117
mobility, 28–34; politics of, 13, 173–78
Monahan, Torin, 3–4
Mountz, Allison, 175
Mulvey, Laura, 82
Murdoch, Jonathan, 192n35

Naccara, George, 121
Nakamura, Lisa, 31–32, 58
Napolitano, Janet, 158–59, 160–61, 172
National Opt-Out Day, 87, *88*
National Security Administration (NSA), 15
National Security Entry-Exit Registration System (NSEERS), 100
Negri, Antonio, 166
New Yorker (magazine), 83, *84*, 85–86, *86*
New York Times (newspaper), 79–80, 81, 126
NEXUS program, 92, 93
9/11 attacks. *See* September 11, 2001, terrorist attacks

No Joking Zone (KC Improv Company), 170–72
No-Joking Zones, 169–70, 203n35
Northwest Flight 253 (2009), 72, 158–60, 200n1
NSA. *See* National Security Administration
NSEERS. *See* National Security Entry-Exit Registration System

Obama, Barack, 78, 160
OBIM. *See* Office of Biometric Identity Management
object relations, 34–37
Office of Biometric Identity Management (OBIM), 91
opacity: diabolical, 57–58, 75, 81; of enemy bodies, 57–58; in Guantanamo Bay video, 66–72; in photography, 58, 65, 68, 72–75, 175; strategic, 15, 16; terrorist embodiment and, 7–8, 21, 57–76, 81–82, 90
O'Sullivan, Maureen, 139
Othello error, 145–47
othered bodies: criminalization of, 12–13; surveillance of, 83

Packer, Jeremy, 75, 166
Padilla, Jose, 147
Panopticon, 34, 183n37
Parks, Lisa, 6–7, 104–5, 188n17
Passport Photos (Kumar), 16
pat-down procedures, 1–2, 22, 86–87, 89, 123–25
Patriot Act. *See* USA PATRIOT Act (2001)
Pelli, Cesar, 30
performance: authenticity and, 189n11; biopolitics and, 4; of citizenship, 49; cultural, 1–2, 3, 4, 10–11, 192n35; of innocence, 148–49; of space, 192n35; theory of, 180n15
personal data protection, 164
Peters, Jeremy, 126

shoe bomber incident (2002), 11, 147
Shohat, Ella, 60
Simmel, Georg, 186n60
SimpliLFY campaign, 112–17, 113, 127, 128
Skooba Designs, 46
Sky (Delta magazine), 47
Slutzky, Robert, 29, 32
Smart Entry Service (SeS), 93
Smithsonian (magazine), 25, 26, 27
Snowden, Edward, 14
social networking sites, 20, 109–10
Sontag, Susan, 55
special assistance lane, 122–25
Spitler, Robert, 142
SPOT program. *See* Screening Passengers by Observation Techniques
Stam, Robert, 60
Stand Your Ground law, 168
Staples, Brent, 155
stop-and-frisk policies, 167
stress, signs of, 132
Sturken, Maria, 186n61, 187n6
Superman (film), 84–85
Support Our Law Enforcement and Safe Neighborhoods Act. *See* Arizona Senate Bill 1070
surveillance: capacity and, 4; critique of, 16; interactivity in, 110; sexualization of, 85–86; spaces, 16, 185n24; technologies, 4, 5, 10, 21–22, 55, 75–76, 77–80, 83–84, 103, 107. *See also specific technologies*
Surveillance in the Time of Insecurity (Monahan), 3–4
Sydney Morning Herald (newspaper), 161

Taylor, Diana, 11, 185n20, 187n2
television commercials, security and sex in, 103–7
Telling Lies (Ekman), 153
terrorism embodiment: cultural

stereotypes in, 155; female grotesque and, 81–82; media depictions of, 57–59, 61, 72–75; opacity and, 7–8, 21, 57–76, 81–82, 90; spectacles of, 77
terrorism prevention, 1–2; biopolitics and, 4, 79, 155–56; effectiveness of, 102; flying checkpoints, 167–68; media representation of, 105–6; as national emergency, 124; opacity/embodiment and, 7–8, 21, 57–76, 81–82, 90; risk management approach, 5, 42, 47, 90; threat and, 5–6, 11–12, 21–22, 32–34, 49, 55, 76, 82–83, 90–91, 110–11; voluntary transparency in, 10–11, 32–33, 75–76, 79, 149. *See also* specific programs; specific technologies
Terrorist Assemblages (Puar), 4
terrorist grotesque, 72–75, 77, 81–83
terror of suspicion, 145–47
3-1-1 policy, 37–41, 39
Tomkins, Sylvan, 138
Toronto Star (newspaper), 159
Tracking Transience (Elahi), 16–17
Transit Security Grant Program (DHS), 172
transnationality, 32, 103, 165, 182n26
transparency: aesthetics of, 9, 20, 33, 48, 53–56, 57, 101, 128, 157, 165, 174–75; affective, 149; asymmetrical, 14–23, 107, 157, 165, 167, 173, 175–76; chic, 20, 25, 27, 57–58, 83, 173, 177–78; compulsory, 7–8, 10–13; defined, 14, 29–30; in Guantanamo Bay video, 66–72; involuntary, 9–10, 153; privilege of, 75–76; in security cultures, 20–21, 45, 75–76, 82, 110, 149, 157, 165, 167–68; symmetrical, 15; of trusted travelers, 94, 100; types of, 28–29; voluntary, 6, 8, 10–11, 32–33, 58, 79, 82, 110–11, 122, 149, 155–56, 177